Presbyterian Church in the U.S.A.

The appeal in the Briggs heresy case before the General assembly of the Presbyterian church in the U.S.A.

Presbyterian Church in the U.S.A.

The appeal in the Briggs heresy case before the General assembly of the Presbyterian church in the U.S.A.

ISBN/EAN: 9783337260255

Printed in Europe, USA, Canada, Australia, Japan

Cover: Foto ©Lupo / pixelio.de

More available books at **www.hansebooks.com**

THE APPEAL

IN

THE BRIGGS HERESY CASE

BEFORE THE

GENERAL ASSEMBLY OF THE PRESBYTERIAN
CHURCH IN THE UNITED STATES
OF AMERICA.

COMPILED BY

JOHN J. McCOOK,

A MEMBER OF THE PROSECUTING COMMITTEE.

NEW YORK:
JOHN C. RANKIN CO., PRINTERS.
1893.

Table of Contents.

	PAGE
I.—Introduction	5
II.—Notice of appeal	11
III.—Appeal with specifications of error	12
History of the case prior to the appeal	13
Judgment of General Assembly of 1892, reversing the decision of the Presbytery dismissing the case	18
Final judgment of the Presbytery of New York, January 9th, 1893	20
Grounds of the appeal with the specifications of error alleged	26-41
IV.—Proceedings of the Presbytery of New York during the trial below	43
Mandate of General Assembly of 1892, ordering a new trial	43
Status of Prosecuting Committee questioned	47
Decision of Moderator as to status of Committee with reasons therefor	48
Moderator's decision appealed from and sustained by Presbytery	49
Amended charges and specifications	50
Evidence introduced by Prosecuting Committee	92-94
Evidence introduced by Dr. Briggs	95
Exception by Prosecution as to matter improperly entered upon the stenographic record	105
Protest as to same	110
Answer to the protest	122
Order of procedure in taking the vote upon the charges and specifications	138
Motion to exclude Professors and Trustees of Union Theological Seminary from voting	141
Drs. George Alexander and Henry Van Dyke and Elder Jaffray, appointed Committee to prepare the judgment of Presbytery	143
Vote of thanks to Moderator, etc.	144
Vote of each member of Presbytery in detail on the charges and specifications	145

	PAGE
Protest as to Rev. Mr. Mingin's vote	165
Answer to the protest	166
Report of Committee and form of final judgment	166
Report adopted and the final judgment entered by the Presbytery	169
Exception of Prosecuting Committee as to stenograpic report of the trial	170
Exception of Prosecuting Committee to the final judgment	170

V.—Appellant's opening argument in favor of entertaining the appeal presented by Dr. Birch, Chairman of the Prosecuting Committee................................. 172

VI.—Appellant's closing argument in favor of entertaining the appeal presented by Mr. McCook, a member of the Prosecuting Committee 190

VII.—Preliminary statement submitted by Mr. McCook, as to procedure and designating the portions of the record to be used by the Appellant during the argument of the appeal 259

VIII.—Appellant's opening argument on the merits and in favor of sustaining the appeal presented by Dr. Lampe, a member of the Prosecuting Committee............. 264

IX.—Appellant's closing argument in favor of sustaining the appeal, being Mr. McCook's reply to Dr. Briggs' argument upon the merits of the appeal 347

X.—Appendix containing the judgment of the General Assembly and vote of thanks to the Prosecuting Committee 374

I.

INTRODUCTION.

This volume contains the printed documents and arguments submitted by the Prosecuting Committee, representing the Appellant, in the case of the Presbyterian Church in the United States of America, Appellant, against the Rev. Charles A. Briggs, D. D., Appellee, before the One Hundred and Fifth General Assembly of the Presbyterian Church, in session at Washington, D. C., May, 1893, together with the Judgment of the Assembly therein.

The case came before the General Assembly upon appeal from the final judgment of the Presbytery of New York, entered on the 9th day of January, 1893.

The history of the case prior to the hearing before the General Assembly is given in the appeal as printed at page 13.

The proceedings before the Assembly in the judicial case were as follows:

On May 23d, the Judicial Committee, by its Chairman, the Rev. George D. Baker, D. D., brought in its report upon the appeal, which was entitled "Judicial Case Number I." A minority report was presented by the Rev. Samuel J. Niccolls, D. D. The report of the Committee was amended by the General Assembly and adopted as a whole, as follows:

"In the case of the Presbyterian Church in the United States of America against the Rev. Charles A. Briggs, D. D., being an appeal to the General Assembly from a decision and final judgment of the Presbytery of New York, rendered January 9, 1893, the Judicial Committee beg leave respectfully to report that they have examined the papers pertaining to this case, and find : "

" 1. That the Appellant in this case is the Presbyterian Church in the United States of America, represented by its Prosecuting Committee, appointed by the Presbytery of New York, and, as such Appellant, has a right of Appeal to this Assembly as an original party, and said Prosecuting Committee is entitled to conduct the prosecution, in all its stages, in whatever judicatory, until the final issue be reached."

" 2. That the notice of appeal in this case has been given, and the Appeal and specifications of error alleged, and the record in the case, have been filed in due time, in accordance with the provisions of the Book of Discipline, Secs. 96 and 97, and that said Appeal is accordingly in order."

" 3. They, therefore, respectfully recommend that the Appeal be entertained and the case be issued."

" In order to the determination of this recommendation, your Committee submit the following resolutions : "

"*Resolved*, 1. That the General Assembly finds that due notice of the Appeal in this case has been given, and that the Appeal and the specifications of the errors alleged have been filed in due time, and that the Appeal is in order, in accordance with the provisions of the Book of Discipline."

"*Resolved*, 2. That after the judgment, the notice of appeal, the Appeal, and specifications of errors alleged have been read, then the parties shall be heard respectively as to whether said Appeal shall be entertained."

"*Resolved*, 3. That the Appellants be allowed, if they so desire, one hour in which to present their case at the beginning."

"*Resolved*, 4. The appellee having informed the Chairman of the Judicial Committee that he would probably need five hours to present his defence of the action of the Presbytery and his reply to the Appellants, that five hours shall be allowed him, should he wish to occupy so much time."

"*Resolved*, 5. That the Appellants be allowed two hours to reply to the Appellee, the time to be extended should they request it, not to exceed, however, the limit of time allowed to the Appellee."

"*Resolved*, 6. That four hours be given to the members of the judicatory to discuss the question pending, ten minutes being allowed to each speaker; and that at the end of that time a vote shall be taken as to whether the Appeal shall be entertained. (Minutes General Assembly, 1893, p. 104.)"

The General Assembly was constituted and charged as

a Court on May 23d, and thereupon, in compliance with Section 99 of the Book of Discipline, the judgment of the lower Court, the notice of appeal, the appeal and the specifications of the errors alleged were read by the Stated Clerk.

On the 24th and 25th of May, the parties were heard; the Rev. George W. F. Birch, D. D., Chairman of the Prosecuting Committee, representing the Appellant, presented the opening argument in support of the entertainment of the Appeal, page 172.

The Rev. Charles A. Briggs, D. D., the Appellee, was then heard in argument against entertaining the Appeal.*

At the close of Dr. Briggs's argument, Mr. McCook of the Prosecuting Committee presented the Appellant's closing argument in favor of entertaining the Appeal, which will be found at page 190.

On May 26th, the General Assembly, by a vote of 410 to 145, determined to entertain the appeal. (Minutes General Assembly, 1893, p. 95.)

On May 29th the Judicial Committee presented a further report, fixing the time to be allowed to the Appellant and the Appellee for their arguments upon the merits of the appeal, and outlined the order of procedure to be followed by the Court. (Minutes General Assembly, 1893, p. 132.) This report having been received and adopted by the Assembly, Mr. McCook, of the Prosecuting Committee, made a preliminary statement as to procedure and designating the portions of the Record to be used by the Appellant during the argument of the appeal, page 259.

---

* The Defence of Prof. Briggs before the General Assembly, page 35.

The Rev. Joseph J. Lampe, D. D., of the Prosecuting Committee, then presented the Appellant's opening argument upon the merits of and in favor of sustaining the appeal, page 264.

On May 29th and 30th Dr. Briggs presented his argument to the General Assembly upon the merits of and against sustaining the appeal.*

At the close of Dr. Briggs's argument, Mr. McCook, of the Prosecuting Committee, presented his argument in reply, closing the case for the Appellant, page 347.

In compliance with the provisions of Section 99 of the Book of Discipline, the parties having been heard, the members of the Presbytery of New York, the Judicatory appealed from, were then heard, and upon the call of the roll an opportunity was given for all the members of the General Assembly to be heard.

A vote was then taken on each specification of error alleged, and all of the thirty-four specifications of error, excepting specifications first and fifth, under the fourth ground of appeal, were sustained, and the appeal was sustained by a vote of 379 to 116. (Minutes of General Assembly, 1893, p. 140.)

A Committee was then appointed, of which the Rev. Thomas A. Hoyt, D. D., was Chairman, to formulate the Judgment of the Assembly in the case. On June 1st, the Committee reported to the Assembly, when the

---

* The Defence of Prof. Briggs before the General Assembly, p. 138.

form of Judgment recommended by the Committee was adopted by the Assembly and was ordered to be entered upon the records of the Assembly and of the Presbytery of New York, as the Judgment in the case. (Minutes General Assembly, 1893, pp. 163-5.)

The report of the Committee and the form of the Judgment will be found at page 374.

The action of the Assembly expressing its approval of the conduct of the case by the Prosecuting Committee, is given at page 378.

120 Broadway,
New York, July, 1893.

II.

NOTICE OF APPEAL.

NEW YORK, January 18th, 1893.

To the REV. SAMUEL D. ALEXANDER, D. D.,
Stated Clerk of the Presbytery of New York.

DEAR SIR:

The Presbyterian Church in the United States of America, represented by the undersigned Prosecuting Committee, in the case of the Presbyterian Church in the United States of America, against the Rev. Charles A. Briggs, D.D., hereby gives written notice of appeal, with specifications of the errors alleged, in the said case, to the General Assembly of the Presbyterian Church in the United States of America, to meet at Washington, D. C., on the third Thursday of May, A. D. 1893, from the decision and final judgment of the Presbytery of New York, sitting in a judicial capacity, given on the ninth day of January, 1893. The grounds of this appeal and the specifications of the errors alleged, are hereto attached and made a part of this notice.

The Presbyterian Church in the United States of America, represented by

GEORGE W. F. BIRCH,
JOSEPH J. LAMPE,
ROBERT F. SAMPLE,
JOHN J. STEVENSON,
JOHN J. McCOOK,

Prosecuting Committee,
Appellant.

III.

APPEAL TO THE GENERAL ASSEMBLY.

NEW YORK, January 18th, 1893.

TO THE VENERABLE THE GENERAL ASSEMBLY OF THE PRESBYTERIAN CHURCH IN THE UNITED STATES OF AMERICA, GREETING:

The Presbyterian Church in the United States of America, represented by the undersigned Prosecuting Committee, in the case of the said Presbyterian Church against the Rev. Charles A. Briggs, D. D., presents the following Appeal from the final judgment in this case, rendered by the Presbytery of New York on the ninth day of January, 1893, with the grounds therefor, and the specifications of the errors alleged. Believing that the trial of the said Dr. Briggs is one of the most important in the history of the Presbyterian Church, by reason of the dangerous errors alleged to be contained in the Address of the said Dr. Briggs at his inauguration as Professor of Biblical Theology in Union Theological Seminary, delivered on the 20th day of January, 1891, upon which Inaugural Address charges and specifications were tabled and prosecution, in compliance with Sections 10 and 11 of the Book of Discipline, was initiated by the Presbytery of New York in the name of the Presbyterian Church in the United States of America; and believing that the distinct and definite condemnation of those alleged errors, by the Supreme Judicatory of the said Presbyterian Church, is necessary in order to prevent their spread and influence in the denomination; and, while having the highest respect for the Synod of New York, believing that a special responsibility rests upon the General Assembly which is charged with the duty of deciding in all controversies respecting doctrine; of reproving, warning or bearing testimony against error in doctrine in any Church, Presbytery or Synod, and in cases that affect or concern the promotion of truth and holiness through all the Churches under its care, as set forth in Chapter XII., Sections IV. and V., of the Form of Government; and in view of the desirableness of the speediest settlement of this most important case, do hereby appeal to and request your Venerable Body to enter immediately upon the consideration and judicial investigation of the appeal hereby presented, to issue the case, and to finally determine the important questions involved, so as to secure the purity and the peace of the Church at the earliest possible day.

In the further prosecution of the case on the part of the said Presbyterian Church, the Appellant, represented by the said Prosecuting Committee, respectfully sets forth:

That on the thirteenth day of April, A. D. 1891, the Presbytery of New York appointed a Committee to consider the Inaugural Address of the Rev. Charles A. Briggs, D. D., in its relation to the Confession of Faith, and that on May eleventh, A. D. 1891, the said Committee presented to said Presbytery a report which was accepted, and its recommendation, "that the Presbytery enter at once upon the judicial investigation of the case," was adopted by the said Presbytery, and thereupon it was "*Resolved*, That a Committee be appointed to arrange and prepare the necessary proceedings appropriate in the case of Dr. Briggs"; and the Rev. G. W. F. Birch, D. D., Rev. Joseph J. Lampe, D. D., Rev. Robert F. Sample, D. D., and Ruling Elders John J. Stevenson and John J. McCook were appointed such Committee in conformity with the provisions of Section 11 of the Book of Discipline.

That after the initiation of the prosecution by the said Judicatory, the Presbytery of New York, as above recited, the said Prosecuting Committee entered upon its duties.

That as said prosecution was initiated by a Judicatory and not by individual prosecutors, in compliance with the provisions of Section 10 of the Book of Discipline, the Presbyterian Church in the United States of America became the prosecutor, and an original party in the case, and was represented by the said Prosecuting Committee, which said Committee, under Section 11 of the Book of Discipline, was charged with the duty of conducting the prosecution in all its stages in whatever judicacatory, until the final issue be reached.

That at the meeting of said Presbytery, held on the fifth day of October, A. D. 1891, the said Prosecuting Committee presented charges and specifications in the case of the Presbyterian Church in the United States of America against the Rev. Charles A. Briggs, D. D., which were read in the presence of the Judicatory, and were then served by the Moderator upon the said Rev. Charles A. Briggs, D. D,, together with a citation, citing him to appear and plead to the said charges and specifications at a meeting of the said Presbytery, to be held on November fourth, A. D. 1891.

That after said charges and specifications had been presented to the said Presbytery and had been read, the Presbytery entertained a motion made by the Rev. George Alexander, D. D., to arrest the judicial proceedings and to discharge the Prosecuting Committee from further consideration of the case, as follows :

"*Whereas*, the Presbytery of New York, at its meeting in May last, on account of utterances contained in an inaugural address delivered January 20th, 1891, appointed a Committee to formulate charges against the author of that address, Rev. Charles A. Briggs, D. D., and whereas, since that action was taken, the accused has supplemented those utterances by responding to certain categorical questions. * * *

"*Therefore, Resolved*, that Presbytery, without pronouncing on the sufficiency of these later declarations to cover all the points concerning which the accused has been called in question, with hearty appreciation of the faithful labors of the Committee, deems it expedient to arrest the judicial proceedings at this point, and hereby discharges the Committee from further consideration of the case."

On the aforesaid motion to dismiss the case, as expressed specifically in the words "to arrest the judicial proceedings" and "hereby discharges the Committee from further consideration of the case," the Presbytery by a yea and nay vote refused to adopt the above resolution and to dismiss the case.

That on the said fifth day of October, A. D. 1891, the said Presbytery adjourned to meet on the fourth day of November, A. D. 1891, the day upon which the said citation was made returnable, and that at said meeting on the fourth day of November, A. D. 1891, the said Presbytery was charged as a Judicatory in accordance with Rule XL. of General Rules for Judicatories, and thereupon the said Presbytery proceeded in the case of the Presbyterian Church in the United States of America against the Rev. Charles A. Briggs, D.D., and the said Dr. Briggs then presented a paper purporting to be objections to the sufficiency of the said charges and specifications in form and legal effect; that said paper was largely an answer to said charges or an argument upon the merits of the case, and was denominated by the said Dr. Briggs himself, a "Response to the Charges and Specifications submitted to the Presbytery of New York, by Prof. Charles Augustus Briggs, D. D.," and that the said Presbytery thereupon permitted members of the said Presbytery to discuss the merits of the main question on behalf of the accused before and without permitting the Prosecuting Committee to be heard on the merits of the case.

That a question as to the status of the Prosecuting Committee was raised, and the Moderator decided that the Committee was properly a Committee of Prosecution in view of the previous action of the Presbytery, and was in the house as an original party under the provisions of Section 10 of the Book of Discipline. That an appeal was taken from the decision of the Moderator, the question was divided, and the Moderator was sustained in the point, that the Committee was in the house as a properly appointed Committee of Prosecution, and also sustained in the point that the Committee, as representing the Presbyterian Church in the United States of America, was an original party in the case.

That on said November fourth, A. D. 1891, the said Presbytery, after fully hearing Dr. Briggs' "Response to the Charges and Specifications," and without permitting the Prosecuting Committee to be heard on the merits of the case, upon the motion of the Rev. Henry Van Dyke, D. D., made and entered on its records its decision and final judgment dismissing the said case in the following words, to wit:

"*Resolved*, that the Presbytery of New York, having listened to the paper of the Rev. Charles A. Briggs, D.D., in the case of the Presbyterian Church in the United States of America against him as to the sufficiency of the charges and specifications in form and legal effect; and without approving of the positions stated in his Inaugural Address, at the same time desiring earnestly the peace and quiet of the Church, and in view of the declarations made by Dr. Briggs touching his loyalty to the Holy Scriptures and the Westminster Standards, and of his disclaimers of interpretations put on some of his words, deems it best to dismiss the case, and hereby does so dismiss it."

From the aforesaid action of the said Presbytery of New York on the said fourth day of November, A.D. 1891, in dismissing the case, the Prosecuting Committee took an appeal in the name and on behalf of the said Presbyterian Church to the General Assembly of the Presbyterian Church in the United States of America, in accordance with the provisions of Sections 94 to 102, inclusive, of the Book of Discipline.

The said Appeal was made upon six different grounds, supported by twenty-five specifications of error, and together with the written notice of Appeal required by Section 96 of the Book of Discipline, was given to the

Stated Clerk of the Presbytery of New York, and lodged with the Stated Clerk of the General Assembly, within the time required by Sections 96 and 97 of the Book of Discipline.

The Appeal, the Record and other documents in the case were referred to the Judicial Committee of the General Assembly of 1892 at Portland, Oregon, and the following action was had thereon:

"The Judicial Committee presented its report in the case of the Presbyterian Church in the U. S. of A. vs. Rev. Charles A. Briggs, D. D., which was accepted, as follows:

The Judicial Committee respectfully reports that it has carefully considered the documents submitted to it in this case, and adopted the following resolutions:

1. That, in the opinion of this Committee, the Appeal taken by the Presbyterian Church in the United States of America, an original party represented by the "Committee of Prosecution," appointed under Section 11 of the Book of Discipline, has been taken from the final judgment of the Presbytery in dismissing the case; and that the said Committee had the right to take this Appeal representing the said original party.

2. That it finds that the notice of the Appeal has been given, and that the Appeal, Specifications of Error, and Record have been filed in accordance with Sections 96 and 97 of the Book of Discipline, and the appeal is in order.

3. That, in the judgment of the Committee, the Appeal should be entertained, and a time set apart for the hearing of the case.

In view of these considerations, the Committee reports that the Appeal is in order, and that the General Assembly should proceed, in accordance with the provisions of Section 99 of the Book of Discipline, by causing the judgment appealed from, the notice of Appeal, the Appeal and the specifications of the errors alleged, to be read; then to hear the appellant by the Committee of Prosecution; then the defendant in person, or by his counsel; then the appellant by the Committee of Prosecution in reply, upon the question, "Whether the Appeal shall be entertained?" (Minutes of General Assembly, 1892, page 90.)

The General Assembly was then constituted and charged, in accordance with Rule XL. of the General Rules for Judicatories, and during its sessions, on the 25th and 26th days of May, 1892, heard the Arguments of the Appellant and the Appellee upon the question whether the Appeal should or should not be entertained, the Assembly adopted the report of the Judicial Committee and the Appeal was entertained. (Minutes of General Assembly, 1892, pp. 118 and 119.)

Against this action of the Assembly, "in entertaining the Appeal of the Prosecuting Committee, * * * and so giving the Committee which preferred the Charges against Dr. Briggs, standing before the Assembly and right of Appeal as an original party," a protest was presented by the Rev. S. J. McPherson, D.D., and others, which protest was ordered to be entered on the Minutes of the Assembly without answer. (Minutes of General Assembly, 1892, pp. 153, 205.)

The Appeal, upon its merits, was then fully argued by the Appellant and the Appellee before the General Assembly, on May 28th, 1892 (Minutes of General Assembly, 1892, p.140), and the provisions of Section 99 of the Book of Discipline having been fully complied with, each of the twenty-five specifications of error was sustained. The yeas and nays were ordered upon the question, "Shall the Appeal be sustained?" and 431 Commissioners voted to sustain the Appeal and 87 voted not to sustain. (Minutes of General Assembly, 1892, p. 141.)

On May 30th, 1892, the Committee appointed to draft a form of Judgment to be entered in the said case submitted its report and recommended the form of decree or order, which was adopted, (Minutes of the General Assembly, 1892, p. 152) and is as follows :

"THE PRESBYTERIAN CHURCH IN THE UNITED STATES OF AMERICA *vs.* REV. CHARLES A. BRIGGS, D. D. } Appeal from the judgment of the Presbytery of New York, dismissing the case.

"The General Assembly having, on the 28th day of

May, 1892, duly sustained all the specifications of error alleged and set forth in the appeal and specifications in this case,

"It is now, May 30, 1892, ordered, that the judgment of the Presbytery of New York, entered November 4, 1891, dismissing the case of the Presbyterian Church in the United States of America against Rev. Charles A. Briggs, D. D., be, and the same is hereby, reversed. And the case is remanded to the Presbytery of New York for a new trial, with directions to the said Presbytery to proceed to pass upon and determine the sufficiency of the charges and specifications in form and legal effect, and to permit the Prosecuting Committee to amend the specifications or charges, not changing the general nature of the same, if, in the furtherance of justice, it be necessary to amend, so that the case may be brought to issue and tried on the merits thereof as speedily as may be practicable.

"And it is further ordered, that the Stated Clerk of the General Assembly return the record, and certify the proceedings had thereon, with the necessary papers relating thereto, to the Presbytery of New York."

This mandate of the General Assembly was received by the Stated Clerk of the Presbytery of New York and submitted to the Presbytery at its meeting held on the 13th day of June, 1892, when the Presbytery

"*Resolved*, That in the judgment of Presbytery, the issue of the case is impracticable during the Summer, but will receive the attention of Presbytery on its reassembling in the Fall."

On the 9th day of November, 1892, the Presbytery of New York met, was constituted and charged, in accordance with Rule XL. of the General Rules for Judicatories. During the first day's session of the said Judicatory, in compliance with the said mandate of the General Assembly, and the provisions of Section 22 of the Book of Discipline, the said Judicatory permitted the Prosecuting Committee to amend the Charges and Specifications theretofore submitted in this case, and the Prosecuting

Committee thereupon submitted amended Charges and Specifications. In the furtherance of justice, and with an earnest desire to fairly and fully meet and conform to the suggestions and objections raised by Dr. Briggs in his response to the original Charges and Specifications, so far as such objections were valid or well taken, the Prosecuting Committee, without departing from or changing the general nature of the original Charges, made such amendments as appeared to them to be necessary to secure clearness and certainty as to what was charged; also to prevent the Charges from covering more than one offence and to make the Specifications, and the proofs cited in support thereof, germane and pertinent to the Charges they were intended to sustain. The sessions of said Judicatory were continued with certain interruptions for a number of days, during which certain proceedings were taken as recorded in the minutes of said Judicatory, which minutes are hereby referred to as a part of the record of the proceedings in this case, which culminated in the decision and final Judgment from which this Appeal is taken.

On the 9th day of January, 1893, a committee consisting of the Rev. George Alexander, D. D., the Rev. Henry Van Dyke, D. D. and Elder Robert Jaffray, appointed to bring in a minute to express the action of the said Judicatory, made its report, which was adopted by the Judicatory, and the said Presbytery, sitting in a judicial capacity, made and entered its decision and final judgment in this case, in the following words, to wit:

FINAL JUDGMENT OF THE PRESBYTERY OF NEW YORK.

"The case of the Presbyterian Church in the United States of America against the Reverend Charles A. Briggs, D. D., having been dismissed by the Presbytery of New York on November 4th, 1891, was remanded by the General Assembly of 1892 to the same Presbytery, with instructions that 'it be brought to issue and tried on the merits thereof as speedily as possible.'"

"In obedience to this mandate the Presbytery of New York has tried the case. It has listened to the evidence and argument of the Committee of Prosecution, acting in fidelity to the duty committed to them. It has heard the defense and evidence of the Rev. Charles A. Briggs, presented in accordance with the rights secured to every minister of the church.

"The Presbytery has kept in mind these established principles of our polity, 'that no man can rightly be convicted of heresy by inference or implication'; that 'in the interpretation of ambiguous expressions candor requires that a court should favor the accused by putting upon his words the more favorable rather than the less favorable construction,' and 'there are truths and forms with respect to which men of good character may differ.'

"Giving due consideration to the defendant's explanation of the language used in his Inaugural Address, accepting his frank and full disclaimer of the interpretation which has been put upon some of its phrases and illustrations, crediting his affirmations of loyalty to the Standards of the church and to the Holy Scriptures as the only infallible rule of faith and practice, the Presbytery does not find that he has transgressed the limits of liberty allowed under our Constitution to scholarship and opinion.

"Therefore, without expressing approval of the critical or theological views embodied in the Inaugural Address or the manner in which they have been expressed and illustrated, the Presbytery pronounces the Rev. Charles A. Briggs, D. D., fully acquitted of the offences alleged against him, the several charges and specifications accepted for probation having been 'not sustained' by the following vote:

		SUSTAINED.			NOT SUSTAINED.		
		MINISTERS.	ELDERS.	TOTAL.	MINISTERS.	ELDERS.	TOTAL.
I.	1 Specification,	41	17	58	55	15	70
	2 "	42	17	59	54	15	69
	Charge { a	42	17	59	54	15	69
	{ b	42	17	59	54	15	69
II.	1 Specification,	39	16	55	56	16	72
	2 "	39	16	55	56	16	72
	Charge { a	39	16	55	56	16	72
	{ b	39	16	55	56	16	72
III.	Specification,	44	17	61	52	15	67
	Charge { a	44	17	61	52	15	67
	{ b	42	17	59	54	15	69
	{ c	44	17	61	52	15	67
IV.	Specification,	39	15	54	55	17	72
	Charge { a	39	15	54	55	17	72
	{ b	39	15	54	55	17	72
V.	Specification,	35	14	49	57	16	73
	Charge { a	35	14	49	57	16	73
	{ b	35	14	49	57	16	73
VI.	Specification,	41	16	57	55	14	69
	Charge,	41	16	57	55	14	69

"Accordingly, the Presbytery, making full recognition of the ability, sincerity and patience with which the Committee of Prosecution have performed the onerous duty assigned them, does now, to the extent of its constitutional power, relieve said Committee from further responsibility in connection with this case. In so doing, the Presbytery is not undertaking to decide how far that Committee is subject to the authority of the body appointing it, but intends by this action to express an earnest conviction that the grave issues involved in this case will be more wisely and justly determined by calm investigation and fraternal discussion than by judicial arraignment and process.

"In view of the present disquietude in the Presbyterian Church, and of the obligation resting upon all Christians to walk in charity and to have tender concern for the consciences of their brethren, the Presbytery earnestly counsels its members to avoid on the one hand hasty or over-confident statement of private opinion on points concerning which profound and reverent students of God's word are not yet agreed, and, on the other hand, suspicions and charges of false teaching which are not clearly capable of proof.

"Moreover, the Presbytery advises and exhorts all subject to its authority to regard the many and great things in which we agree rather than the few and minor things in which we differ; and, turning from the paths of controversy, to devote their energies to the great and urgent work of the Church, which is the proclamation of the Gospel and the edifying of the Body of Christ."

From the aforesaid action, decision and final judgment of the said Presbytery of New York, sitting in a judicial capacity, taken on the ninth day of January, 1893, being the final judgment of the said Presbytery in the case of the Presbyterian Church in the United States of America against the Rev. Charles A. Briggs, D. D., in behalf of the Presbyterian Church in the United States of America, we, the undersigned, the Prosecuting Committee in the said case, do hereby appeal to your Venerable Body, the General Assembly of the Presbyterian Church in the United States of America, in accordance with the provisions of Sections 94 to 102, inclusive, of the Book of Discipline.

Under the provisions of Section IV. of Chapter XI. of the Form of Government of said Presbyterian Church, the decision of a Synod on an Appeal which affects the doctrine of the Church, is not final.

Section V. of Chapter XII. of the said Form of Government devolves upon the General Assembly "the power of deciding in all controversies respecting doctrine and discipline; of reproving, warning, or bearing testimony against error in doctrine * * * in any church, presbytery or synod."

Section IV. of the same Chapter provides that "The General Assembly shall receive and issue all Appeals * * * that affect the doctrine or constitution of the Church, which may be regularly brought before them from the inferior judicatories."

Under these Sections of the Form of Government and Section 102 of the Book of Discipline, the Appeal from the former Judgment dismissing this case was taken by the Prosecuting Committee, in behalf of the said Presbyterian Church, directly from the Presbytery of New York to the General Assembly. The Supreme Court of the Church, after full discussion, assumed jurisdiction of the case, entertained the Appeal, and, after further full argument, sustained the same.

The General Assembly, in reversing the former Judgment of the Presbytery, directed that the case should be tried upon its merits by the Presbytery of New York, and from the result of that trial it is proper that the Appeal should be made directly to the higher Judicatory, which has already entertained jurisdiction of the case.

The status of the Prosecuting Committee, as representing the Presbyterian Church in the United States of America, as an original party, under Sections 10 and 11 of the Book of Discipline, having been sustained by the General Assembly of 1892, the Committee is charged with conducting the prosecution in all its stages, in whatever Judicatory, until the final issue be reached.

The Prosecuting Committee cannot accept the decision of the Presbytery of New York as final, and not take an appeal therefrom, inasmuch as it would thereby assume the responsibility of acting for the entire Church and would surrender the Church's rights and the only opportunity of securing a final determination, by the General Assembly, of the questions at issue which involve most important and fundamental doctrines.

As the Book of Discipline, Section 96, provides that written Notice of Appeal, with the specifications of the errors alleged, shall be given within ten days after the Judgment has been rendered, the Prosecuting Committee must act promptly, and without being able to obtain in advance the instruction or wishes of the only body representing the entire Church, namely, the General Assembly.

If the action of the Committee in taking this Appeal does not commend itself to the court of last resort it need not be entertained, and the Appeal can be dismissed without prejudice to any interest.

Under ordinary conditions the Prosecuting Committee would have taken this Appeal to the Synod of New York, but it does not appear to be best to do so in this exceptional case for the following reasons:

1. To secure the peace and quiet of the Church it is essential that a final determination of the fundamental and important questions involved should be reached by the Court of last resort at the earliest practicable date.

2. As this case involves doctrine, it must be finally determined by the General Assembly. The delay in reaching an ultimate decision through an appeal by way of the Synod could not be less than a year, during which the character of instruction given our candidates for the gospel ministry might be unfavorably affected. By securing the speedy decision of the Court of last resort in this case, neither the rights nor the interests of any individual would suffer.

3. If the Appeal should go to the Synod of New York and be passed upon by that Judicatory, when the case reaches the General Assembly by appeal from the decision of the Synod, all of the Presbyteries constituting that Synod would be excluded from representation in the final determination of these important questions. If the Appeal goes directly to the Assembly, the Commissioners from only one Presbytery in the entire Church would be excluded from sitting, deliberating and voting in the final decision. In the Synod of New York there are thirty-two Presbyteries, nearly fifteen per cent. of the

whole number of Presbyteries in the Church. Inasmuch as all these Presbyteries, excepting one, would be fully represented and heard in the General Assembly, and the General Assembly alone can give a final decision, we believe the time and the interests of the Synod of New York will be best conserved if the Assembly should entertain the Appeal according to the Committee's request. This important consideration of having these questions finally determined by the representatives of substantially the entire Church, apart from the other reasons above mentioned, would seem to require, in the interest of fairness and justice to all concerned, that the Prosecuting Committee should take an Appeal directly to the General Assembly, and that the General Assembly should entertain said Appeal.

The grounds of this appeal are as follows:

FIRST GROUND OF APPEAL.

IRREGULARITY IN THE PROCEEDINGS OF SAID PRESBYTERY OF NEW YORK.

(Section 95, Book of Discipline.)

SPECIFICATION FIRST.

In this, that in consideration of objections offered by the accused the Presbytery of New York, sitting in a judicial capacity, required the Prosecuting Committee to amend the Amended Charges and Specifications submitted to said Presbytery on the 9th day of November, 1892, by striking out Charge IV., said Charge IV. being in substance an essential part of the original Charges and Specifications in the case sent down by the last General Assembly to the said Presbytery, with instructions that the said case be brought to issue and tried on the merits thereof.

SPECIFICATION SECOND.

In this, that in consideration of objections offered by the accused the said Presbytery required the said Prosecuting Committee to amend the Amended Charges and Specifications by striking out Charge VII.; said Charge VII. being in substance an essential part of the original Charges and Specifications in the case sent down by the last General Assembly to the said Presbytery, with instructions that the said case be brought to issue and tried on the merits thereof.

SPECIFICATION THIRD.

In this, that the said Presbytery, before proceeding to trial, directed the transference of the proofs cited by the Prosecuting Committee from the Scriptures, the Confession of Faith and the Catechisms, to sustain the several Specifications, from the Specifications to the Charges, by the following action, to wit: "Without sustaining the general objection to the relevancy of the proofs from the Scriptures, Catechisms and Confession, the Presbytery directs the transference of these proofs from the Specifications to the Charges."

SPECIFICATION FOURTH.

In this, that the Moderator of the Presbytery, the Rev. John C. Bliss, D. D., without submitting the question to the Judicatory, ruled that the Rev. Joseph J. Lampe, D. D., speaking as a member of the Prosecuting Committee, introduced new matter in his argument in reply to the argument of the accused, and without specifying the alleged new matter, the Presbytery, after the close of the argument of the said Rev. Joseph J. Lampe, D. D., on behalf of the Prosecuting Committee, took the following action, to wit:

"Resolved, that the Presbytery now give the defendant an opportunity to reply."

SPECIFICATION FIFTH.

In this, that by the ruling of the Moderator, referred to in Specification Fourth, the said Prosecuting Committee were refused the opportunity to close the case, contrary to the practice and precedents in such cases in the Judicatories of the Presbyterian Church in the United States of America.

SPECIFICATION SIXTH.

In this, that, notwithstanding the fact that the said Dr. Briggs declined to be sworn as a witness when called upon, the said Presbytery accepted statements or explanations of the language used by the said accused, or disclaimers on the part of the said accused, and gave to said statements, explanations or disclaimers in the final judgment of the said Presbytery, the force of such sworn, approbated and subscribed testimony, as is described or referred to in Sections 61 and 62 of the Book of Discipline.

SPECIFICATION SEVENTH.

In this, that there was placed upon or in the Official Stenographic Report of the proceedings of the said Judicatory, of December 5th, 1892, as furnished to the parties by the Stenographer, beginning at the last line on page 448 (erased page No. 461) to a point below the middle of page 468 (erased page No. 481), about twenty pages, which said twenty pages contain words and matter which were not spoken upon the floor of the Presbytery, and, as is stated by the Stenographer, were introduced into the Stenographic Report upon the request or suggestion of Prof. Briggs, with the approval of the Moderator, and after it had been announced to the Judicatory that both of the parties had fully presented their evidence, and after the argument of the Prosecuting Committee had been begun.

SPECIFICATION EIGHTH.

In this, that there was placed upon or in the Official Stenographic Report of the proceedings of the said Judicatory, beginning at page 468 of said Official Stenographic Report of the proceedings of the said Presbytery, held on Monday, December 5th, 1892, fifteen or more additional printed sheets, which said fifteen or more additional printed sheets contain words and matter which were not spoken upon the floor of the Presbytery, and were introduced by the Stenographer into the official Stenographic Report of the proceedings, as said Stenographic Report of December 6, 1892 shows, (page 578), upon the request or suggestion of Prof. Briggs and by direction of the Moderator, and after it had been announced to the Judicatory that both of the parties had fully presented their evidence, and after the argument of the Prosecuting Committee had been begun.

SPECIFICATION NINTH.

In this, that the request of the Prosecuting Committee that such part of the Stenographic Report described and referred to in Specifications Seventh and Eighth as twenty pages and fifteen or more additional printed sheets, respectively, should be stricken out and that the accused should not be permitted to refer to or use any portion of such matter, or the books or documents therein referred to, as evidence upon the trial, was refused by the said Judicatory, and in this, that the record of said request was stricken from the Minutes of the said Presbytery. (See Records of the New York Presbytery, Vol. 14, pp. 395, 396.)

SPECIFICATION TENTH.

In this, that after the Prosecuting Committee had objected to the insertion into the Official Stenographer's Report of certain words and matter, said matter being upon about twenty pages of the Stenographer's notes, and fifteen or more printed sheets being the pages and printed sheets referred to in Specification Seventh and Eighth, which said words and matter were not spoken on the floor of the Presbytery, and after the said Prosecuting Committee had requested that the said twenty pages and the said fifteen or more printed sheets should be stricken out, and that the accused should not be permitted to refer to or to use any portion of such matter or the books or documents therein referred to, as evidence upon the trial, and in this, that the said Presbytery, while retaining as a part of the Stenographer's Report, the said twenty pages and the said fifteen or more printed sheets, voted to strike out of the Minutes the said record of the request of the said Prosecuting Committee.

SPECIFICATION ELEVENTH.

In this, that when the vote was taken on the said Charges and Specifications, the said Presbytery refused to permit any of the members of the said Judicatory to vote, to "Sustain in part," contrary to the precedents and practice of the judicial procedure of the Presbyterian Church in the United States of America.

SPECIFICATION TWELFTH.

In this, that the said Presbytery required that each item in Charges I., II., III., V. and VI. should be voted upon separately, thereby implying and proceeding upon the theory, which was not warranted by the facts, that each of said Charges contained more than one offence. (See Records of the New York Presbytery, Vol. 14, p. 368.)

SECOND GROUND OF APPEAL.

RECEIVING IMPROPER TESTIMONY.

(Section 95, Book of Discipline.)

SPECIFICATION FIRST.

In this, that notwithstanding the fact that the said accused declined to be sworn as a witness when called upon, the said Presbytery accepted statements or explanations of the language used by the said accused or disclaimers on the part of the said accused and gave to said statements, explanations or disclaimers, in the final judgment of the said Presbytery, the force of such sworn, approbated and subscribed testimony as is described or referred to in Sections 61 and 62 of the Book of Discipline.

SPECIFICATION SECOND.

In this, that the Moderator, at the request of the said accused, instructed the Stenographer, as appears by page 578 of the Stenographer's Report of the proceedings of December 6th, 1892, to insert, beginning at the last line on page 448 (erased page No. 461), to a point below the middle of page 468 (erased page No. 481) of the Official

Stenographer's Report of the proceedings of the Judicatory at its session on Monday, December 5th, about twenty pages of stenographic notes, and also fifteen or more additional printed sheets beginning at page 468 of the Official Stenographic Report, the statements and matter contained in the said twenty pages of said Stenographer's notes, and in the said fifteen or more additional printed sheets, being matter or statements which were not spoken upon the floor of the Presbytery, and which were permitted to remain as a part of the Stenographer's Official Report and were received by the said Judicatory as competent evidence.

SPECIFICATION THIRD.

In this, that the Presbytery admitted as lawful and competent testimony any part of the quotations made by the accused, in so far as they were writings or extracts from the writings of the said accused, without his having first taken the oath or affirmation required by Section 61 of the Book of Discipline.

THIRD GROUND OF APPEAL.

DECLINING TO RECEIVE IMPORTANT TESTIMONY.

(Section 95, Book of Discipline.)

SPECIFICATION FIRST.

In this, that the said Presbytery instructed the said Prosecuting Committee to strike out Amended Charge IV., thereby declining to permit the said Committee to prove said Charge IV. by competent evidence.

SPECIFICATION SECOND.

In this, that the said Presbytery instructed the said Prosecuting Committee to strike out Amended Charge VII., thereby declining to permit the said Committee to prove said Charge VII. by competent evidence.

FOURTH GROUND OF APPEAL.

Manifestation of Prejudice in the Conduct of the Case.

(Section 95, Book of Discipline.)

SPECIFICATION FIRST.

In this, that several members, hereinafter named, of the said Presbytery, sitting in a judicial capacity, who afterwards voted not to sustain each and every one of the Specifications and Charges, made statements upon the floor of the Presbytery, respectively, as hereinafter set forth, to wit:

Rev. George Alexander, D. D., said:

"What seems to me strange, Mr. Moderator, is that one of Dr. Shedd's acknowledged logical faculty should be so blind to the distinction that ought to be made. I could adopt as my own every word of that which he quoted from Dr. Briggs, and I am not a Restorationist. The Lord has done great things for me whereof I am glad, and I confidently believe that he is going to do a great deal more for me hereafter. But that has nothing to do with the question as to whether Dr. Briggs holds that there is redemption in the world to come for those who die in sin. The difficulty is, that this Charge imputes to Dr. Briggs views which he distinctly says he does not hold." * * * "When Dr. Briggs intimated a suspicion that the Prosecuting Committee might be holding back deliberately with testimony or evidence in order to crush him with it after the opportunity for response had gone by, I resented that suspicion, and if it had been in order I should have risen in my place and asked him to withdraw those words because it seemed to me an unworthy suspicion. Now, that the suspicion seems to be justified by the event, I am at a loss what to say. I am puzzled and distressed. The members of this Prosecuting Committee are my personal friends; I cannot believe that there is one of them that would consciously do an injustice. I won't believe it, but I cannot shrink from the fact that a wrong has been done in some way and the more I think of it and the more I think of the defendant, from whom I differ so widely, worn out and weak and suffering from this terrific strain, required now to meet this fresh assault—why, the more every drop of Anglo-Saxon blood in me protests against it. We cannot remedy the wrong. All that we can do is to give the defendant, if he desires it (I hope he will not desire it), an opportunity to meet this fresh evidence and this fresh argument; giving him reasonable time to prepare his defense, and, if need be, giving the prosecution the last word. I should not object to that at all. But, having spent so much time, we cannot afford to seem, even, to do an injustice to any one."

Rev. Antonio Arreghi, said:

"An engagement made long before this Court, and made out of fidelity to my work, renders it impossible for me to attend at the sessions of this Court to-morrow and the day after. I therefore ask the unanimous consent of the House to excuse me for those two days. It seems to me a great injustice because I have an engagement, over which I have no control in the least, and if I am not enrolled, it deprives me of the right to vote on this trial. I may say right here that it is well known by the Brethren on which side of the House each man stands on this floor." [Cries of No! no!].

Rev. Henry M. Field, D.D., said:

"I wish at the beginning of this trial we might have one vote that could be unanimous. We are all anxious to hurry on this matter as much as possible. I believe our excellent friends of the Prosecuting Committee would be very glad if this Presbytery would relieve them of the necessity of pressing these two portions of their Charges. Let us be unanimous. I do not think Col. McCook would be at all sorry to have these two Charges stricken out. There are enough Charges left any way to sink a ship. Let us go to trial on them and, if possible, unite in this first disposal of these two Charges, which will be a most happy and auspicious omen for all the rest."

Rev. Thomas S. Hastings, D.D., said:

"The change is radical, in my judgment, between this amended Charge IV. and what was in the former Charges. It gives the lie direct. That is the plain English of it and there is no getting around that by any casuist. Dr. Briggs has told this Presbytery that he does not hold such views, and in his demurrer he has reiterated it. Now, to bring before such a body as this a Charge to try a man upon, assuming that it is doctrinal, when it is really moral—being a question whether he lies or not—is certainly a very serious and a very radical change. * * * * I said that the charge does give him the lie direct and I adhere to it. I did not say, however, that the Committee called Dr. Briggs a liar. * * * And I take it that he himself is to be accepted as an authority as to what he meant in that Inaugural Address and in anything else that he has said or published, and what has seemed to me extremely unfair and ungenerous on the part of some is the persistent effort to read into his language what he says distinctly was not in his mind and was not his intention. A man must be his own interpreter, and, as I understand it, Dr. Briggs is before this body saying that he intended no such thing as is charged against him. When a man says that about a charge, it seems to me that it is utterly out of character and out of keeping for the Presbytery to insist upon that Charge. Accept the man's disclaimer and denial and let the Charge be withdrawn."

Rev. Henry Van Dyke, D.D., said:

"I can very readily specify some new matter that has been introduced. It is quite evident that new matter has been introduced [cries of "No! no!"]. Those who do not yet see it will see it when the Court comes to vote upon it. So it is simply a matter of fairness and justice that we should allow the defendant, if he wishes it, to reply. It would be an unheard of thing in any civil Court that a prosecution should be allowed to traverse new ground and that the accused should not be allowed to be heard or to offer evidence in rebuttal. It is a thing to cause the blood of an Anglo-Saxon to boil within him, every drop of it, too. Moreover, Mr. Moderator, it is not simply that new matter has been introduced, but that statements which have been made by the defendant again and again upon this floor in respect to doctrines which he rejects, have been again attributed to him. And I maintain that it is simply a matter of fairness and candor that we should make this offer to Dr. Briggs, whether he will accept it or not, for the sake of the honor of this House and in the way of decency."

SPECIFICATION SECOND.

In this, that while the said Presbytery in obedience to the mandate of the last General Assembly has issued and tried the case, it has not tried it fully on the merits thereof, as is evinced by the striking out of Charges IV. and VII. of the Amended Charges and Specifications.

SPECIFICATION THIRD.

In this, that said Presbytery, in said final judgment, by attempting to relieve the said Prosecuting Committee from further responsibility in connection with this case appears to hinder and prevent the attainment of the ends of discipline, apparently aiming to now terminate the said case, and thus secure the same result that the said Presbytery attempted to reach on November 4th, A. D. 1891, by voting to dismiss the said case.

SPECIFICATION FOURTH.

In this, that the said Presbytery, in said final judgment, expresses "an earnest conviction that the grave issues involved in this case will be more wisely and justly determined by calm investigation and fraternal discussion than by judicial arraignment and process," notwithstanding the fact that the General Assembly directed the case to be tried on the merits thereof and thereby expressed a no less earnest conviction that the grave issues involved should be determined by judicial arraignment and process.

SPECIFICATION FIFTH.

In this, that sundry members of the said Presbytery, to wit: Rev. Francis Brown, D. D., Rev. Henry M. Field, D. D., Rev. Thomas S. Hastings, D. D., Rev. J. Hall McIlvaine, D. D., and Rev. Henry Van Dyke, D. D., sat and deliberated in the trial of this case and voted to acquit the said accused, upon each and every specificacation and charge, after manifestations of prejudice in the conduct of the case, on the part of the said members was charged in the appeal to and sustained by the General Assembly of 1892.

SPECIFICATION SIXTH.

In this, that sundry Directors, Officers and Professors of Union Theological Seminary, to wit: Rev. Francis Brown, D. D., Rev. Edward L. Clark, D. D., Rev. Charles R. Gillett, D. D., Rev. Thomas S. Hastings, D. D., Rev. J. Hall McIlvaine, D. D., Rev. Philip Schaff, D. D., Rev. W. M. Smith, D. D., Rev. Marvin R. Vincent, D. D., and William A. Wheelock, Esq., sat and deliberated in the said trial and voted to acquit the said accused upon each and every specification and charge, said Directors, Officers and Professors having previously approved and published the said Inaugural Address, as appears in the first edition which bears the imprint : " Printed for The Union Theological Seminary, New York, 1891," "Copyright, 1891, by The Union Theological Seminary," and as also appears in the second edition of said Inaugural Address, which was also " Copyright, 1891, by The Union Theological Seminary," which said Inaugural Address contained the alleged erroneous doctrines for the holding and publishing of which doctrines the accused was then on trial.

FIFTH GROUND OF APPEAL.

MISTAKE OR INJUSTICE IN THE DECISION.

SPECIFICATION FIRST.

In this, that the said Presbytery having declared the

said Amended Charges and Specifications sufficient in form and legal effect and the said accused having repeatedly admitted the facts as set forth in the said several Specifications, the said Presbytery was inconsistent and erred in not accepting the said admissions of the said accused and in not sustaining the said Charges as its final judgment.

SPECIFICATION SECOND.

In this, that the said final judgment of the said Presbytery was not warranted by the law and the evidence, because the Court had decided that the Charges were sufficient in form and legal effect; that is, it had already substantially determined that if the accused had taught the doctrine with which he was charged, he was guilty of an offence. The several Charges alleged an offence and the several allegations were proved by extracts from the Inaugural Address cited in the several Specifications, and said extracts were admitted as authentic by the accused, and were not retracted by him. The proof was therefore complete. Said accused also introduced his own writings as evidence, which writings, so introduced, contained the extracts recited by the Prosecuting Committee in the several Specifications. If the accused had brought evidence to show that he had made no such utterances as were contained in the specifications, then and then only should he have been "fully acquitted." The indictment had been found in order. The evidence was unchallenged and the judgment should have been "guilty as charged."

SPECIFICATION THIRD.

In this, that the said final judgment of the said Presbytery, which disclaims to be an expression of the approval of the critical or theological views embodied in the said Inaugural Address, is, in fact, an approval of said critical or theological views and will have the effect of encouraging the dissemination of said views and will further increase the present disquietude in the said Presbyterian Church and practically sets at naught the declaration of the General Assembly of 1892, as found on page 179 of its Minutes, in which said General Assembly "reminds all under its care that it is a fundamental doctrine that the Old and New Testaments are the inspired and infallible word of God," and that "our Church holds that the inspired Word, as it came from God, is without error. The assertion of the contrary cannot but shake the confidence of the people in the sacred Books."

SPECIFICATION FOURTH.

In this, that the said final judgment is vague and uncertain, inasmuch as said judgment gives due consideration to the defendant's explanation of the language used in his Inaugural Address and accepts his disclaimer of the interpretation which has been put upon some of its phrases and illustrations, but does not specify which explanations, phrases or illustrations, or whether such explanations or disclaimers relate to the portions of the said Inaugural Address upon which the Charges and Specifications are based, and the said judgment is also vague and uncertain in the statement that the said accused has not transgressed the limits of liberty allowed under our Constitution to scholarship and opinion.

SPECIFICATION FIFTH.

In this, that the said final judgment is based wholly, or in part, on the affirmation of loyalty made by the said defendant to the Standards of the Church and to the Holy Scriptures, as the only infallible rule of faith and practice, when such affirmations consisted only of unsworn statements, which statements were not competent evidence and should have had no greater weight or influence in shaping the final judgment than the ordinary and technical plea of "not guilty."

SPECIFICATION SIXTH.

In this, that the said Presbytery received and was moved by unsworn and improper testimony in making its decision or final judgment, said improper testimony being statements and arguments for the defence of said accused, touching the merits of the case and being explanations made by the accused of the language used in his Inaugural Address and also statements referred to in the said final judgment, as a frank and full disclaimer of the interpretation which has been put upon some of its phrases and illustrations and in giving to the argument of the said accused, as counsel in his own behalf, the consideration due to sworn and approbated testimony as provided for in Sections 61 and 62 of the Book of Discipline.

SPECIFICATION SEVENTH.

In this, that said final judgment is vague and misleading and confounds unjustifiable controversy with useful and constitutional discipline, ignoring the fact that "The ends of Discipline are the maintenance of the truth, the vindication of the authority and honor of Christ, the removal of offences, the promotion of the purity and edification of the Church, and the spiritual good of offenders." (Book of Discipline, Sec. 2.)

SPECIFICATION EIGHTH.

In this, that said final judgment is misleading and unjust, because it evidently but erroneously aims to set forth that there has been an effort to convict the accused by inference or implication, and in quoting the words "there are truths and forms with respect to which men of good character may differ," seems to deny and make light of the well-established principle of our polity, that there are also truths and forms with respect to which men of good character, who have assumed the ordination vows of a Minister in the Presbyterian Church in the United States of America, should not differ.

SPECIFICATION NINTH.

In this, that upon December 28th, 1892, when the Rev. George Alexander, D. D., offered a resolution as follows, to wit:

"The Court deems it proper to declare that a vote by any member of this Court not to sustain the charges preferred against Rev. Charles A. Briggs, D. D., does not denote approval of his theological or critical views or of the manner in which they have been advanced, but only a judgment that the specific charges have not been established," and after the said resolution had been discussed, it was laid on the table, and subsequently, after the vote on the Charges and Specifications had been taken the said resolution of Dr. Alexander was again taken up and referred to the Committee appointed to prepare the final judgment.

SPECIFICATION TENTH.

In this, that the said Presbytery, on January 9th, A. D. 1893, sitting in private session, refused to strike out of the resolution offered by Rev. Geo. Alexander, D.D., and referred to in Specification Ninth, the words, "does not denote approval of his theological or critical views or of the manner in which they have been advanced."

SPECIFICATION ELEVENTH.

In this, that the said final judgment of the said Presbytery is contradictory in form and effect, because in said final judgment the said Judicatory disclaimed agreement with the critical or theological views held by the accused, which were pronounced by said Judicatory when they voted not to sustain the charges, as in agreement with the Scriptures and the Standards. By reason of their ordination vows and obligations, the views of all the members of the said Judicatory must be assumed to have been in agreement with the Scriptures and Standards. Therefore, if the views of the accused were in agreement with the Scriptures and the Standards, and if the views of the majority of the members of the said Judicatory were not in agreement with those of the accused, then the views of the majority of the members of the said Judicatory must, according to the final judgment, have been in disagreement with the Scriptures and the Standards.

It cannot be urged that there was room for the agreement of both the views of the accused and the views of the majority of the members of the said Judicatory with the Scriptures and the Standards, because said Judicatory had already determined when the charges were pronounced sufficient in form and legal effect, that the said views, if held by the accused, constituted an offence. The Judicatory was therefore shut up to one of two legal and proper courses, either to declare that they agreed with the views of the accused, or to declare that the views of the accused disagreed with the Scriptures and the Standards. In the former case they should have refrained from disclaiming agreement with the views of the accused; in the latter case they should have voted to sustain the charges. There is, therefore, a contradiction in the form and effect of the final judgment.

And in conclusion your Appellant prays your Venerable Body, the General Assembly of the Presbyterian Church in the United States of America, to receive and issue this appeal, and to take therein such action as in your wisdom may seem best, in order to secure and preserve the purity and peace of our Church.

The Presbyterian Church in the United States of America, represented by

GEORGE W. F. BIRCH,
JOSEPH J. LAMPE,
ROBERT F. SAMPLE,
JOHN J. STEVENSON,
JOHN J. McCOOK,

Prosecuting Committee, Appellant.

PRESBYTERY OF NEW YORK.

153 East 78th Street, New York,
January 19th, 1893.

Rev. G. W. F. BIRCH, D. D.,
Chairman Prosecuting Committee.

Dear Sir:

I have received, in due time, from the Prosecuting Committee representing the Presbyterian Church in the United States of America, in the case of the said Presbyterian Church against the Rev. Charles A. Briggs, D. D., written Notice of Appeal, with specifications of the errors alleged in the said case, to the General Assembly, from the decision and final judgment of the Presbytery of New York, entered on the ninth day of January, 1893, and have placed the same on file.

Very truly yours,

S. D. ALEXANDER,
Stated Clerk.

IV.

THE FOLLOWING IS A RECORD OF ALL PROCEEDINGS HAD IN THE PRESBYTERY OF NEW YORK, AS SHOWN BY THE MINUTES OF THE JUDICATORY DURING THE TRIAL OF THE CASE.

THE MARGINAL NUMBERS INDICATE THE PAGES OF THE WRITTEN RECORD OF MINUTES OF THE PRESBYTERY.

LECTURE ROOM, SCOTCH CHURCH,

JUNE 13, 1892.

The following attested copy of the judgment of the General Assembly in the case of the Presbyterian Church in the United States of America against the Rev. Charles A. Briggs, D. D., being an appeal from the Presbytery of New York dismissing the case, was received from the Stated Clerk of the General Assembly.

THE PRESBYTERIAN CHURCH IN THE UNITED STATES OF AMERICA *against* REV. CHARLES A. BRIGGS, D. D.	*Appeal from the judgment of the Presbytery of New York, dismissing the case.*

The General Assembly having on the 28th day of May, 1892, duly sustained all of the specifications of error alleged and set forth in the appeal and specifications in this case,

It is now, May 30, 1892, ordered that the judgment of the Presbytery of New York, entered November 4, 1891, dismissing the case of the Presbyterian Church in the United States of America against Rev. Charles A. Briggs, D. D., be, and the same is hereby, reversed, and the case is remanded to the Presbytery of New York for a new trial, with directions to said Presbytery to proceed

228 to pass upon and determine the sufficiency of the charges and specifications in form and legal effect, and to permit the Prosecuting Committee to amend the specifications or charges, not changing the general nature of the same, if, in the furtherance of justice, it be necessary to amend, so that the case may be brought to issue and tried on the merits thereof as speedily as may be practicable.

And it is further ordered, that the Stated Clerk of the General Assembly return the record and certify the proceedings had thereon, with the necessary papers relating thereto, to the Presbytery of New York.

Presbytery, on motion, adopted the following:

229 *Whereas*, Presbytery has received the official notice of the action of the General Assembly in the matter of the appeal against the Presbytery in dismissing the case against the Rev. Charles A. Briggs, D. D.,

Resolved, that in the judgment of Presbytery the issue of the case is impracticable during the summer, but will receive the attention of Presbytery on its re-assembling in the fall.

---

253   BRIGGS CASE.

NEW YORK, 9TH NOVEMBER, 1892.

SCOTCH CHURCH, 2 P. M.

Presbytery met, in accordance with the direction of the General Assembly, to take up the judicial case of the Presbyterian Church in the United States of America against the Rev. Charles A. Briggs, D. D.

Constituted by prayer.

Present: Ministers—John C. Bliss, Mod'r; Geo. Alexander, Sam. D. Alexander, Anson P. Atterbury, W. Wallace Atterbury, Geo. W. F. Birch, Nicholas Bjerring, Robert R. Booth, Samuel Boult, Saml. Bowden, Thomas S. Bradner, Charles A. Briggs, Francis Brown, John M. Buchanan, Walter D. Buchanan, James Chambers, Henry B. Chapin, Edward L. Clark, John B. Devins, Ira S. Dodd, D. Stuart Dodge, Conrad Doench, Wm. Durant, Thomas

Douglas, Howard Duffield, John H. Edwards, Frank F.
Ellinwood, Henry B. Elliot, Wm. T. Elsing, Henry M.
Field, Walter B. Floyd, Jesse F. Forbes, Herbert Ford, 254
Charles H. Gardner, Charles R. Gillett, Henri Grand-
lienard, James Hall, A. Woodruff Halsey, Wm. R. Har-
shaw, Thomas S. Hastings, Spencer L. Hillier, Edward
W. Hitchcock, James H: Hoadley, James Hunter, A. D.
Lawrence Jewett, Albert B. King, Saml. M. Jackson, A.
Dunlap King, Joseph J. Lampe, Sidney G. Law, Theo-
dore Leonhard, Joseph P. Lestrade, Milton S. Littlefield,
John C. Lowrie, Daniel L. Lorenz, Geo. C. Lucas, Wm.
M. Martin, Charles P. Mallery, Francis H. Marling,
Henry M. McCracken, Henry T. McEwen, James H.
McIlvaine, Alexander H. McKinney, Alex. McLain,
Horace G. Miller, Geo. J. Mingins, William L. Moore,
James C. Nightingale, Israel H. Northrup, Geo. Nixon,
Daniel H. Overton, Charles H. Parkhurst, Levi H.
Parsons, James G. Patterson, John R. Paxton, Wm. M.
Paxton, Edward P. Payson, Geo. S. Payson, Geo. L.
Prentiss, Daniel Redmon, James S. Ramsey, Charles S.
Robinson, Stealy B. Rossiter, Albert G. Ruliffson,
Robert F. Sample, Joseph Sanderson, Wm. A. Rice,
Joseph A. Saxton, Philip Schaff, Adolphus F. Schauffler,
J. Balcom Shaw, Geo. L. Shearer, Andrew Shiland, 255
David G. Smith, Roswell D. Smith, Wilton M. Smith,
John M. Stevenson, Wm. C. Stitt, Charles A. Stoddard,
J. Ford Sutton, Alex. W. Sproull, Geo. L. Spining,
Charles L. Thompson, John J. Thompson, Charles H.
Tyndall, Henry M. Tyndal, Henry VanDyke, Marvin R.
Vincent, Abbott L. R. Waite, Thomas G. Wall, W. Scott
Watson, Geo. S. Webster, Erskine N. White, Gaylord S.
White, John T. Wilds, Livingston Willard, Geo. W.
Wood, David G. Wylie, Duncan J. McMillan.

Elders—Moses P. Brown, Adams Mem'l; James 256
Tompkins, Bethany; Albert R. Ledoux, Brick; A. P.
Ketcham, Calvary, Wm. Mickens, Central; Andrew
Robinson, Christ; James McDowell, East Harlem;
H. Edward Rowland, Fifth Ave.; Wm. McJimp-
sey, First; Geo. P. Hotaling, First Union; John

McWilliam, Fourth ; Geo. E. Sterry, Fourth Ave. ; Saml. H. Willard, Harlem ; Joseph Moorhead, Knox ; Charles H. Woodbury, Madison Square ; Robert Johnson, Morrisania First ; Thomas Anderson, New York ; G. C. King, North ; Henry Q. Hawley, Park ; James E. Ware, Phillips ; Geo. C. Lay, Puritans ; Cleveland H. Dodge, Riverdale ; Wm. M. Onderdonk, Rutgers ; Robert Houston, Scotch ; John Denham, Sea and Land ; Joseph La Boyteaux, Seventh ; James L. Wilson, Spring St. ; Wm. R. Worrall, Thirteenth St. ; Thomas Bond, University Place ; Robert Gentle, Union Tabernacle ; Wm. A. Wheelock, Washington Heights ; Robert Jaffray, West ; Clarence P. Leggett, West End ; Alex'r Wilson, W. Fifty-First St. ; Thomas Anderson, New York.

The Committee of Arrangements appointed at the last regular meeting of the Presbytery reported as follows :

257 The Committee of Arrangements would report that the instructions of Presbytery relative to the appointment of an official stenographer has been fully carried out.

We have secured the services of Mr. Charles A. Morrison, who agrees to furnish three type-written copies of the stenographic report daily, it being understood that the official report is the exclusive property of the Presbytery.

The Committee also reports that sufficient space has been reserved for members of the Presbytery and visiting clergymen, and the families of those most interested in the proceedings ; the remainder of the space to be open to the public.

The report was accepted and adopted.

258 By direction of Presbytery, the Moderator appointed, as an additional temporary clerk, the Rev. Thomas Douglas.

The Moderator now announced that the Body was now about to be constituted a Court of Jesus Christ, and he solemnly admonished the members of Presbytery to recollect and regard the high character of the position they were to occupy as Judges.

The following action of the General Assembly was then read. (See page 227 of this volume.)

Whereupon the Moderator asked if the Charges and Specifications, before presented, were to be those upon which the trial was to proceed, or if the Prosecuting Committee wished to present amended Charges and Specifications.

Dr. Briggs then submitted the following objections to the procedure:

I do hereby submit to Presbytery the following objections to the procedure: 259

1. A Committee originally appointed to "arrange and prepare the necessary proceedings appropriate in the case of Dr. Briggs," appears before you claiming to be a *Committee of Prosecution*, and they are recognized as such by the Moderator, giving them the floor to act in that capacity. But their right so to act is legally questioned by complaint to the Synod of New York, and it has not yet been lawfully determined by the Synod.

2. This Committee appeared before the last General Assembly as *an original party*, and acted as such by presenting an appeal against the judgment of the Presbytery in dismissing the case against me. They now appear before you as an original party, successful in their appeal. Their right to act as an original party is questioned in the said complaint, and it has not been lawfully 260 determined by the Synod.

3. This Committee claims to represent the Presbyterian Church in the United States of America, and to be *independent of this Presbytery which appointed them*. They acted independently of the Presbytery by appealing to the General Assembly against the judgment of the Presbytery in dismissing the case against me. They now appear before you with a reversal of the judgment of the Presbytery which they have obtained. Their right to act independently of the Presbytery is questioned in the said complaint and it has not yet been lawfully determined by the Synod.

261 4. This Committee appears before you, having acted, as is claimed, in violation of the Constitution of the Church, which provides that when a complaint has been signed by more than one-third of those present and voting in the Presbytery, it acts *as a stay to further proceedings*. The above-mentioned complaint, signed by a majority of the voters, has been filed with the Synod of New York, and has been found in order by the Synod of New York, and is now in possession of that Synod. Until the questions raised in such complaint have been determined, this Committee cannot legally take any action in the matters complained of. They cannot act as a Prosecuting Committee, or as an original party, or as independent of the Presbytery, and you cannot allow them so to act without a violation of the law of complaint embedded in the Constitution of the Church.

Inasmuch as the Synod of New York suggested that the complainants, being, according to the number of signers in the complaint, a majority of the Presbytery, "may have the remedy in their own hands," the Presbytery are respectfully requested to apply the said remedy and in accordance with the provision of the Book of Discipline, to determine these preliminary objections.

[Signed.] C. A. BRIGGS.

262 Elder John J. McCook, of the Prosecuting Committee, was then heard in reply to these objections.

A point of order was here raised as to whether anything is in order except the consideration of the specific action of the General Assembly.

The Moderator decided that the point of order was well taken. That the raising of the question of the status of the Prosecuting Committee and of its right to appear and continue the conduct of this case is not now in order for these reasons:

1st. That this whole question was fully discussed and decided by the Judicial Committee of the General Assembly.

2d. That the recognition of the status of the Committee and its powers as defined in the appeal were embodied in the Judicial Committee's report, recommending the entertainment of the appeal.

3d. That in the minutes of the General Assembly, giving its findings in the case, the Committee's status is clearly recognized.

4th. That the protest recorded in the minutes of the General Assembly by those objecting to its action, was based, on the fact, that its action in entertaining the appeal gave the committee the standing and powers claimed for it; and

Lastly. That the order sending the case again to this Presbytery, requiring us to proceed to pass upon and determine the sufficiency of the Charges and Specifications, as to form and legal effect, and to proceed with the trial, this being the single point before us to be acted upon, therefore the Moderator's decision is, that this question is out of order.

An appeal to the house against the Moderator's decision was then taken. On a vote being taken, a division was called for, which resulted in 78 to 58 in favor of the Moderator's decision.

Dr. Briggs then gave notice of an appeal and complaint to the Synod.

The Prosecuting Committee now declared that they were ready to present Amended Charges and Specifications.

Dr. Briggs assented.

On motion they were permitted to present such Amended Charges and Specifications as follows:

PRESBYTERY OF NEW YORK.

The Presbyterian Church in the United States
of America
AGAINST
The Rev. Charles A. Briggs, D. D.

AMENDED CHARGES AND SPECIFICATIONS.

CHARGE I.

The Presbyterian Church in the United States of America charges the Rev. Charles A. Briggs, D. D., being a Minister of the said Church and a member of the Presbytery of New York, with teaching that the Reason is a fountain of divine authority which may and does savingly enlighten men, even such men as reject the Scriptures as the authoritative proclamation of the will of God and reject also the way of salvation through the mediation and sacrifice of the Son of God as revealed therein; which is contrary to the essential doctrine of the Holy Scripture and of the Standards of the said Church, that the Holy Scripture is most necessary, and the rule of faith and practice.

SPECIFICATION I.

In an Inaugural Address, which the said Rev. Charles A. Briggs, D. D., delivered at the Union Theological Seminary in the City of New York, January 20th, 1891, on the occasion of his induction into the Edward Robinson Chair of Biblical Theology, which Address has been published and extensively circulated with the knowledge and approval of the said Rev. Charles A. Briggs, D. D., and has been republished by him in a second edition with a preface and an appendix, there occur the following sentences:

Page 24, lines 7-10 and 31-33 :

"Divine authority is the only authority to which man can yield implicit obedience, on which he can rest in loving certainty and build with joyous confidence. * * * There are historically three great fountains of divine authority—the Bible, the Church, and the Reason."

Page 27, lines 9 to 21 :

"Martineau could not find divine authority in the Church or the Bible, but he did find God enthroned in his own soul. There are those who would refuse these rationalists a place in the company of the faithful. But they forget that the essential thing is to find God and divine certainty, and if these men have found God without the mediation of Church and Bible, Church and Bible are means and not ends ; they are avenues to God, but are not God. We regret that these rationalists depreciate the means of grace so essential to most of us, but we are warned lest we commit a similar error, and depreciate the reason and the Christian consciousness."

Inaugural Address, Appendix, Second Edition, pages 88, 89 :

"(c.) Unless God's authority is discerned in the forms of the Reason, there is no ground upon which any of the heathen could ever have been saved, for they know nothing of Bible or Church. If they are not savingly enlightened by the Light of the World in the forms of the Reason the whole heathen world is lost forever."

SPECIFICATION II.

In an Inaugural Address, which the said Rev. Charles A. Briggs, D. D., delivered at the Union Theological Seminary in the City of New York, January 20th, 1891, on the occasion of his induction into the Edward Robinson Chair of Biblical Theology, which Address has been published and extensively circulated with the knowledge and approval of the said Rev. Charles A. Briggs, D. D., and has been republished by him in a second edition with a preface and an appendix, there occur the following sentences:

Page 28, lines 1 to 22:

"(3.) *The Authority of Holy Scripture.*—We have examined the Church and the Reason as seats of divine authority in an introduction to our theme, *the Authority of the Scriptures*, because they open our eyes to see mistakes that are common to the three departments. Protestant Christianity builds its faith and life on the divine authority contained in the Scriptures, and too often depreciates the Church and the Reason. Spurgeon is an example of the average modern Evangelical, who holds the Protestant position, and assails the Church and Reason in the interest of the authority of Scripture. But the average opinion of the Christian world would not assign him a higher place in the kingdom of God than Martineau or Newman. May we not conclude, on the whole, that these three representative Christians of our time, living in or near the world's metropolis, have, each in his way, found God and rested on divine authority? May we not learn from them not to depreciate any of the means whereby God makes himself known to men? Men are influenced by their temperaments and environments which of the three ways of access to God they may pursue."

These declarations are contrary to Scripture:

Isaiah viii. 20. To the law and to the testimony: if they speak not according to this word, *it is* because *there is* no light in them.

Matt. x. 32, 33.—32 Whosoever therefore shall confess me before men, him will I confess also before my Father which is in heaven. 33 But whosoever shall deny me before men, him will I also deny before my Father which is in heaven.

Luke xvi. 29–31.—29 Abraham saith unto him, They have Moses and the prophets; let them hear them. 30 And he said, Nay, father Abraham: but if one went unto them from the dead, they will repent. 31 And he said unto him, If they hear not Moses and the prophets, neither will they be persuaded, though one rose from the dead.

John v. 39. Search the Scriptures; for in them ye think ye have eternal life; And they are they which testify of me.

John xiv. 6. Jesus saith unto him, I am the way, and the truth, and the life: no man cometh unto the Father, but by me.

1 John v. 10. He that believeth on the Son of God hath the witness in himself: he that believeth not God hath made him a liar, because he believeth not the record that God gave of his Son.

Gal. i. 9. As we said before, so say I now again, If any *man* preach any other gospel unto you than that ye have received, let him be accursed. 271

2 Timothy iii. 15-17.—15 And that from a child thou hast known the Holy Scriptures, which are able to make thee wise unto salvation through faith which is in Christ Jesus. 16 All Scripture *is* given by inspiration of God, and *is* profitable for doctrine, for reproof, for correction, for instruction in righteousness: 17 That the man of God may be perfect, thoroughly furnished unto all good works.

2 Peter i. 19-21.—19 We have also a more sure word of prophecy; whereunto ye do well that ye take heed, as unto a light that shineth in a dark place, until the day dawn, and the day star arise in your hearts: 20 Knowing this first, that no prophecy of the Scripture is of any private interpretation. 21 For the prophecy came not in old time by the will of man: but holy men of God spake *as they were* moved by the Holy Ghost.

These declarations are contrary to the Standards: 272
Confession of Faith, Chap. I., Secs. I., V., VI., X.

I. Although the light of nature, and the works of creation and providence, do so far manifest the goodness, wisdom, and power of God, as to leave men inexcusable; *yet they are not sufficient to give that knowledge of God, and of his will, which is necessary unto salvation; therefore it pleased the Lord*, at sundry times, and in divers manners, to reveal himself, and *to declare that his will* unto his church; *and afterwards*, for the better preserving and propagating of the truth, and for the more sure establishment and comfort of the church against the corruption of the flesh, and the malice of Satan and of the world, *to commit the same wholly unto writing: which maketh the Holy Scripture to be most necessary;* those former ways of God's revealing his will unto his people being now ceased.

V. We may be moved and induced by the testimony of the church to an high and reverent esteem for the Holy Scripture; and the heavenliness of the matter, the efficacy of the doctrine, the majesty of the style, the consent of all the parts, the scope of the whole, (which is to give all glory to God,) the full discovery it makes of *the only way of man's salvation,* the many other incomparable excellencies, and the entire perfection thereof, are arguments whereby it doth abundantly evidence itself to be the word of God; yet, notwithstanding, our full persuasion and assurance of the infallible truth, and divine authority thereof, is from the inward work of the Holy Spirit, *bearing witness by and with the word in our hearts.*

VI. *The whole counsel of God, concerning all things necessary for his own glory, man's salvation, faith, and life, is either expressly set down in Scripture, or by good and necessary consequence may be deduced from Scripture: unto which nothing at any time is to be added, whether by new revelations of the Spirit, or traditions of men.* Nevertheless we acknowledge the inward illumination of the Spirit of God to be necessary for the saving understanding of such things as are revealed in the word; and that there are some circumstances concerning the worship of God, and government of the church, common to human actions and societies, which are to be ordered by the light of nature and Christian prudence, according to the general rules of the word, which are always to be observed.

X. *The Supreme Judge,* by which all controversies of religion are to be determined, and all decrees of councils,

opinions of ancient writers, doctrines of men, and private 275
spirits, are to be examined, and in whose sentence we
are to rest, *can be no other but the Holy Spirit speaking
in the Scripture.*

Larger Catechism.

Q. 2. *How doth it appear that there is a God?*

A. The very light of nature in man, and the works of
God, declare plainly that there is a God; *but his word
and Spirit only,* do sufficiently and effectually reveal
him unto men for their salvation.

Q. 3. *What is the Word of God?*

A. The Holy Scriptures of the Old and New Testament are the word of God, *the only rule of faith and obedience.*

Shorter Catechism.

Q. 2. *What rule hath God given to direct us how we may glorify and enjoy him?*

A. The word of God, which is contained in the Scriptures of the Old and New Testaments, is the *only rule to direct us how we may glorify and enjoy him.*

CHARGE II. 319

The Presbyterian Church in the United States of
America charges the Rev. Charles A. Briggs, D. D., being
a Minister of the said. Church and a member of the
Presbytery of New York, with teaching that the Church
is a fountain of divine authority which, apart from the
Holy Scripture, may and does savingly enlighten men;
which is contrary to the essential doctrine of the Holy
Scripture and of the Standards of the said Church, that
the Holy Scripture is most necessary and the rule of faith
and practice.

SPECIFICATION I.

In an inaugural address, which the said Rev. Charles
A. Briggs, D. D., delivered at the Union Theological Seminary in the City of New York, January 20, 1891, on the 320

occasion of his induction into the Edward Robinson Chair of Biblical Theology, which Address has been published and extensively circulated with the knowledge and approval of the said Rev. Charles A. Briggs, D. D., and has been republished by him in a second edition with a preface and an appendix, there occur the following sentences :

Page 24, lines 7-10 and 31-33 :

" Divine authority is the only authority to which man can yield implicit obedience, on which he can rest in loving certainty and build with joyous confidence. * * * There are historically three great fountains of divine authority—the Bible, the Church, and the Reason.

Page 25, lines 1 to 14, inclusive :

"(1.) *The Authority of the Church.*—The majority of Christians from the apostolic age have found God through the Church. Martyrs and Saints, Fathers and Schoolmen, the profoundest intellects, the saintliest lives, have had this experience. Institutional Christianity has been to them the presence-chamber of God. They have therein and thereby entered into communion with all saints. It is difficult for many Protestants to regard this experience as any other than pious illusion and delusion. But what shall we say of a modern like Newman, who could not reach certainty, striving never so hard, through the Bible or the Reason, but who did find divine authority in the institutions of the Church ? "

SPECIFICATION II.

In an Inaugural Address, which the said Rev. Charles A. Briggs, D. D., delivered at the Union Theological Seminary in the City of New York, January 20, 1891, on the occasion of his induction into the Edward Robinson Chair of Biblical Theology, which Address has been published and extensively circulated with the knowledge and approval of the said Rev. Charles A. Briggs, D. D., and has been republished by him in a second edition with a preface and an appendix, there occur the following sentences:

Page 28, lines 1 to 22, are:

"(3.) *The Authority of Holy Scripture.*—We have examined the Church and the Reason as seats of divine authority in an introduction to our theme, the *Authority of the Scriptures*, because they open our eyes to see mistakes that are common to the three departments. Protestant Christianity builds its faith and life on the divine authority contained in the Scriptures, and too often depreciates the Church and the Reason. Spurgeon is an example of the average modern Evangelical, who holds the Protestant position, and assails the Church and Reason in the interest of the authority of Scripture. But the average opinion of the Christian world would not assign him a higher place in the kingdom of God than Martineau or Newman. May we not conclude, on the whole, that these three representative Christians of our time, living in or near the world's metropolis, have, each in his way, found God and rested on divine authority? May we not learn from them not to depreciate any of the means whereby God makes himself known to men? Men are influenced by their temperaments and environments which of the three ways of access to God they may pursue."

These declarations are contrary to the Holy Scripture.

Isaiah viii. 20. To the law and to the testimony: if they speak not according to this word, *it is* because *there is* no light in them.

Matt. x. 32, 33.—32 Whosoever therefore shall confess me before men, him will I confess also before my Father which is in heaven. 33 But whosoever shall deny me before men, him will I also deny before my Father which is in heaven.

Luke xvi. 29-31.—29 Abraham saith unto him, They have Moses and the prophets; let them hear them. 30 And he said, Nay, father Abraham: but if one went unto them from the dead, they will repent. 31 And he said unto him, If they hear not Moses and the prophets, neither will they be persuaded, though one rose from the dead.

John v. 39. Search the Scriptures; for in them ye think ye have eternal life; And they are they which testify of me.

John xiv. 6. Jesus saith unto him, I am the way, and the truth and the life: no man cometh unto the Father but by me.

1 John v. 10. He that believeth on the Son of God hath the witness in himself: he that believeth not God, hath made him a liar, because he believeth not the record that God gave of his Son.

Gal. i. 9. As we said before, so say I now again, if any *man* preach any other gospel unto you than that ye have received, let him be accursed.

2 Timothy iii. 15-17.—15 And that from a child thou hast known the Holy Scriptures, which are able to make thee wise unto salvation through faith which is in Christ Jesus. 16 All Scripture *is* given by inspiration of God, and *is* profitable for doctrine, for reproof, for correction, for instruction in righteousness: 17 That the man of God may be perfect, thoroughly furnished unto all good works.

2 Peter i. 19-21.—19 We have also a more sure word of prophecy; whereunto ye do well that ye take heed, as unto a light that shineth in a dark place, until the day dawn, and the day star arise in your hearts: 20 Knowing this first, that no prophecy of the Scripture is of any private interpretation. 21 For the prophecy came not in old time by the will of man: but Holy men of God spake *as they were* moved by the Holy Ghost.

These declarations are contrary to the Standards:

Confession of Faith, Chap. 1., Secs. I., V., VI., X.

I. Although the light of nature, and the works of creation and providence, do so far manifest the goodness, wisdom, and power of God, as to leave men inexcusable; *yet they are not sufficient to give that knowledge of God, and of his will, which is necessary unto salvation; therefore it pleased the Lord*, at sundry times, and in divers manners, to reveal himself, and *to declare that his will* unto his church; *and afterwards,* for the better preserving and propagating of the truth, and for the more sure establishment and comfort of the church against the corruption of the flesh, and the malice of Satan and of the world, to *commit the same wholly unto writing: which maketh the Holy Scripture to be most necessary;* those former ways of God's revealing his will unto his people being now ceased. 327

V. We may be moved and induced by the testimony of the church to an high and reverent esteem for the Holy Scripture; and the heavenliness of the matter, the efficacy of the doctrine, the majesty of the style, the consent of all the parts, the scope of the whole, (which is to give all glory to God,) the full discovery it makes of *the only way of man's salvation,* the many other incomparable excellencies, and the entire perfection thereof, are arguments whereby it doth abundantly evidence itself to be the word of God; yet, notwithstanding, our full persuasion and assurance of the infallible truth, and divine authority thereof, is from the inward work of the Holy Spirit, *bearing witness by and with the word in our hearts.* 328

VI. *The whole counsel of God, concerning all things necessary for his own glory, man's salvation, faith, and life, is either expressly set down in Scripture, or by good and necessary consequence may be deduced from Scripture: unto which nothing at any time is to be added, whether by new revelations of the Spirit, or traditions of men.* Nevertheless we acknowledge the inward illumination of the Spirit of God to be necessary for the saving understanding of such things as are revealed in the word; and that there are some circumstances concerning the worship of God, and government of the church, common to human actions and societies, which are to be ordered by the light of nature and Christian prudence, according to the general rules of the word, which are always to be observed. 329

X. *The Supreme Judge,* by which all controversies of religion are to be determined, and all decrees of councils, opinions of ancient writers, doctrines of men, and private spirits, are to be examined, and in whose sentence we are to rest, *can be no other but the Holy Spirit speaking in the Scripture.*

Larger Catechism.

Q. 2. *How doth it appear that there is a God?*

A. The very light of nature in man, and the works of God, declare plainly that there is a God ; *but his word and Spirit only,* do sufficiently and effectually reveal him unto men for their salvation.

Q. 3. *What is the word of God?*

A. The Holy Scriptures of the Old and New Testament are the word of God, *the only rule of faith and obedience.*

330 Shorter Catechism.

Q. 2. *What rule hath God given to direct us how we may glorify and enjoy him?*

A. The word of God, which is contained in the Scriptures of the Old and New Testaments, is the *only rule to direct us how we may glorify and enjoy him.*

CHARGE III.

276 The Presbyterian Church in the United States of America charges the Rev. Charles A. Briggs, D. D., being a Minister of the said Church and a member of the Presbytery of New York, with teaching that errors may have existed in the original text of the Holy Scripture, as it came from its authors, which is contrary to the essential doctrine taught in the Holy Scripture and in the Standards of the said Church, that the Holy Scripture is the Word of God written, immediately inspired, and the rule of faith and practice.

SPECIFICATION.

In an Inaugural Address, which the said Rev. Charles A. Briggs, D. D., delivered at the Union Theological Seminary in the City of New York, January 20, 1891, on the occasion of his induction into the Edward Robin-

son Chair of Biblical Theology, which Address has been
published and extensively circulated with the knowledge
and approval of the said Rev. Charles A. Briggs, D. D.,
and has been republished by him in a second edition with
a preface and an appendix, there occur the following
sentences, beginning with line 4 of page 35 :

"I shall venture to affirm that, so far as I can see,
there are errors in the Scriptures that no one has
been able to explain away ; and the theory that they
were not in the original text is sheer assumption, upon
which no mind can rest with certainty. If such errors
destroy the authority of the Bible, it is already destroyed
for historians. Men cannot shut their eyes to truth and
fact. But on what authority do these theologians drive
men from the Bible by this theory of inerrancy ? The
Bible itself nowhere makes this claim. The creeds of the
Church nowhere sanction it. It is a ghost of modern
evangelicalism to frighten children. The Bible has maintained its authority with the best scholars of our time,
who with open minds have been willing to recognize any
error that might be pointed out by Historical Criticism ;
for these errors are all in the circumstantials and not in
the essentials ; they are in the human setting, not in the
precious jewel itself; they are found in that section of
the Bible that theologians commonly account for from
the providential superintendence of the mind of the author, as distinguished from divine revelation itself. It
maybe that this providential superintendence gives infallible guidance in every particular ; and it may be that it differs but little, if at all, from the providential superintendence of the fathers and schoolmen and theologians of the
Christian Church. It is not important for our purpose that
we should decide this question. If we should abandon
the whole field of providential superintendence so far as
inspiration and divine authority are concerned and limit
divine inspiration and authority to the essential contents of the Bible, to its religion, faith, and morals, we
would still have ample room to seek divine authority
where alone it is essential, or even important, in the teach-

ing that guides our devotions, our thinking, and our conduct."

These declarations are contrary to the statements of Scripture:

Zech. vii. 12. Yea, they made their hearts as an adamant stone, lest they should hear the law, and the words which the Lord of hosts hath sent in his Spirit by the former prophets: therefore came a great wrath from the Lord of hosts.

Mark vii. 13. Making the word of God of none effect through your tradition, which ye have delivered: and many such like things do ye.

Romans iii. 1, 2.—1 What advantage then hath the
280 Jew? or what profit *is there* of circumcision? 2 Much every way: chiefly, because that unto them were committed the oracles of God.

1 Cor. ii. 13. Which things also we speak, not in the words which man's wisdom teacheth, but which the Holy Ghost teacheth; comparing spiritual things with spiritual.

Galatians iii. 8. And the Scripture, foreseeing that God would justify the heathen through faith, preached before the Gospel unto Abraham, *saying*, In thee shall all nations be blessed.

2 Pet. i. 20, 21.—20 Knowing this first, that no prophecy of the Scripture is of any private interpretation. 21 For the prophecy came not in old time by the will of man: but holy men of God spake *as they were* moved by the Holy Ghost.

2 Tim. iii. 16. All Scripture *is* given by inspiration of God, and *is* profitable for doctrine, for reproof, for correction, for instruction in righteousness.

281 These statements are contrary to the Standards.

Confession of Faith, Chap. I., Secs. I., II., IV., VIII.

I. Although the light of nature, and the works of creation and providence do so far manifest the goodness, wisdom, and power of God, as to leave men inexcusable; yet are they not sufficient to give that knowledge of God, and of his will, which is necessary unto salvation; *there-*

fore it pleased the Lord, at sundry times, and in divers manners, to reveal himself, and to declare that his will unto his church; and afterwards, for the better preserving and propagating of the truth, and for the more sure establishment and comfort of the church against the corruption of the flesh, and the malice of Satan and of the world, to commit the same wholly unto writing; which maketh the Holy Scripture to be most necessary; those former ways of God's revealing his will unto his people being now ceased.

II. Under the name of Holy Scripture, or *the word of God written*, are now contained all the books of the Old and New Testament, which are these: 282

OF THE OLD TESTAMENT.

Genesis.	II. Chronicles.	Daniel.
Exodus.	Ezra.	Hosea.
Leviticus.	Nehemiah.	Joel.
Numbers.	Esther.	Amos.
Deuteronomy.	Job.	Obadiah.
Joshua.	Psalms.	Jonah.
Judges.	Proverbs.	Micah.
Ruth.	Ecclesiastes.	Nahum.
I. Samuel.	The Song of Songs.	Habakkuk.
II. Samuel.	Isaiah.	Zephaniah.
I. Kings.	Jeremiah.	Haggai.
II. Kings.	Lamentations.	Zechariah.
I. Chronicles.	Ezekiel.	Malachi.

OF THE NEW TESTAMENT.

The Gospels according to Matthew, Mark, Luke, John.	Corinthians II. Galatians. Ephesians. Philippians. Colossians. Thessalonians I.	The Epistle to the Hebrews. The Epistle of James. The first and second Epistles of Peter.
The Acts of the Apostles.	Thessalonians II. To Timothy, I.	The first, second and third Epistles of John.
Paul's Epistles to the Romans. Corinthians I.	To Timothy, II. To Titus. To Philemon.	The Epistle of Jude. 283 The Revelation.

All which are given by inspiration of God to be the rule of faith and life.

IV.—*The authority of the Holy Scripture*, for which it ought to be believed and obeyed, *dependeth* not upon the testimony of any man or church, *but wholly upon God*, (who is truth itself,) *the author thereof; and therefore it is to be received, because it is the word of God.*

284 VIII.—The Old Testament in Hebrew, (which was the native language of the people of God of old,) and the New Testament in Greek, (which at the time of the writing of it was most generally known to the nations,) *being immediately inspired by God*, and by his singular care and providence, kept pure in all ages, are therefore authentical; so as in all controversies of religion the Church is finally to appeal unto them. But because these original tongues are not known to all the people of God who have right unto, and interest in the Scriptures, and are commanded, in the fear of God, to read and search them, therefore they are to be translated into the vulgar language of every nation unto which they come, that the word of God dwelling plentifully in all, they may worship him in an acceptable manner, and, through patience and comfort of the Scriptures, may have hope.

CHARGE IV.

285 The Presbyterian Church in the United States of America charges the Rev. Charles A. Briggs, D.D., being a Minister in said Church and a member of the Presbytery of New York, with teaching that many of the Old Testament predictions have been reversed by history, and that the great body of Messianic prediction has not been and cannot be fulfilled, which is contrary to the essential doctrine of Holy Scripture and of the Standards of the said Church, that God is true, omniscient and unchangeable.

SPECIFICATION.

In an Inaugural Address, which the said Rev. Charles A. Briggs, D.D., delivered at the Union Theological Seminary in the City of New York, January 20, 1891, on the occasion of his induction into the Edward Robinson Chair

of Biblical Theology, which Address has been published
and extensively circulated with the knowledge and approval of the said Rev. Charles A. Briggs, D. D., and has
been republished by him in a second edition with a preface and an appendix, there occur the following sentences:

Page 38, lines 20 to 30 :

"(6.) *Minute Prediction.*—Another barrier to the
Bible has been the interpretation put upon *Predictive
Prophecy* making it a sort of history before the time, and
looking anxiously for the fulfillment of the details of
Biblical prediction. Kuenen has shown that if we insist
upon the fulfillment of the details of the predictive
prophecy of the Old Testament, many of these predictions
have been reversed by history ; and the great body of the
Messianic prediction has not only never been fulfilled, but
cannot now be fulfilled, for the reason that its own time
has passed forever."

This declaration is contrary to Scripture :

Matt. v. 17, 18.—17 Think not I am come to destroy the
law, or the prophets: I am not come to destroy, but to
fulfill. 18 For verily I say unto you, Till heaven and
earth pass, one jot or one tittle shall in no wise pass from
the law, till all be fulfilled.

Matt. xxiv. 15. When ye, therefore, shall see the
abomination of desolation, spoken of by Daniel the
prophet, stand in the holy place, (whoso readeth, let him
understand.)

Dan. xii. 11. And from the time *that* the daily *sacrifice*
shall be taken away, and the abomination that maketh
desolate set up, *there shall be* a thousand two hundred
and ninety days.

Luke xxiv. 44. And he said unto them, These *are* the
words which I spake unto you, while I was yet with you,
that all things must be fulfilled which were written in the
law of Moses, and *in* the prophets, and *in* the psalms,
concerning me.

Exodus xxxiv. 6. And the Lord passed by before him,
and proclaimed, The Lord, The Lord God, merciful and

gracious, long suffering, and abundant in goodness and truth.

Hebrews iv. 13. Neither is there any creature that is not manifest in his sight: but all things *are* naked and opened unto the eyes of him with whom we have to do.

James i. 17. Every good gift and every perfect gift is from above, and cometh down from the Father of lights, with whom is no variableness, neither shadow of turning.

This declaration is contrary to the Standards:

Confession of Faith, Chap. I., Section IV.

The authority of the Holy Scripture, for which it ought to be believed and obeyed, *dependeth* not upon the testimony of any man or church, but *wholly upon God, (who is truth itself,) the author thereof;* and therefore it is to be received, because it is the word of God.

289 Chap. II., Sec. I., II.

I. There is but one only living and true God, who is infinite in being and perfection, a most pure spirit, invisible, without body, parts, or passions, *immutable*, immense, eternal, incomprehensible, almighty, *most wise*, most holy, most free, most absolute, *working all things according to the counsel of his own immutable and most righteous will*, for his own glory; most loving, gracious, merciful, long suffering, *abundant in goodness and truth*, forgiving iniquity, transgression, and sin; the rewarder of them that diligently seek him; and withal most just and terrible in his judgments; hating all sin, and who will by no means clear the guilty.

II. God hath all life, glory, goodness, blessedness, in and of himself; and is alone in and unto himself all-sufficient, not standing in need of any creatures which he hath made, nor deriving any glory from them, but only
290 manifesting his own glory in, by, unto and upon them: he is the alone fountain of all being, of whom, through whom, and to whom, are all things: and hath most sovereign dominion over them, to do by them, for them, or upon them, whatsoever himself pleaseth. *In his sight all things are open and manifest; his knowledge is in-*

finite, infallible, and independent upon the creature, so as nothing is to him contingent or uncertain. He is most holy in all his counsels, in all his works, and in all his commands. To him is due from angels and men, and every other creature, whatsoever worship, service, or obedience, he is pleased to require of them.

Shorter Catechism.

Q. 4. *What is God?*

A. God is a Spirit, infinite, eternal, and unchangeable, in his being, wisdom, power, holiness, justice, goodness, and truth.

CHARGE V.

The Presbyterian Church in the United States of America charges the Rev. Charles A. Briggs, D. D., being a Minister of the said Church and a member of the Presbytery of New York, with teaching that Moses is not the author of the Pentateuch, which is contrary to direct statements of Holy Scripture and to the essential doctrines of the Standards of the said Church, that the Holy Scripture evidences itself to be the word of God by the consent of all the parts, and that the infallible rule of interpretation of Scripture is the Scripture itself.

SPECIFICATION.

In an Inaugural Address, which the said Rev. Charles A. Briggs, D. D., delivered at the Union Theological Seminary in the City of New York, January 20, 1891, on the occasion of his induction into the Edward Robinson Chair of Biblical Theology, which Address has been published and extensively circulated with the knowledge and approval of the said Rev. Charles A. Briggs, D. D., and has been republished by him in a second edition with a preface and an appendix, there occurs the following sentence:

Page 33, lines 6–8.

"It may be regarded as the certain result of the science of the Higher Criticism that Moses did not write the Pentateuch."

This declaration is contrary to direct statements of Scripture.

Ex. xxiv. 4. And Moses wrote all the words of the Lord, and rose up early in the morning, and builded an altar under the hill, and twelve pillars according to the twelve tribes of Israel.

Num. xxxiii. 2. And Moses wrote their goings out according to their journeys by the commandment of the Lord: and these *are* their journeys according to their goings out.

Deut. v. 31. But as for thee, stand thou here by me, and I will speak unto thee all the commandments, and the statutes, and the judgments, which thou shalt teach them, that they may do *them* in the land which I gave them to possess it.

Deut. xxxi. 9. And Moses wrote this law, and delivered it unto the priests the sons of Levi, which bare the ark of the covenant of the Lord, and unto all the elders of Israel.

Josh. i. 7, 8.—7 Only be thou strong and very courageous, that thou mayest observe to do according to all the law which Moses my servant commanded thee: turn not from it *to* the right hand or *to* the left, that thou mayest prosper whithersoever thou goest. 8 This book of the law shall not depart out of thy mouth; but thou shalt meditate therein day and night, that thou mayest observe to do according to all that is written therein: for then thou shalt make thy way prosperous, and then thou shalt have good success.

1 Kings, ii. 3. And keep the charge of the Lord thy God, to walk in his ways, to keep his statutes, and his commandments, and his judgments, and his testimonies, as it is written in the law of Moses that thou mayest prosper in all that thou doest, and whithersoever thou turnest thyself:

1 Chron. vi. 49. But Aaron and his sons offered upon the altar of the burnt offering, and on the altar of incense, *and were appointed* for all the work of the *place* most holy, and to make an atonement for Israel, according to all that Moses the servant of God had commanded.

Ezra iii. 2. Then stood up Jeshua, the son of Jozadak, and his brethren the priests, and Zerubbabel the son of Shealtiel, and his brethren, and builded the altar of the God of Israel, to offer burnt offerings thereon, as *it is* written in the law of Moses, the man of God.

Ezra vi. 18. And they set the priests in their divisions, and the Levites in their courses, for the service of God, which *is* at Jerusalem; as it is written in the book of Moses. 295

Neh. i. 7. We have dealt very corruptly against thee, and have not kept the commandments, nor the statutes, nor the judgments, which thou commandedst thy servant Moses.

Luke xxiv. 27, 44.—27 And beginning at Moses, and all the prophets, he expounded unto them in all the Scriptures the things concerning himself. 44 And he said unto them, These *are* the words which I spake unto you, while I was yet with you, that all things must be fulfilled which were written in the law of Moses, and *in* the prophets, and *in* the psalms, concerning me. 296

John v. 45 to 47.—45 Do not think that I will accuse you to the Father: there is *one* that accuseth you, *even* Moses, in whom ye trust. 46 For had ye believed Moses, ye would have believed me: for he wrote of me. 47 But if ye believe not his writings, how shall ye believe my words?

Acts vii. 38. This is he that was in the church in the wilderness with the angel which spoke to him in the Mount Sina, and *with* our fathers: who received the lively oracles to give unto us.

Acts xv. 21. For Moses of old time hath in every city them that preach him, being read in the synagogues every sabbath day.

This declaration is contrary to the Standards.

Confession of Faith, Chap. 1, Secs. V. and IX.

V. We may be moved and induced by the testimony of the church to an high and reverent esteem for the Holy Scripture; and the heavenliness of the matter, the efficacy of the doctrine, the majesty of the style, *the consent of all* 297 *the parts*, the scope of the whole, (which is to give all glory to God,) the full discovery it makes of the only way of man's salvation, the many other incomparable excellencies, *and the entire perfection thereof, are arguments whereby it doth abundantly evidence itself to be the word of God;* yet, notwithstanding, our full persuasion and assurance of the infallible truth, and divine authority thereof, is from the inward work of the Holy Spirit, bearing witness by and with the word in our hearts.

IX. *The infallible rule of interpretation of Scripture is the Scripture itself;* and therefore, when there is a question about the true and full sense of any scripture, (which is not manifold, but one,) it may be searched and known by other places that speak more clearly.

CHARGE VI.

The Presbyterian Church in the United States of America charges the Rev. Charles A. Briggs, D. D., being a Minister of the said Church and a member of the Presbytery of New York, with teaching that Isaiah is not the author of half of the book that bears his name, which is contrary to direct statements of Holy Scripture and to the essential doctrines of the Standards of the said Church that the Holy Scripture evidences itself to be the word of God by the consent of all the parts, and that the infallible rule of interpretation of Scripture is the Scripture itself.

SPECIFICATION.

In an Inaugural Address, which the said Rev. Charles A. Briggs, D. D., delivered at the Union Theological Seminary in the City of New York, January 20, 1891, on the occasion of his induction into the Edward Robinson Chair of Biblical Theology, which Address has been published and extensively circulated with the knowledge and approval of the said Rev. Charles A. Briggs, D. D., and has been republished by him in a second edition with a preface and an appendix, there occurs the following sentence:

Page 33, lines 14-15:

"Isaiah did not write half of the book that bears his name."

This declaration is contrary to direct statements of Scripture:

Matt. iv. 14, 15.—14 That it might be fulfilled which was spoken by Esaias the prophet, saying, 15 The land of Zabulon, and the land of Nepthalim, *by* the way of the sea, beyond Jordan, Galilee of the Gentiles:

Matt. xii. 17, 18.—17 That it might be fulfilled which was spoken by Esaias the prophet, saying, 18 Behold my servant, whom I have chosen; my beloved, in whom my soul is well pleased: I will put my Spirit upon him, and he shall shew judgment to the Gentiles.

Luke iii. 4.—As it is written in the book of the words of Esaias the prophet, saying, The voice of one crying in the wilderness, Prepare ye the way of the Lord, make his paths straight.

Acts xxviii. 25, 26.—25 And when they agreed not among themselves they departed, after that Paul had spoken one word, Well spake the Holy Ghost by Esaias the prophet unto our fathers, 26 Saying, Go unto this people, and say, Hearing ye shall hear, and shall not understand; and seeing ye shall see, and not perceive.

John xii. 38, 41.—38 That the saying of Esaias the prophet might be fulfilled, which he spake, Lord, who hath believed our report? and to whom hath the arm of the Lord been revealed? 41 These things said Esaias, when he saw his glory and spake of him.

Rom. x. 16, 20.—16 But they have not all obeyed the gospel. For Esaias saith, Lord, who hath believed our report? 20 But Esaias is very bold, and saith, I was found of them that sought me not; I was made manifest unto them that asked not after me.

This declaration is contrary to the Standards.

Confession of Faith, Chap. 1, Secs. V. and IX.

V. We may be moved and induced by the testimony of the church to an high and reverent esteem for the Holy

Scripture; and the heavenliness of the matter, the efficacy of the doctrine, the majesty of the style, *the consent of all the parts;* the scope of the whole, (which is to give all glory to God,) the full discovery it makes of the only way of man's salvation, the many other incomparable excellencies, *and the entire perfection thereof, are arguments whereby it doth abundantly evidence itself to be the word of God;* yet, notwithstanding, our full persuasion and assurance of the infallible truth, and divine authority thereof, is from the inward work of the Holy Spirit,
302 bearing witness by and with the word in our hearts.

IX. *The infallible rule of interpretation of Scripture is the Scripture itself;* and therefore, when there is a question about the true and full sense of any scripture, (which is not manifold, but one,) it may be searched and known by other places that speak more clearly.

CHARGE VII.

The Presbyterian Church in the United States of America charges the Rev. Charles A. Briggs, D. D., being a Minister of said Church, and a member of the Presbytery of New York, with teaching that the processes of redemption extend to the world to come in the case of many who die in sin; which is contrary to the essential doctrine of Holy Scripture and the Standards of the said Church, that the processes of redemption are limited to this world.

SPECIFICATION.

303 In an Inaugural Address, which the said Rev. Charles A. Briggs, D. D., delivered at the Union Theological Seminary in the City of New York, January 20, 1891, on the occasion of his induction into the Edward Robinson Chair of Biblical Theology, which address has been published and extensively circulated with the knowledge and approval of the said Rev. Charles A. Briggs, D. D., and has been republished by him in a second edition with a preface and an appendix, there occur the following sentences:

Page 50: "The processes of redemption ever keep the *race* in mind. The Bible tell us of a race origin, a race sin, a race ideal, a race Redeemer, and a race redemption."

Page 53: "(c.) Another fault of Protestant theology is in its limitation of the process of redemption to this world, and its neglect of those vast periods of time which have elapsed for most men in the Middle State between death and the resurrection."

Pages 55 and 56. "The Bible does not teach universal salvation, but it does teach the salvation of the world, of the race of man, and that cannot be accomplished by the selection of a limited number of individuals from the mass. The holy arm that worketh salvation does not contract its hand in grasping only a few; it stretches its loving fingers so as to comprehend as many as possible—a definite number, but multitudes that no one can number. The salvation of the world can only mean the world as a whole, compared with which the unredeemed will be so few and insignificant, and evidently beyond the reach of redemption by their own act of rejecting it and hardening themselves against it, and by descending into such depths of demoniacal depravity in the Middle State, that they will vanish from the sight of the redeemed as altogether and irredeemably evil, and never more disturb the harmonies of the saints."

Inaugural Address, Appendix, 2d ed.

Page 104. This raises the question whether any man is irretrievably lost ere he commits this unpardonable sin, and whether those who do not commit it in this world ere they die are, by the mere crisis of death, brought into an unpardonable state; and whether, when Jesus said that this sin against the Holy Spirit was unpardonable here and also hereafter, he did not imply that all other sins might be pardoned hereafter as well as here.

These declarations are contrary to direct statements of Scripture:

Prov. xi. 7. When a wicked man dieth, *his* expectation shall perish: and the hope of unjust *men* perisheth.

Luke xvi. 22, 23.—22 And it came to pass that the beggar died, and was carried by the angels into Abraham's bosom : the rich man also died, and was buried ; 23 And in hell he lifted up his eyes, being in torments, and seeth Abraham afar off, and Lazarus in his bosom.

John viii. 24. For if ye believe not that I am *He*, ye shall die in your sins.

II. Cor. vi. 2. Behold, now *is* the accepted time ; behold, now *is* the day of salvation.

Heb. iv. 7. To-day, if ye will hear his voice, harden not your hearts.

These declarations are contrary to the Standards :

Confession of Faith, Chap. XXXII., Sec. I.

I. The bodies of men, after death, return to dust, and see corruption ; but their souls, (which neither die nor sleep,) having an immortal subsistence, immediately return to God who gave them. The souls of the righteous, being then made perfect in holiness, are received into the highest heavens, where they behold the face of God in light and glory, waiting for the full redemption of their bodies : *and the souls of the wicked are cast into hell, where they remain in torments and utter darkness, reserved to the judgment of the great day.* Besides these two places for souls separated from their bodies, the Scripture acknowledgeth none.

Larger Catechism.

Q. 83. *What is the communion in glory with Christ, which the members of the invisible church enjoy in this life ?*

A. The members of the invisible church have communicated to them, in this life, the first-fruits of glory with Christ, as they are members of him their head, and so in him are interested in that glory which he is fully possessed of ; and as an earnest thereof, enjoy the sense of God's love, peace of conscience, joy in the Holy Ghost, and hope of glory. As, on the contrary, sense of God's revenging wrath, horror of conscience, and a fearful expectation of judgment, are to the wicked the beginning of the torments, which they shall endure after death.

Q. 86. *What is the communion in glory with Christ, which the members of the invisible church enjoy immediately after death?*

A. The communion in glory with Christ, which the members of the invisible church enjoy immediately after death, is in that their souls are then made perfect in holiness, and received into the highest heavens, where they behold the face of God in light and glory; waiting for the full redemption of their bodies, which even in death continue united to Christ, and rest in their graves as in their beds, till at the last day they be again united to their souls. *Whereas the souls of the wicked are at their death cast into hell, where they remain in torments and utter darkness;* and their bodies kept in their graves, as in their prisons, until the resurrection and judgment of the great day.

CHARGE VIII.

The Presbyterian Church in the United States of America charges the Rev. Charles A. Briggs, D. D., being a Minister of the said Church and a member of the Presbytery of New York, with teaching that Sanctification is not complete at death, which is contrary to the essential doctrine of Holy Scripture and of the Standards of the said Church that the souls of believers are at their death at once made perfect in holiness.

SPECIFICATION.

In an Inaugural Address, which the said Rev. Charles A. Briggs, D. D., delivered at the Union Theological Seminary in the City of New York, January 20, 1891, on the occasion of his induction into the Edward Robinson Chair of Biblical Theology, which Address has been published and extensively circulated with the knowledge and approval of the said Rev. Charles A. Briggs, D. D., and has been republished by him in a second edition with a preface and an appendix, there occur the following sentences:

Pages 53, 54, 55:

"(c.) Another fault of Protestant theology is in its limitation of the process of redemption to this world, and its neglect of those vast periods of time which have elapsed for most men in the Middle State between death and the resurrection. The Roman Catholic Church is firmer here, though it smears the Biblical doctrine with not a few hurtful errors. The reaction against this limitation, as seen in the theory of second probation, is not surprising. I do not find this doctrine in the Bible, but I do find in the Bible the doctrine of a Middle State of conscious higher life in the communion with Christ and the multitude of the departed of all ages; and of the necessity of entire sanctification, in order that the work of re-
311 demption may be completed. There is no authority in the Scriptures, or in the creeds of Christendom, for the doctrine of immediate sanctification at death. The only sanctification known to experience, to Christian orthodoxy, and to the Bible, is progressive sanctification. Progressive sanctification after death is the doctrine of the Bible and the Church; and it is of vast importance in our times that we should understand it, and live in accordance with it. The bugbear of a judgment immediately after death, and the illusion of a magical transformation in the dying hour should be banished from the world. They are conceits derived from the Ethnic religions, and without basis in the Bible or Christian experience as expressed in the symbols of the Church. The former makes death a terror to the best of men, the latter makes human life and experience of no effect; and both cut the nerves of Chris-
312 tian activity and striving after sanctification. Renouncing them as hurtful, unchristian errors, we look with hope and joy for the continuation of the processes of grace, and the wonders of redemption in the company of the blessed, to which the faithful are all hastening."

Inaugural Address, Appendix, 2d ed., pages 107, 108:
"Sanctification has two sides—a negative and a positive—mortification and vivification; the former is manward, the latter is Godward. Believers who enter the middle state,

enter guiltless; they are pardoned and justified; they are mantled in the blood and righteousness of Christ; and nothing will be able to separate them from His love. They are also delivered from all temptations such as spring from without, from the world and the devil. They are encircled with influences for good such as they have never enjoyed before. But they are still the same persons, 313 with all the gifts and graces, and also the same habits of mind, disposition, and temper they had when they left the world. Death destroys the body. It does not change the moral and religious nature of man. It is unpsychological and unethical to suppose that the character of the disembodied spirit will all be changed in the moment of death. It is the Manichean heresy to hold that sin belongs to the physical organization and is laid aside with the body. If this were so, how can any of our race carry their evil natures with them into the middle state and incur the punishment of their sins? The eternal punishment of a man whose evil nature has been stripped from him by death and left in the grave, is an absurdity. The Plymouth Brethren hold that there are two natures in the redeemed—the old man and the new. In accordance with such a theory, the old man might be cast off at death. But this is only a more subtle kind of Manicheism, which 314 has ever been regarded as heretical. Sin, as our Saviour teaches, has its source in the heart—in the higher and immortal part of man. It is the work of sanctification to overcome sin in the higher nature."

These declarations are contrary to Scripture :

1 Cor. xv. 51, 52.—51 Behold I shew you a mystery; We shall not all sleep, but we shall all be changed. 52 In a moment, in the twinkling of an eye, at the last trump : for the trumpet shall sound, and the dead shall be raised incorruptible, and we shall be changed.

Heb. xii. 23.—To the general assembly and church of the firstborn, which are written in heaven and to God the Judge of all, and to the spirits of just men made perfect.

315 These declarations are contrary to the Standards: Confession of Faith, Chap. XXXII., Sec. I.

I. The bodies of men, after death, return to dust, and see corruption; *but their souls* (which neither die nor sleep), having an immortal subsistence, *immediately return to God who gave them. The souls of the righteous, being then made perfect in holiness, are received into the highest heavens*, where they behold the face of God in light and glory, waiting for the full redemption of their bodies; and the souls of the wicked are cast into hell, where they remain in torments and utter darkness, reserved to the judgment of the great day, besides these two places for souls separated from their bodies, the Scripture acknowledgeth none.

316 Larger Catechism.

Q. 86. *What is the communion in glory with Christ, which the members of the invisible church enjoy immediately after death?*

A. The communion in glory with Christ, which the members of the invisible church *enjoy immediately after death, is in that their souls are then made perfect in holiness, and received into the highest heavens, where they behold the face of God in light and glory;* waiting for the full redemption of their bodies, which even in death continue united to Christ, and rest in their graves as in their beds, till at the last day they be again united to their souls. Whereas the souls of the wicked are at their death cast into hell, where they remain in torments and utter darkness; and their bodies kept in their graves, as in their prisons, until the resurrection and judgment of the great day.

Shorter Catechism.

317 Q. 37. *What benefit do believers receive from Christ at their death?*

A. *The souls of believers are at their death made perfect in holiness, and do immediately pass into glory;* and their bodies, being still united in Christ, do rest in their graves till the resurrection.

The Presbyterian Church in the United States of America, represented by the undersigned Prosecuting Committee, offers in evidence the whole of the said Inaugural Address, both the first and second editions, and all the works of the said Rev. Charles A. Briggs, D. D., quoted therein, in so far as they bear upon this case; also the appendix to the second edition of said Address, and all the works of the said Rev. Charles A. Briggs, D. D., quoted therein, in so far as they bear upon this case; 318 the whole of the Holy Scriptures and the whole of the Standards of the Presbyterian Church in the United States of America.

      GEORGE W. F. BIRCH, D. D.,
      JOSEPH J. LAMPE, D. D.,
      ROBERT F. SAMPLE, D. D.,
      JOHN J. STEVENSON,
      JOHN J. McCOOK,
        Prosecuting Committee.

It was, on motion, resolved that a copy of these Charges 330 and Specifications be served on Dr. Briggs. This having been done, Dr. Briggs asked for the time allowed by the Book. Whereupon it was resolved that we now take a recess, to meet on Monday, the 27th, at 2 P. M.

A recess was now taken.

Concluded with prayer.

The minutes were read and approved.

      S. D. ALEXANDER,
        Stated Clerk.

NEW YORK, 28TH NOVEMBER.

BRIGGS CASE.   344

SCOTCH CHURCH, 2 P. M.

After a recess from November 9th, Presbytery met and was constituted with prayer, and proceeded to consider the case of Rev. C. A. Briggs, D. D.

Present: Ministers—John C. Bliss, Mod.; Geo. Alexander, S. D. Alexander, Antonio Arreghi, Anson P. Atterbury, W. Wallace Atterbury, Geo. W. F. Birch, Robert R. Booth, Samuel Bowden, Charles A. Briggs, Francis Brown, Walter D. Buchanan, James Chambers, Edward L. Clark, Nathaniel W. Conkling, Wilbur F. Crafts, John B. Devins, Ira S. Dodd, D. Stuart Dodge, Conrad Doench, William Durant, Thomas Douglas, Howard Duffield, John H. Edwards, Frank F. Ellinwood, Henry B. Elliot, Wm. T. Elsing, Charles P. Fagnani, Henry M. Field, Walter B. Floyd, Jesse F. Forbes, Herbert Ford, Charles R. Gillett, Henri Grandlienard, James Hall, A. Woodruff Halsey, Wm. R. Harshaw, Thomas S. Hastings, Spencer L. Hillier, Edward W. Hitchcock, James H. Hoadley, James Hunter, Sam. W. Jackson, A. D. Lawrence Jewett, Albert B. King, A. Dunlop King, Joseph J. Lampe, Sidney G. Law, Theodore Leonhard, Milton S. Littlefield, John C. Lowrie, Daniel E. Lorenz, Wm. M. Martin, Charles P. Mallery, Henry T. McEwen, James H. McIlvaine, Alex. H. McKinney, Alex. McLean, Duncan J. McMillan, Horace G. Miller, William L. Moore, James C. Nightingale, Geo. Nixon, Israel H. Northrup, Daniel H. Overton, Charles H. Parkhurst, Levi H. Parsons, James G. Patterson, John R. Paxton, Wm. M. Paxton, Edward P. Payson, Geo. S. Payson, Geo. L. Prentiss, James S. Ramsey, Daniel Redmon, Charles S. Robinson, Stealy B. Rossiter, Albert G. Ruliffson, Wm. A. Rice, Robert F. Sample, Joseph A. Saxton, Adolphus F. Schauffler, J. Balcom Shaw, Geo. L. Shearer, Wm. G. T. Shedd, Andrew Shiland, David G. Smith, Wilton M. Smith, John M. Stevenson, Wm. C. Stitt, Charles A. Stoddard, J. Ford Sutton, Alex. W. Sproull, Geo. L. Spining, Charles L. Thompson, John J. Thompson, Charles L. Tyndall, Henry M. Tyndall, Henry Van Dyke, Marvin R. Vincent, Thomas G. Wall, Abbott L. R. Waite, W. Scott Watson, Geo. S. Webster, Erskine N. White, Gaylord S. White, John T. Wilds, Livingston Willard, David G. Wylie, Fred. G. Beebe, Hugh Pritchard, Vincent Pisek.

345

Elders—Moses P. Brown, Adams' Memorial; James 346
Tompkins, Bethany; Albert R. Ledoux, Brick; A. P.
Ketcham, Calvary; William Mickens, Central; Andrew
Robinson, Christ; James McDowell, East Harlem; H.
Edward Rowland, Fifth Avenue; Eugene McJimpsey,
First; John McWilliam, Fourth; Geo. E. Sterry, Fourth
Avenue; Samuel Reeve, Fourteenth Street; Samuel H.
Willard, Harlem; Joseph Moorhead, Knox; Henry D.
Nicoll, Madison Avenue; Charles H. Woodbury, Madison Square; Robert Johnson, First Morrisania; G. C.
King, North; Henry Q. Hawley, Park; James E. Ware,
Phillips; Cleveland H. Dodge, Riverdale; Wm. M. Onderdonk, Rutgers; Robert Houston, Scotch; John Denham, Sea and Land; Wm. R. Worrall, Thirteenth Street;
Thomas Bond, University Place; Robert Gentle, Union
Tabernacle; Wm. A. Wheelock, Washington Heights; 347
Robert Jaffray, West; Clarence P. Leggett, West End;
Alex. Wilson, West Fifty-first Street; Robert Drummond,
Westminster; James Anderson, Seventh; W. C. Humbly,
Mt. Tabor; Geo. C. Lay, Puritans; James L. Birdsall,
Spring Street; C. E. Garey, Tremont; John Cepek,
Bohemian.

On motion, the Committee of Arrangements were authorized to give such persons as they approve copies of
the stenographic reports, at the expense of the applicants.

The Moderator, Stated Clerk and Rev. Charles R. Gillette were appointed a committee to supervise the official
stenographer's reports of the proceedings.

The Moderator charged the brethren to remember that 348
they are now in the attitude of a Court, and he then made
the following statement, viz.: In view of certain expressions of opinions which have come to me from sources
both religious and secular, I would make a statement
bearing on both sides of the case now before us.

1st. As to the action and spirit of the defendant and his
immediate friend or friends, respecting the interpretation
of the law and methods of procedure in this case. In
raising the questions and in making the objections which
they have presented here, or which they may yet present,

and in their complaints carrying these points to the Synod, they are not to be considered as desiring merely to obstruct the progress of the trial on its merits, or to act in any way so as to cause needless hindrance or delay. Instead of this their course is to be viewed in the light of the strong convictions which they hold against some of the methods pursued, and certain decisions made in this case and in the light of their honest desire to conserve great and important principles in the constitution and government of our Church.

In this case your Moderator is thoroughly convinced that they are perfectly conscientious and sincere.

Then, on the other hand, as to the position, purpose and animus of the Prosecuting Committee, your Moderator is as thoroughly convinced that they are not in that position, because they have sought or enjoy it; that their aim is not that of mere "heresy hunters," and that they have no unkind personal feelings whatever toward him who has been arraigned; but they are just acting under the obligations laid upon them from a deep sense of duty to the truth and to the Church ; and because they believe that they represent a very large portion of our Church in a most serious and earnest feeling of alarm over the effects of the views set forth by the defendant, and in this course they are as conscientious and sincere as the defendant. Now, of this view of both sides of the case, I would have every one in this Court, and all outside of it, fully assured.

And further, let me avouch the confidence that every member of this Court will endeavor to hold his judgment as close to a perfect balance as possible in the hearing of this whole case, so that, without any previous bias, he may reach the decision that shall be most just, and that therefore there be all effort on the part of all to avoid raising points which may cause unnecessary discussion or delay in the conduct of our proceedings.

The Moderator then stated that the Amended Charges and Specifications had been placed in the hands of the defendant at the last meeting, and he now called upon Dr. Briggs to answer.

Whereupon he proceeded to file preliminary objections.
The Moderator then declared that the next step was to 351
hear from the other party, when Dr. Lampe, of the Prosecuting Committee, was heard.

It was moved that Presbytery, in consideration of objections offered by the accused, require the Committee to amend the Charges and Specifications by striking out Charges IV. and VII.

Pending the consideration of this motion, after the approval of the minutes so far as read, and after prayer, Presbytery took a recess.

S. D. ALEXANDER,
Stated Clerk.

SCOTCH CHURCH, TUESDAY, NOV. 29, 2 P. M.

BRIGGS CASE.

After recess Presbytery convened and was opened with prayer.

Present: Ministers—John C. Bliss, Mod.; Geo. Alex- 352
ander, S. D. Alexander, Antonio Arreghi, Anson P. Atterbury, W. Wallace Atterbury, Frederick G. Beebe, Geo. W. F. Birch, Robert R. Booth, Charles A. Briggs, Francis Brown, Samuel Bowden, Walter D. Buchanan, James Chambers, Edward L. Clark, Nathaniel W. Conkling, Wilbur F. Crafts, John B. Devins, Ira S. Dodd, D. Stuart Dodge, Conrad Doench, Wm. Durant, Thomas Douglas, Howard Duffield, John H. Edwards, Frank F. Ellinwood, Henry B. Elliot, Wm. T. Elsing, Charles P. Fagnani, Henry M. Field, Walter B. Floyd, Jesse F. Forbes, Herbert Ford, Charles R. Gillett, Henri L. Grandlienard, James Hall, A. Woodruff Halsey, Wm. R. Harshaw, Thomas S. Hastings, Spencer L. Hillier, Edward W. Hitchcock, James H. Hoadley, James Hunter, Saml. M. Jackson, Joseph R. Kerr, Albert B. King, A. Dunlop King, Joseph J. Lampe, Sidney G. Low, Theodore Leonhard, Milton S. Littlefield, John C. Lowrie, Daniel E. Lorenz, William M. Martin, Charles

P. Mallery, Alex. H. McKinney, Alex. McLean, Duncan J. McMillan, Horace G. Miller, Wm. L. Moore, James C. Nightingale, Geo. Nixon, Israel H. Northrup, Dan. H. Overton, Charles H. Parkhurst, Levi H. Parsons, James G. Patterson, John R. Paxton, Wm. M. Paxton, Edward
353 P. Payson, Geo. S. Payson, Vincent Pisek, Geo. L. Prentiss, Hugh Pritchard, James S. Ramsay, Daniel Redmon, Charles S. Robinson, Stealy B. Rossiter, Albert G. Ruliffson, Robert F. Sample, Wm. A. Rice, Joseph A. Saxton, Adolphus F. Schauffler, J. Balcom Shaw, Geo. L. Shearer, Wm. G. T. Shedd, Andrew Shiland, David G. Smith, Wilton M. Smith, Wm. C. Stitt, Charles A. Stoddard, J. Ford Sutton, Alex. W. Sproull, Geo. L. Spining, Charles L. Thompson, John J. Thompson, Charles H. Tyndall, Henry M. Tyndall, Henry Van Dyke, Marvin R. Vincent, Frederick E. Voegelin, Abbott L. R. Waite, Thomas G. Wall, W. Scott Watson, Geo. S. Webster, Erskine N. White, John T. Wilds, Livingston Willard, David G. Wylie.

Elders: Moses P. Brown, Adams Memorial; James Tompkins, Bethany; John Cepek, Bohemian; Albert R. Ledoux, Brick; A. P. Ketcham, Calvary; Andrew Robinson, Christ; Wm. Mickens, Central; James Mc-
354 Dowell, East Harlem; H. Edward Rowland, Fifth Avenue; Eugene McJimpsey, First; John McWilliam, Fourth; Geo. E. Sterry, Fourth Avenue; Saml. Reeve, Fourteenth Street; Saml. H. Willard, Harlem; Joseph Moorhead, Knox; Henry D. Nicoll, Madison Avenue; Charles H. Woodbury, Madison Square; Robert Johnson, First Morrisiana; G. C. King, North; Henry Q. Hawley, Park; James E. Ware, Phillips; Cleveland H. Dodge, Riverdale; Wm. M. Onderdonk, Rutgers, Riverside; Robert Houston, Scotch; John Denham, Sea and Land; Wm. R. Worrall, Thirteenth Street; Thomas Bond, University Place; Robert Gentle, Union Tabernacle; Wm. A. Wheelock, Washington Heights; Robert Jaffray, West; Clarence P. Leggett, West End; Alex. Wilson, West Fifty-first Street; Richard Drummond, Westminster; James L. Birdsall, Spring Street;

James Anderson, Seventh; Wm. C. Humbly, Mount 355
Tabor; Caleb E. Garey, Tremont; Geo. E. Lay, Puritans.

The resolution pending at the close of the last meeting was then taken up and Mr. McCook, of the Prosecuting Committee, was heard.

At this point Dr. Briggs wished the following objections recorded, viz.: That the Prosecuting Committee were heard yesterday in response to his objections and the Committee is now being heard again without his consent.

A motion to lay the pending resolution on the table was lost by a vote of 47 to 67.

At this point the resolution was divided in order to take action respecting Charges IV. and VII. separately.

The resolution requiring the Committee to strike out Charge IV. was sustained by a vote of 70 to 49.

The Committee of Prosecution take exception and ask 356 to have entered upon the record an exception to the action of the Presbytery in requiring the Committee to amend the Charges and Specifications by striking out Charge IV.

The resolution to require the Committee to strike out Charge VII. was sustained by a vote of 74 to 54.

The Prosecuting Committee take exception and ask to have entered upon the record an exception to the action of the Presbytery in requiring the Committee to amend the Charges and Specifications by striking out Charge VII.

It was resolved that when Presbytery convene tomorrow, we proceed at once to take up the objections in their order.

The minutes were read and approved.

Presbytery now took a recess until to-morrow at 2 P. M. Concluded with prayer.

S. D. ALEXANDER,

Stated Clerk.

NEW YORK, 30TH NOVEMBER, 1892.

357 BRIGGS CASE.

SCOTCH CHURCH, Wednesday, Nov. 30, 2 P. M.

Presbytery convened after recess and was opened with prayer.

Present: Ministers—John C. Bliss, Moderator; Geo. Alexander, Saml. D. Alexander, Antonio Arreghi, Anson P. Atterbury, W. Wallace Atterbury, Frederick G. Beebe, Geo. W. F. Birch, Nicholas Bjerring, Robert R. Booth, Saml. Bowden, Thomas S. Bradner, Charles A. Briggs, Francis Brown, Walter D. Buchanan, James Chambers, Edward L. Clark, Nathaniel W. Conkling, Wilbur F. Crafts, John B. Devins, Ira S. Dodd, D. Stuart Dodge, Conrad Doench, William Durant, Howard Duffield, John H. Edwards, Frank F. Ellinwood, Henry B. Elliott, Wm. T. Elsing, Charles P. Fagnani, Henry M. Field, Walter B. Floyd, Jesse F. Forbes, Herbert Ford, Charles R. Gillett, Henri Grandlienard, James Hall, A. Woodruff Halsey, Wm. R. Harshaw, Thomas S. Hastings, Edward W. Hitchcock, James H. Hoadley, James Hunter, Saml. M. Jackson, Joseph R. Kerr, Albert B. King, A. Dunlap King, Joseph J. Lampe, Sidney G. Law, Theodore Leon-
358 hard, Wilton S. Littlefield, John C. Lowrie, Daniel E. Lorenz, Wm. M. Martin, Charles P. Mallery, Francis H. Marling, Henry T. McEwen, James H. McIlvaine, Alex. H. McKinney, Alex. McLean, Duncan J. McMillan, Horace G. Miller, Geo. J. Mingins, Wm. L. Moore, James C. Nightingale, Geo. Nixon, Israel H. Northrup, Daniel H. Overton, Charles H. Parkhurst, Levi H. Parsons, James G. Patterson, John R. Paxton, Edward P. Payson, Geo. S. Payson, George L. Prentiss, Hugh Pritchard, James S. Ramsay, Daniel Redmon, Charles S. Robinson, Stealy B. Rossiter, Albert G. Ruliffson, William A. Rice, Robert F. Sample, Joseph A. Saxton, Adolphus F. Schauffler, J. Balcom Shaw, Geo. L. Shearer, Wm. G. T. Shedd, Andrew Shiland, David G. Smith, Wilton M.

Smith, Wm. C. Stitt, Charles A. Stoddard, J. Ford Sutton, Alex. W. Sproull, Geo. L. Spining, Charles L. Thompson, John J. Thompson, Charles H. Tyndall, Henry M. Tyndall, Henry Van Dyke, Marvin R. Vincent, Frederick E. Voegelin, Thomas G. Wall, Abbott L. R. Waite, W. Scott Watson, Geo. S. Webster, Erskine N. White, John T. Wilds, Livingston Willard, David G. Wylie.

Elders—Moses P. Brown, Adams Memorial; James 359 Tompkins, Bethany; Albert R. Ledoux, Brick; A. P. Ketcham, Calvary; Wm. Mickens, Central; Andrew Robinson, Christ; James McDowell, East Harlem; H. Edward Rowland, Fifth Avenue; Eugene McJimpsey, First; John McWilliam, Fourth; Geo. E. Sterry, Fourth Avenue; Saml. Reeve, Fourteenth Street; Saml. H. Willard, Harlem; Joseph Moorhead, Knox; Henry D. Nicoll, Madison Avenue; Charles H. Woodbury, Madison Square; Robert Johnson, Morrisania First; G. C. King, North; Henry Q. Hawley, Park; James E. Ware, Phillips; Geo. C. Lay, Puritans; Cleveland H. Dodge, Riverdale; Wm. M. Onderdonk, Rutgers, etc.; Robert Houston, Scotch; James Anderson, Seventh; James L. Birdsall, Spring Street; Wm. R. Worrell, Thirteenth 360 Street; Caleb E. Garey, Tremont; Thomas Bond, University Place; Robert Gentle, Union Tabernacle; Wm. A. Wheelock, Washington Heights; Robert Jaffray, West; Clarence P. Leggett, West End; Alexr. Wilson, West Fifty-first Street; Richd. Drummond, Westminster.

The resolution offered at the close of the session yesterday afternoon, to proceed at once to take up the objections in their order, was taken up.

The first objection of Dr. Briggs to the charges and specifications was not sustained.

The second objection of Dr. Briggs to the charges and specifications was not sustained.

Dr. Briggs reserved his rights (page 251 in the stenographer's report) to apply them to the specific charges.

It was, on motion, resolved that without sustaining the 361 general objection to the relevancy of the proofs from

Scripture, catechisms and confession, the Presbytery direct the transference of these proofs from the specifications to the charges.

A division of the house being called for, the above resolution was sustained by a vote of 71 to 56.

The Committee of Prosecution took exception, and asked to have entered upon the record an exception to the action of the Presbytery in directing the transference of the proofs from Scripture, catechisms and confession from the specifications to the charges.

It was moved, that in view of the fifth objection of the defendant that the last paragraph of the amended charges from the words "The Presbyterian Church, etc." at the bottom of page 35 be stricken out. It was then moved to amend the resolution by instructing the Committee to amend the last clause of the Charges by stating what portion of the Holy Scriptures, the works of Rev. Charles A. Briggs, D. D., and the Standards they intend to present as evidence in the case.

This amendment was lost by a vote of 23 to 84.

The resolution being voted upon was lost. The ayes and noes being called for, the resolution was lost by the following 68 persons in the affirmative, and the following 70 persons in the negative:

Ministers: Aye—Geo. Alexander, Antonio Arreghi, Anson P. Atterbury, W. Wallace Atterbury, Frederick G. Beebe, Francis Brown, James Chambers, Edward L. Clark, Ira S. Dodd, D. Stuart Dodge, Wm. Durant, John H. Edwards, Frank F. Ellinwood, Wm. T. Elsing, Charles P. Fagnani, Henry M. Field, Herbert Ford, Charles R. Gillett, Henri L. Grandlienard, Wm. R. Harshaw, Thomas S. Hastings, Edward W. Hitchcock, James H. Hoadley, James Hunter, Saml. M. Jackson, Milton S. Littlefield, Danl. E. Lorenz, Wm. M. Martin, Francis H. Marling, Henry T. McEwen, James H. McIlvaine, Duncan McMillan, Geo. J. Mingins, Daniel H. Overton, Charles H. Parkhurst, Geo. S. Payson, Geo. L. Prentiss, James S. Ramsay, Daniel Redmon, Stealy B. Rossiter, Albert

G. Ruliffson, Wm. A. Rice, Joseph A. Saxton, Philip Schaff, J. Balcom Shaw, David G. Smith, Wilton M. Smith, Geo. L. Spining, Charles L. Thompson, Henry Van Dyke, Marvin R. Vincent, Geo. S. Webster—52.

Elders: Aye—Moses P. Brown, Albert L. Ledoux, Wm. Mickens, Saml. Reeve, Charles H. Woodbury, Robert Johnson, G. C. King, Henry Q. Hawley, James E. Ware, Geo. C. Lay, Cleveland H. Dodge, Thomas Bond, Robert Gentle, Wm. A. Wheelock, Robert Jaffray, Clarence P. Leggett—16.

Ministers: Nay—Sam'l D. Alexander, Nicholas Bjerring, Robert R. Booth, Samuel Bowden, Thomas S. Bradner, Walter D. Buchanan, Nathaniel W. Conkling, Wilbur F. Crafts, Conrad Doench, Thomas Douglas, Howard Duffield, Henry B. Elliot, Jesse F. Forbes, James Hall, A. Woodruff Halsey, Joseph R. Kerr, Albert B. King, Alex. D. King, Sidney G. Low, Theodore Leonhard, John C. Lowrie, Charles P. Mallery, Alexander McLean, Horace G. Miller, Wm. L. Moore, James C. Nightingale, George Nixon, Israel H. Northrup, Levi H. Parsons, James G. Patterson, Edward P. Payson, Hugh Pritchard, Charles S. Robinson, Adolphus F. Schauffler, George L. Shearer, Wm. G. T. Shedd, Andrew Shiland, Wm. C. Stitt, Charles A. Stoddard, J. Ford Sutton, Alex. W. Sproull, John J. Thompson, Henry M. Tyndall, Frederick E. Voegelin, Thomas G. Wall, Abbott L. R. Waite, W. Scott Watson, Erskine N. White, John T. Wilds, Livingston Willard, David G. Wylie, Walter B. Floyd—52.

Elders: Nay—James Tompkins, A. P. Ketcham, Andrew Robinson, James McDowell, H. Edwards Rowland, Eugene McJimpsey, John McWilliam, Geo. E. Sterry, Samuel H. Willard, Joseph Moorhead, Henry D. Nicoll, Wm. M. Onderdonk, Robert Houston, James Anderson, James L. Birdsall, William R. Worrall, Caleb E. Garey, Richard Drummond—18.

Dr. Briggs gave notice of an exception and notice of an appeal and complaint.

365 It was resolved that the sessions of Presbytery hereafter close on Thursday afternoon instead of on Friday as in the original motion.

The minutes were read and approved as far as written. Presbytery now took a recess until to-morrow at 2 P. M.

S. D. ALEXANDER,
Stated Clerk.

SCOTCH CHURCH, DECEMBER 1ST, 2 P. M.

BRIGGS CASE.

Presbytery convened after recess and was opened with prayer.

Present: Ministers—John C. Bliss, Mod'r; Geo. Alexander, Saml. D. Alexander, Antonio Arreghi, Anson P. Atterbury, W. Wallace Atterbury, Wm. H. Beach, Frederick G. Beebe, Geo. W. F. Birch, Nicholas Bjerring, Robert R. Booth, Samuel Bowden, Thomas S. Bradner, Charles A. Briggs, Francis Brown, Walter D. Buchanan, James Chambers, Edward L. Clark, Nathl. W. Conkling, Wilbur F. Crafts, John B. Devins, Ira S. Dodd, D. Stuart Dodge, Conrad Doench, Wm. Durant, Thomas Douglas, Howard Duffield, John H. Edwards, Frank F. Ellinwood,
366 Henry B. Elliot, Wm. T. Elsing, Charles P. Fagnani, Henry M. Field, Walter B. Floyd, Jesse F. Forbes, Herbert Ford, Charles R. Gillett, Henri L. Grandlienard, James Hall, A. Woodruff Halsey, Wm. R. Harshaw, Thomas S. Hastings, Edward W. Hitchcock, James H. Hoadley, James Hunter, Samuel M. Jackson, Joseph H. Kerr, Albert B. King, Alex. D. King, Jos. J. Lampe, Sidney G. Law, Theodore Leonhard, Milton S. Littlefield, John C. Lowrie, Daniel E. Lorenz, William M. Martin, Charles P. Mallery, Francis H. Marling, Henry T. McEwen, James H. McIlvaine, Alex. McKinney, Alex. McLean, Duncan J. McMillan, Horace G. Miller, Geo. J. Mingins, Wm. L. Moore, James C. Nightingale, Geo. Nixon, Israel H. Northrup, Daniel H. Overton, Charles H. Parkhurst, Levi Parsons, James G. Patterson, John R. Paxton, Wm. M. Paxton, Edward P. Payson, Geo.

S. Payson, Geo. L. Prentiss, Hugh Pritchard, James S. Ramsay, Daniel Redmon, Charles S. Robinson, Stealy B. Rossiter, Albert G. Ruliffson, Wm. A. Rice, Robert F. Sample, Joseph Sanderson, Joseph A. Saxton, Philip Schaff, Adolphus F. Schauffler, J. Balcom Shaw, Geo. L. Shearer, Wm. G. T. Shedd, Andrew Shiland, Wilton M. Smith, Wm. C. Stitt, Charles A. Stoddard, J. Ford Sutton, Alex. W. Sproull, Geo. L. Spining, Charles L. Thompson, John J. Thompson, Charles H. Tyndall, Henry M. Tyndall, Marvin R. Vincent, Frederick E. Voegelin, Thomas G. Wall, Abbott L. R. Waite, W. Scott Watson, Geo. S. Webster, Erskine N. White, John T. Wilds, Livingston Willard, David G. Wylie.

Elders—Moses P. Brown, Adams Memorial; James Tompkins, Bethany; Albert R. Ledoux, Brick; A. P. Ketcham, Calvary; Wm. Mickens, Central; James McDowell, East Harlem; H. Edwards Rowland, Fifth Avenue; Eugene McJimpsey, First; John McWilliam, Fourth; Geo. E. Sterry, Fourth Avenue; Samuel Reeve, Fourteenth Street; Samuel H. Willard, Harlem; Joseph Moorhead, Knox; Henry D. Nicoll, Madison Avenue; Charles H. Woodbury, Madison Square; Robert Johnson, Morrisania First; Thomas Anderson, New York; G. C. King, North; Henry Q. Hawley, Park; James E. Ware, Phillips; Geo. C. Lay, Puritans; Cleveland H. Dodge, Riverdale; Wm. M. Onderdonk, Rutgers; Robert Houston, Scotch; James L. Birdsall, Spring Street; James Anderson, Seventh; Caleb E. Garey, Tremont; Thomas Bond, University; Robert Gentle, Union Tabernacle; Wm. A. Wheelock, Washington Heights; Robert Jaffray, West; Clarence P. Leggett, West End; Alex. Wilson, West Fifty-first Street; Richard Drummond, Westminster.

The objections of Dr. Briggs were again taken up, when it was resolved that in view of the conditional waiver made by the defendant, Presbytery, Presbytery without passing upon his objection to Charges I., II., III., V. and VI., rules that in taking the vote, each of the items in those charges as indicated by numerals in the objections filed, shall be voted upon separately.

369 The Committee of Prosecution take exception and ask to have entered upon the record an exception to the action of the Presbytery in view of the conditional waiver made by the defendant, Presbytery, without passing upon his objections to Charges I., II., III., V. and VI., rules that in taking the vote each of the items in those Charges as indicated by numerals in the objections filed, shall be voted upon separately.

It was then resolved that the proceedings are found in order, and that the Charges and Specifications in their amended form be considered sufficient to put the accused on his defense.

Whereupon Dr. Briggs was called upon to plead guilty or not guilty.

He pleaded not guilty.

The accused then waived the notice of testimony under Section 23 of the Book of Discipline.

The Prosecuting Committee then took up the case, and put in evidence pamphlets marked A and B, being the
370 1st and 2d editions of the Inaugural Address, and the Preface and Appendix to the 2d edition; and all the works of the said Rev. Charles A. Briggs, D. D., quoted therein, in so far as they bear upon this case, the whole of the Holy Scriptures and the whole of the Standards of the Presbyterian Church in the United States of America.

Here the Prosecution rested its evidence.

It was resolved that the evidence offered by the Prosecution be considered competent.

Dr. Briggs then gave notice of an exception and appeal.

It was resolved that we take recess until Monday afternoon next at 2 P. M.

After the reading and approval of the minutes so far as written, and prayer, Presbytery took recess as above.

S. D. ALEXANDER,
Stated Clerk.

NEW YORK, 5TH DECEMBER, 1892.

BRIGGS CASE.

SCOTCH CHURCH, MONDAY, 5, 2 P. M.

After recess Presbytery met and was opened with prayer.
Present: Ministers—John C. Bliss, Mod'r; Geo. Alexander, Saml. D. Alexander, Antonio Arreghi, Anson P. Atterbury, W. Wallace Atterbury, Frederick G. Beebe, Geo. W. F. Birch, Nicholas Bjerring, Robert R. Booth, Thomas S. Bradner, Charles A. Briggs, Francis Brown, Walter Buchanan, James Chambers, Edward L. Clark, Nathaniel W. Conkling, John B. Devins, Ira S. Dodd, D. Stuart Dodge, Conrad Doench, William Durant, Thomas Douglas, Howard Duffield, John H. Edwards, Frank F. Ellinwood, Henry B. Elliot, Wm. T. Elsing, Charles P. Fagnani, Henry M. Field, Walter B. Floyd, Jesse F. Forbes, Herbert Ford, Charles R. Gillett, Henri L. Grandlienard, James Hall, A. Woodruff Halsey, Wm. R. Harshaw, Thomas S. Hastings, Edward W. Hitchcock, James H. Hoadley, James Hunter, Saml. M. Jackson, A. D. Lawrence Jewett, Joseph R. Kerr, Albert B. King, A. Dunlop King, Joseph J. Lampe, Sidney G. Law, Theodore Leonhard, Milton S. Littlefield, John C. Lowrie, Daniel E. Lorenz, Wm. M. Martin, Charles P. Mallery, Francis H. Marling, Henry T. McEwen, Alex. H. McKinney, Alex. McLean, Duncan J. McMillan, Horace G. Miller, Geo. J. Mingins, Wm. L. Moore, James C. Nightingale, Geo. Nixon, Israel H. Northrup, Daniel H. Overton, Charles H. Parkhurst, Levi H. Parsons, James G. Patterson, Edward P. Payson, Vincent Pisek, George L. Prentiss, Hugh Pritchard, James S. Ramsay, Daniel Redmon, Charles S. Robinson, Stealy B. Rossiter, Albert G. Ruliffson, Wm. A. Rice, Robert F. Sample, Joseph Sanderson, Joseph A. Saxton, Philip Schaff, Adolphus Schauffler, J. Balcom Shaw, Geo. L. Shearer, Wm. G. T. Shedd, Andrew Shiland, Wilton M. Smith, Wm. C. Stitt, Charles A. Stoddard, J. Ford Sutton, Alex. W. Sproull,

Geo. L. Spining, Charles L. Thompson, John J. Thompson, Henry M. Tyndall, Henry Van Dyke, Marvin R. Vincent, Frederick E. Voegelin, A. L. R. Waite, W. Scott Watson, Geo. S. Webster, Erskine N. White, John T. Wilds, Livingston Willard, David G. Wylie.

373 Elders—Moses P. Brown, Adams Memorial; Albert R. Ledoux, Brick; A. P. Ketcham, Calvary; Wm. Mickens, Central; Andrew Robinson, Christ; James McDowell, East Harlem; H. Edwards Rowland, Fifth Avenue; Eugene McJimpsey, First; John McWilliam, Fourth; Geo. E. Sterry, Fourth Avenue; Saml. Reeve, Fourteenth Street; Samuel H. Willard, Harlem; Joseph Moorhead, Knox; Henry D. Nicoll, Madison Avenue; Charles H. Woodbury, Madison Square; Robert Johnson, Morrisania First; Thomas Anderson, New York; Gerardus C. King, North; Henry Q. Hawley, Park; James E. Ware, Phillips; Geo. C. Lay, Puritans; Cleveland H. Dodge, Riverside; Wm. M. Onderdonk, Rutgers R.; Robert Houston, Scotch; James Anderson, Seventh;

374 James L. Birdsall, Spring Street; Wm. R. Worrall, Thirteenth Street; Clarence E. Garey, Tremont; Thomas Bond, University; Robert Gentle, Union Tabernacle; Wm. A. Wheelock, Washington Heights; Robert Jaffray, West; Cl. P. Leggett, West End; Alex. Wilson, West Fifty-first Street; Richard Drummond, Westminster.

The Committee of Prosecution was permitted to introduce the following additional evidence:

(1) The Inaugural Address, 3d Edition, by Charles A. Briggs, D. D.

(2) Newman's Apologia pro vita sua, pages 1 and 4 in volume marked D.

(3) Martineau's Seat of Authority in Religion. Book I., Chapter 1 and 2. Book II., Chapter 2; Book IV., Chapter 2, in volume marked E.

(4) The Constitution of the Presbyterian Church in the
375 United States of America, marked F.

(5) The Holy Bible, marked G.

(6) Messianic Prophecy, by Charles A. Briggs, D. D., marked H (1).

(7) Biblical Study, by Charles A. Briggs, D. D., marked H (2).

(8) Whither, by Charles A. Briggs, D. D., marked H (3).

Dr. Briggs then introduced his evidence as follows:

(1) I offer in evidence the whole of the Holy Scriptures of the Old and New Testaments in the following texts and versions. (*a*) The Hebrew text of the Old Testament. Theile's editions. (*b*) The Septuagint version of the Old Testament, Sweet's edition. (*c*) The Greek text of the New Testament, edition of Westcott & Hort. (*d*) The revised English versions of the Old and New Testaments. (*e*) The authorized version, the variorum reference edition. I submit these, without reading, according to the ruling of Presbytery.

(2) I offer in evidence the Standards of Presbyterian Church in the United States of America in the amended edition, published by the Presbyterian Board of Publication, 1891.

I submit these, without reading, according to the ruling of the Presbytery, with the exception of a few passages which I shall now read. The Westminster Confession, I., i., 4, 5, 6, 7; X., I; XIII., 1; XVIII., 1, 2; XX., 2; XXV., 3; XXVII., 3; Larger Catechism, Ques. 90; Shorter Catechism, Ques. 2; Book of Discipline, Sec. 1.

(3) I shall offer in evidence the Inaugural Address as published in the first edition, with accompanying documents, under the title "The Edward Robinson Chair of Biblical Theology," as published in the second edition with an appendix, and as published in a third and fourth edition with appendices, all under the title "The Authority of Holy Scripture."

I beg leave to put a copy of the third edition of these documents in the hands of every member of the Court, in place of reading them, except so far as the following extracts, which I shall now read, in order to put the citations made by the Prosecution in the light of their context. I shall read p. 4-6; p. 10. I ask the Court to read especially 23-29, 32-36, 52, 55. I shall read from the appendices 85-89, 111.

(4) I offer in evidence the following official documents in so far as they bear upon this case.

(a) The Confession of Faith, together with the Larger and Lesser Catechisms composed by the reverend assembly of divines sitting at Westminster; edition of 1658.

(b) The Minutes of the Sessions of the Westminster Assembly, Nov., 1644, to March, 1649, edited for the Committee of the Church of Scotland, with an introduction by A. F. Mitchell, Edinburgh, 1874.

(c) The Records of the Presbyterian Church in the United States of America, published by Presbyterian Board of Publication.

(d) The Minutes of the Presbyterian Church in the United States of America, 1789-1892.

(e) The Minutes of the Presbytery of New York.

(f) The stenographical report of the meeting of Presbytery, Oct. 5th, 1891.

(g) The stenographical report of the meeting of Presbytery of New York, Nov. 4th, 1891.

(h) Stenographical report of the Sessions of the General Assembly at Portland, May 26-30, 1892.

(i) The Creeds of Christendom, by Dr. Schaff.

I submit these documents, without reading, in accordance with the ruling of the Presbytery, with the exception of the following extracts which I shall read to the Court at this time. Read extract from the Minutes of Presbytery, Oct. 5th, 1891, as given in the Case, pp. 135, 137.

(5) Inasmuch as the Prosecution have put in evidence all the works of Dr. Briggs quoted in the first and second editions of the Inaugural Address, so far as they "bear upon this case," the defendant puts in all the works of Dr. Briggs "in so far as they bear upon this case." These are put in evidence, without reading, in accordance with the ruling of the Presbytery, save the following testimony, which I shall read at the present time.

(a) Address on the occasion of his inauguration as Davenport professor of Hebrew and the cognate languages 379 in the Union Theological Seminary, October, 1876. (Read pp. 6, 7, 15, 16.)

(b) Article in the Presbyterian Review, 1881, on *the right, duty and limits of Biblical criticism*, pp. 242, 243, 138.

(c) Article on Biblical Theology in the Presbyterian Review, 1882, pp. 516–527, which was taken up into Biblical study in 1884 as Chapter XI., pp. 387, 404.

(d) *The Holy Scriptures a means of grace.*
Address before the Sunday School Teachers of the Presbytery of New York in 1883, repeated before the Reformed Theological Seminary at Lancaster and published as Chapter XII. of Biblical Study in 1884. (Read pp. 411, 412, 416, 417.)

(e) Article on, *A Critical Study of the History of the Higher Criticism*, in the Presbyterian Review, 1883. (Read pp. 129, 130.)

(f) Address at the beginning of the term of Union Theological Seminary, September, 1883, in Interpretation 380 of Holy Scripture, published as Chap. 10 of Biblical Study in 1884. (Read pp. 359, 355, 356.)

(g) Biblical Study, first edition 1884, second, third and fourth editions in subsequent years. (Read pp. 136, 137, 222, 227, 228, 240, 241.)

(h) American Presbyterianism, published in 1885. (Read pp. 9, 10.)

(i) Messianic Prophecy, published in 1886. (Read pp. 67, 192, 408.)

(j) Whither, published in 1889, second and third editions, 1890. (Read pp. 11, 285–287.)

(k) Article, *Redemption after Death*, in the Magazine of Christian Literature, Dec., 1889 (pp. 112, 114).

(l) *The Bible, the Church and the Reason*, 1891, consisting of an address at the opening of the term of the Union Theological Seminary, September 19, 1889, on Biblical History; an address delivered at Wellesley College, and before the American Institute of Sacred Litera- 381 ture, at Chicago, on the Messianic Ideal, in 1890, and several lectures delivered in the city of New York, and elsewhere, in order to set forth the defendant's views of the Bible, the Church and the Reason, in 1891. (Read pp. 63, 64, 115, 117.)

I beg leave to put a copy of this volume in the hands of every member of the Presbytery and to ask them to read it as an exposition of the Inaugural for the people in the matter included in the title.

Other passages will be read in the argument for the defense.

(6) I put in evidence all the authorities cited in my writings "in so far as they bear upon this case," and especially the following:

The Synod of New York and Philadelphia Vindicated, 1765.

Eight letters of Antony Tuckney and Benjamin Whichcote, London, 1755.

Wm. G. T. Shedd, Dogmatic Theology, 1888.

Orders and Regulations for Field Officers of the Salvation Army, London, 1891.

Ball, Treatise of Faith, 1837.

Martineau's Seat of Authority in Religion.

Westcott's Commentary on the Epistle of John Newman's Apologia.

A. A. Hodge and B. B. Warfield, Article, Inspiration, in Presbyterian Review, Vol. II.

John Wallis, Sermons, London, 1791.

Schaff, Church History, The German Reformation, 1888.

Lyford, Plain Man's Senses Exercised, 1655.

Best, Commentary on Galatians.

Schaff, Commentary on Galatians.

Lechler, Commentary on Acts.

Evans and Smith, Inspiration and Inerrancy, new edition, 1892.

Alexander, Commentary on Acts.

Delitzsch, Commentary on Genesis, new edition, 1887.

A. B. Davidson, Commentary on Job, 1884.

Delitzsch, Commentary on Ecclesiastes, 1875.
Kirkpatrick, Commentary on Samuel, 1884.
Perowne, Commentary on the Psalter, 6th edition, 1886.
Wesley's Sermons, cxxvi. 383
Calvin's Commentaries on the New Testament.
Westcott, Commentary on Hebrews, 1889.
Cotton Mather, Hades Looked Into, 1717.
Dorner's Future State, edited by Smythe, 1883.
A. F. Mitchell, The Westminster Assembly, 1883.
A. H. Strong, Systematic Theology, 1886.
Dr. Prentiss's Article, Infant Salvation, in the Presbyterian Review, Vol. IV.
G. P. Fisher, Nature and Method of Revelation, 1890.
Lux Mundi, 1890, 1892.
White's Way to the Tree of Life, 1848.
Sunday, Oracles of God, 1891.
A. B. Bruce, Kingdom of God, 1890.
H. B. Smith, System of Theology, 1884.
W. G. T. Shedd, Article, New York Observer, 1891.
W. H. Green, Article, New York Observer, 1891.

Add here the following writers who testify to errors in Holy Scripture, pp. 215, 235, of Bible, Church and Reason.

And also the following writers who testify against the Mosaic authorship of the Pentateuch and the integrity of Isaiah, pp. 236, 247, of Bible, Church and Reason.

These are submitted, without reading, in accordance with the ruling of the Presbytery. All this evidence, whether read or not read, is filed so far as it bears upon this case.

The question was here raised by the Prosecuting Com- 384
mittee of the necessity of putting Dr. Briggs under oath, in order to the admission of the evidence presented by him from his own works, otherwise said quotations should not be accepted as evidence. The parties were heard on this point, and the Moderator decided that because the whole evidence offered in the case was documentary and not personal or oral, and admitted to be authentic, the administration of the oath was not necessary.

From this decision the Prosecuting Committee took exception, and asked to have entered upon the record an exception to the above decision.

It was then resolved that the documentary evidence which has been offered by the defendant be considered competent, whereupon the Prosecuting Committee took exception and asked to have entered upon the record an exception to the decision of the Presbytery in admitting as lawful and competent evidence any part of the quotations made by the accused, in so far as they are writings or extracts from the writings of the accused, without his having first taken the oath or affirmation required by section 61 of the Book of Discipline.

The evidence from both parties having been entered, the Moderator announced that it is now proper to hear from the Prosecuting Committee. Whereupon Dr. Birch, of the Prosecuting Committee, was heard in part.

The minutes were read and approved as far as written.

After prayer, Presbytery took a recess until to-morrow at 2 P. M.

S. D. ALEXANDER,
Stated Clerk.

NEW YORK, 6TH DECEMBER, 1892.

BRIGGS CASE.

SCOTCH CHURCH, TUESDAY, DEC. 6, 2 P. M.

Opened with prayer.

Present: Ministers—John C. Bliss, Moderator ; Geo. Alexander, Samuel D. Alexander, Anson P. Atterbury, W. W. Atterbury, Frederick G. Beebe, Geo. W. F. Birch, Nicholas Bjerring, Robert R. Booth, Samuel Bowden, Thomas S. Bradner, Charles A. Briggs, Francis Brown, Walter D. Buchanan, James Chambers, Edward L. Clark, Nathaniel W. Conkling, Wilbur F. Crafts, John B. Devins, Ira S. Dodd, D. Stuart Dodge, Conrad Doench, Wm. Durant, Thomas Douglas, Howard Duffield, John H. Edwards, Frank F. Ellinwood, Henry B. Elliot, William T. Elsing, Charles P. Fagnani, Henry M. Field,

Walter B. Floyd, Jesse F. Forbes, Herbert Ford, Charles R. Gillett, Henri L. Grandlienard, James Hall, A. Woodruff Halsey, Wm. R. Harshaw, Thomas S. Hastings, Edward W. Hitchcock, James H. Hoadley, James Hunter, Samuel M. Jackson, Joseph R. Kerr, Albert B. King, A. Dunlop King, Joseph J. Lampe, Theodore Leonhard, Milton S. Littlefield, John C. Lowrie, Daniel E. Lorenz, Wm. Martin, Charles P. Mallery, Francis H. Marling, Henry T. McEwen, James H. McIlvaine, Alex. H. McKinney, Alex. McLean, Duncan J. McMillan, Horace G. Miller, Wm. L. Moore, James C. Nightingale, Geo. Nixon, Israel H. Northrup, Daniel H. Overton, Levi Parsons, James G. Patterson, John R. Paxton, Edward P. Payson, Geo. S. Payson, Vincent Pisek, Hugh Pritchard, James S. Ramsay, Daniel Redmon, Charles Robinson, Stealy B. Rossiter, Albert G. Ruliffson, William A. Rice, Robert F. Sample, Joseph Sanderson, Joseph A. Saxton, Philip Schaff, J. Balcom Shaw, Geo. L. Shearer, Wm. G. T. Shedd, Andrew Shiland, Wilton M. Smith, Wm. S. Stitt, Charles A. Stoddard, J. Ford Sutton, Alex. W. Sproull, Geo. L. Spinning, Charles L. Thompson, John J. Thompson, Henry M. Tyndall, Henry Van Dyke, Marvin R. Vincent, Fred. E. Voegelin, Thomas G. Wall, Abbott L. R. Waite, W. Scott Watson, Geo. Webster, Erskine N. White, John T. Wilds, Livingston Willard, David G. Wylie.

Elders—Moses P. Brown, Adams Memorial; James Tompkins, Bethany; Albert R. Ledoux, Brick; A. P. Ketcham, Calvary; Wm. Mickens, Central; Andrew Robinson, Christ; James McDowell, East Harlem; H. Edwards Rowland, Fifth Avenue; Eugene McJimpsey, First; John McWilliam, Fourth; Geo. E. Sterry, Fourth Avenue; Samuel Reeve, Fourteenth Street; Samuel H. Willard, Harlem; Joseph Moorhead, Knox; Charles H. Woodbury, Madison Square; Robert Johnson, Morrisania First; Thomas Anderson, New York; Gerardus C. King, North; Henry Q. Hawley, Park; James E. Ware, Phillips; Geo. C. Lay, Puritans; Cleveland H. Dodge, Riverdale; Wm. M. Onderdonk, Rutgers R.; Robert

Houston, Scotch ; James Anderson, Seventh ; James L. Birdsall, Spring Street ; Wm. R. Worrall, Thirteenth Street ; C. E. Garey, Tremont ; Thomas Bond, University Place ; Robert Gentle, Union Tabernacle ; Wm. A. Wheelock, Washington Heights ; Robert Jaffray, West ; C. P. Leggett, West End ; Richard Drummond, Westminster.

It was resolved that a committee of five be appointed to consider and report a principle which shall guide the Presbytery in the granting of permission to vote after temporary absence, and also to receive the excuses which are offered, and report upon the same to the Presbytery.

The Moderator therefore appointed as this committee Messrs. Henry Van Dyke, Anson P. Atterbury and James C. Nightingale, with elders Geo. E. Sterry and A. P. Ketcham.

Dr. Birch, of the Prosecuting Committee, now continued his argument.

Dr. Briggs asked respecting the evidence submitted by him yesterday, that certain extracts from publications named, as indicated in the pages given, which he offered without reading, in order to save time, be incorporated in the stenographer's notes.

Whereupon the Moderator decided that this should be done.

The Committee on Leave of Absence reported as follows : 1st. That the excuse for absence shall relate to a positive and important duty. 2d. That it shall not involve absence during two consecutive sessions. 3d. That the absentee shall qualify himself for voting by reading the records of the meeting at which he was absent. 4th. Excuses must be in writing.

The minutes were read and approved. Presbytery now took a recess until to-morrow at 2 P. M.

Concluded with prayer.

S. D. ALEXANDER,

Stated Clerk.

New York, 7th December, 1892.

Scotch Church, Dec. 7, 2 p. m.

BRIGGS CASE.

After recess Presbytery met and was opened with prayer.
Present: Ministers—John C. Bliss, Moderator; Geo. Alexander, Samuel D. Alexander, Anson P. Atterbury, W. Wallace Atterbury, Frederick G. Beebe, Geo. W. F. Birch, Nicholas Bjerring, Robert R. Booth, Samuel Bowden, Thomas S. Bradner, Charles A. Briggs, Francis Brown, Walter D. Buchanan, James Chambers, Edward L. Clark, Nathaniel W. Conkling, Wilbur F. Crafts, John B. Devins, Ira S. Dodd, D. Stuart Dodge, Conrad Doench, Wm. Durant, Thomas Douglas, Howard Duffield, John H. Edwards, Frank F. Ellinwood, Henry B. Elliot, Wm. T. Elsing, Charles P. Fagnani, Henry M. Field, Walter B. Floyd, Jesse F. Forbes, Herbert Ford, Charles R. Gillett, Henri L. Grandlienard, James Hall, A. Woodruff Halsey, Wm. R. Harshaw, Thomas S. Hastings, Edward W. Hitchcock, James H. Hoadley, James Hunter, Samuel M. Jackson, A. D. Lawrence Jewett, Joseph R. Kerr, Albert B. King, Alexander Dunlap King, Joseph J. Lampe, The. Leonhard, Milton S. Littlefield, John C. Lowrie, Daniel E. Lorenz, Wm. M. Martin, Charles P. Mallery, Francis H. Marling, Henry T. McEwen, James H. McIlvaine, Alex. H. McKinney, Alex. McLean, Duncan J. McMillan, Horace G. Miller, Wm. L. Moore, James C. Nightingale, George Nixon, Israel H. Northrup, Danl. H. Overton, Charles H. Parkhurst, Levi H. Parsons, James G. Patterson, John R. Paxton, Edward P. Payson, Geo. S. Payson, Hugh Pritchard, James S. Ramsey, Danl. Redmon, Charles S. Robinson, Stealy B. Rossiter, Albert G. Ruliffson, Wm. A. Rice, Robert F. Sample, Joseph Sanderson, Joseph A. Saxton, Philip Schaff, J. Balcom Shaw, Geo. L. Shearer, Wm. G. T. Shedd, Andrew Shiland, Wilton M. Smith, Wm. C. Stitt, Charles A. Stoddard, J. Ford Sutton, Alexander W. Sproull, Geo.

L. Spining, Charles L. Thompson, John J. Thompson, Henry M. Tyndall, Henry Van Dyke, Marvin R. Vincent, Fredk. E. Voegelin, Thomas G. Wall, Abbott L. R. Waite, W. Scott Watson, Geo. S. Webster, John T. Wilds, Livingston Willard, David G. Wylie.

393 Elders—Moses P. Brown, Adams Memorial; James Tompkins, Bethany; Albert R. Ledoux, Brick; A. P. Ketcham, Calvary; Wm. Mickens, Central; Andrew Robinson, Christ; James McDowell, East Harlem; H. Edwards Rowland, Fifth Avenue; Eugene McJimpsey, First; John McWilliam, Fourth; Geo. E. Sterry, Fourth Avenue; Saml. Reeve, Fourteenth Street; Saml. H. Willard, Harlem; Charles H. Woodbury, Madison Square; Robert Johnson, Morrisania First; Thomas Anderson, New York; Gerardus C. King, North; Henry Q. Hawley, Park; James E. Ware, Phillips; Geo. C. Lay, Puritans; Cleveland H. Dodge, Riverdale; Wm. M. Onderdonk, Rutgers; Robert Houston, Knox; James Anderson, Seventh; James L. Birdsall, Spring Street;
394 Wm. R. Worrall, Thirteenth Street; C. E. Garey, Tremont; Thomas Bond, University Place; Robert Gentle, Union Tabernacle; Wm. A. Wheelock, Washington Heights; Robert Jaffray, West; C. P. Leggett, West End; Alex. Wilson, West Fifty-first Street; Richard Drummond, Westminster.

The Committee of Leave of Absence reported, recommending that the following persons have unanimous consent to vote, on condition that they read the evidence submitted during their absence in full.

Rev. Messrs. Stitt, W. D. Buchanan, Arreghi, Shaw, E. N. White, Duffield and W. M. Smith under the rules.

Whereupon, by consent of the parties and Court, they were so excused.

It was resolved that Rev. Messrs. Vincent, Pisek and A. D. Lawrence Jewett, and Elder Alexander Wilson be enrolled.

The Rev. Henry Van Dyke, and Anson P. Atterbury resigned from the committee.

Mr. McCook, of the Prosecuting Committee, then asked the Clerk to read from pages 572 to 578, inclusive, of the stenographer's minutes of the proceedings of yesterday, Dec. 6, 1892, down to and including the sentence in brackets.

The extract called for was read.

Thereupon the following exception was presented, in compliance with Section 25 of the Book of Discipline:

In compliance with Section 25 of the Book of Discipline, the Prosecuting Committee take exception, and ask to have their exception entered upon the record as follows: The stenographic report of the proceedings of the judicatory upon December 5, 1892, as furnished to the parties by the stenographer, beginning at the last line of page 448 (erased page No. 484), being about twenty pages of the stenographer's notes, contain words and matter which were not spoken upon the floor of the Presbytery and were introduced, as is stated by the stenographer, into the stenographic record, upon the request of Prof. Briggs, with the approval of the Moderator.

The Prosecuting Committee further except, and ask leave to have their exception entered upon the record, against the decision and action of the Moderator, taken at the request of Prof. Briggs in instructing the stenographer, as appears by page 578 of the stenographer's report of the proceedings of December 6, 1892, to insert at page 468 of the official stenographic report of the proceedings of this court, had at its sessions Monday, December 5, 1892, fifteen additional printed sheets.

It was resolved that the record of the request of the Prosecuting Committee be stricken out from the minutes, which was done.

The Prosecuting Committee gave notice of exception, viz.:

The Prosecuting Committee except, and ask their exception to be noted on the record, against the action of the judicatory in striking from the minutes as read the request of the Prosecuting Committee to strike out the

matter contained upon pages 448 to a point below the middle of page 468, being about twenty pages of the stenographer's notes, which contain words and mat-
397 ter which were not spoken upon the floor of the Presbytery, and also the request of the Prosecuting Committee, that fifteen additional sheets which contain words and matter which were not spoken upon the floor of the Presbytery, which have been inserted at page 468 of the official stenographic report, be stricken out and that the accused be not permitted to refer to or use any portion of said twenty pages of the stenographer's notes or of the said fifteen additional printed sheets, or the books or documents therein referred to as evidence upon the trial or in any manner whatever before this judicatory.

398 Dr. Birch, of the Prosecuting Committee, now completed his argument, and Mr. McCook, of the Prosecuting Committee, was heard in part.

The Rev. Messrs. Van Dyke and A. P. Atterbury were, on motion, requested to remain on the Committee on Leave of Absence.

After the reading a part of the minutes Presbytery took a recess until Tuesday the 13th, at 2 P. M.

409 NEW YORK, 8th December, 1892.

SCOTCH CHURCH, 2 P. M.

BRIGGS CASE.

Presbytery met after recess (Dec. 7) and was opened with prayer.

Present: Ministers — John C. Bliss, Mod'r; Geo. Alexander, Saml. D. Alexander, Anson P. Atterbury, W. Wallace Atterbury, Frederick G. Beebe, Geo. W. F. Birch, Nicholas Bjerring, Robert R. Booth, Saml. Bowden, Thomas S. Bradner, Charles A. Briggs, Francis Brown, Walter D. Buchanan, James Chambers, Edward L. Clark, Nathaniel W. Conkling, John B. Devins, Ira S. Dodd, D. Stuart Dodge, Conrad Doench, Wm. Durant,

Thomas Douglas, Howard Duffield, John H. Edwards, Frank F. Ellinwood, Henry B. Elliot, Wm. T. Elsing, Charles P. Fagnani, Henry M. Field, Walter B. Floyd, Jesse F. Forbes, Herbert Ford, Charles R. Gillett, Henri L. Grandlienard, James Hall, A. Woodruff Halsey, Wm. R. Harshaw, Thomas S. Hastings, Edward W. Hitchcock, James H. Hoadley, James Hunter, Saml. N. Jackson, A. D. Lawrence, Jos. R. Kerr, Albert B. King, A. Dunlop King, Joseph J. Lampe, Theodore Leonhard, Milton S. Littlefield, John C. Lowrie, Daniel E. Lorenz, W. M. Martin, Charles P. Mallery, Francis H. Marling, Henry T. McEwen, James H. McIlvaine, Alexander H. McKinney, Alexander McLean, Duncan J. McMillan, Horace G. Miller, Wm. L. Moore, James C. Nightingale, Geo. Nixon, Israel H. Northrup, Daniel H. Overton, Charles H. Parkhurst, Levi H. Parsons, James G. Patterson, John R. Paxton, Edward P. Payson, Geo. S. Payson, Vincent Pisek, Hugh Pritchard, James S. Ramsay, Daniel Redmon, Charles S. Robinson, Stealy B. Rossiter, Albert G. Ruliffson, William A. Rice, Robert F. Sample, Joseph Sanderson, Joseph A. Saxton, Philip Schaff, J. Balcom Shaw, Geo. L. Shearer, Wm. G. T. Shedd, Andrew Shiland, Wilton M. Smith, Wm. C. Stitt, Charles A. Stoddard, J. Ford Sutton, Alex. W. Sproull, Geo. L. Spining, Charles L. Thompson, John J. Thompson, Henry M. Tyndall, Henry Van Dyke, Marvin R. Vincent, Frederick E. Voegelin, Thomas G. Wall, Abbott L. R. Waite, W. Scott Watson, Geo. S. Webster, John T. Wilds, Erskine N. White, Livingston Willard, David G. Wylie.

Elders—Moses P. Brown, Adams Memorial; James Tompkins, Bethany; Albert R. Ledoux, Brick; A. P. Ketcham, Calvary; Wm. Mickins, Central; Andrew Robinson, Christ; James McDowell, East Harlem; H. Edwards Rowland, Fifth Avenue; Eugene McJimpsey, First; John McWilliam, Fourth; Geo. E. Sterry, Fourth Avenue; Saml. Reeve, Fourteenth Street; Saml. H. Willard, Harlem; Charles H. Woodbury, Madison Square; Robert Johnson, First Morrisania;

Thomas Anderson, New York; Gerardus C. King, North; Henry Q. Hawley, Park; James E. Ware, Phillips; Geo. C. Lay, Puritans; Cleveland H. Dodge, Riverdale; Wm. M. Onderdonk, Rutgers; Robert Houston, Scotch; James Anderson, Seventh; James L. Birdsall, Spring Street; Wm. R. Worrall, Thirteenth Street; C. E. Garey, Tremont; Thomas Bond, University Place; Robert Gentle, Union Tabernacle; Wm. A. Wheelock, Washington Heights; C. P. Leggett, West End; Alex. Wilson, West Fifty-first Street; Richd. Drummond, Westminster.

412

On a question of privilege, notice of intention to protest against matter inserted in the stenographer's notes, not spoken upon the floor, was then given by Elder A. P. Ketcham.

Mr. McCook, of the Prosecuting Committee, then completed his argument.

It was resolved that when we take recess it be until Tuesday, December 13th, at 2 P. M., in view of the regular monthly meeting of Presbytery on Monday next, at 3 P. M.

The minutes were read and approved as far as written. Concluded with prayer.

Presbytery took recess until Tuesday next.

S. D. ALEXANDER,
Stated Clerk.

NEW YORK, 13TH DECEMBER, 1892.

413

BRIGGS CASE.

Presbytery met after recess December 13th, 2 P. M., in the Scotch Church.

Present: Ministers—John C. Bliss, Moderator; Geo. L. Alexander, Saml. D. Alexander, Antonio Arreghi, Anson P. Atterbury, W. Wallace Atterbury, Frederick G. Beebe, Geo. W. F. Birch, Nicholas Bjerring, Robert R. Booth, Saml. Bowden, Thos. S. Bradner, Charles A. Briggs, Francis Brown, Walter D. Buchanan, James Chambers, Edward L. Clark, Nathaniel W. Conkling, John B. Devins, Ira S. Dodd, D. Stuart Dodge, Conrad

Doench, Wm. Durant, Thomas Douglas, Howard Duffield, John H. Edwards, Frank F. Ellinwood, Henry B. Elliott, Charles P. Fagnani, Henry M. Field, Walter B. Floyd, Jesse F. Forbes, Herbert Ford, Charles R. Gillett, Henri L. Grandlienard, James Hall, A. Woodruff Halsey, Wm. R. Harshaw, Thomas S. Hastings, Edward W. Hitchcock, James H. Hoadley, James Hunter, Saml. M. Jackson, A. D. Lawrence Jewett, Joseph R. Kerr, Albert B. King, A. Dunlop King, Joseph J. Lampe, Theodore Leonhard, Milton S. Littlefield, John C. Lowrie, C. E. Lorenz, Wm. M. Martin, Charles P. Mallery, Francis H. Marling, James H. McIlvaine, Alex. H. McKinney, Alex. McLean, Duncan J. McMillan, Horace G. Miller, Wm. L. Moore, James C. Nightingale, Israel H. Northrup, Daniel H. Overton, Levi H. Parsons, James H. Patterson, John R. Paxton, Edward P. Payson, Vincent Pisek, Hugh Pritchard, James S. Ramsey, Daniel Redmon, Charles S. Robinson, Stealy B. Rossiter, Albert G. Ruliffson, William A. Rice, Robert F. Sample, Joseph Sanderson, Joseph A. Saxton, Philip Schaff, Geo. L. Shearer, Wm. G. T. Shedd, Andrew Shiland, Wilton M. Smith, Wm. C. Stitt, Charles A. Stoddard, J. Ford Sutton, Alex. W. Sproull, Geo. L. Spining, Charles L. Thompson, John J. Thompson, Henry M. Tyndall, Henry Van Dyke, Marvin R. Vincent, Thomas G. Wall, Abbott L. R. Waite, W. Scott Watson, Geo. S. Webster, Erskine N. White, Livingston Willard, David G. Wylie.

Elders—Moses P. Brown, Adams Memorial; James Tompkins, Bethany; Albert R. Ledoux, Brick; A. P. Ketcham, Calvary; William Mickins, Central; Andrew Robinson, Christ; James McDowell, East Harlem; H. Edwards Rowland, Fifth Avenue; Eugene McJimpsey, First; John McWilliam, Fourth; Geo. E. Sterry, Fourth Avenue; Saml. Reeve, Fourteenth Street; Saml. H. Willard, Harlem; Charles H. Woodbury, Madison Square; Robert Johnson, Morrisania First; Thomas Anderson, New York; Gerardus C. King, North; Henry Q. Hawley, Park; James E. Ware, Phillips; Geo. C.

Lay, Puritans ; Cleveland H. Dodge, Riverdale ; Robert Houston, Scotch ; James Anderson, Seventh ; James L. Birdsall, Spring Street ; Wm. R. Worrall, Thirteenth Street ; C. E. Garey, Tremont ; Thomas Bond, University Place ; Robert Gentle, Union Tabernacle ; Wm. A. Wheelock, Washington Heights ; Robert Jaffray, West ; C. P. Leggett, West End ; Richd. Drummond, Westminster.

The Rev. Dr. Briggs now began his defense, and continued his argument until the hour of recess.

The following members of the court were excused, under the rules, for a part of this afternoon, Rev. Messrs. J. Balcom Shaw, Henry T. McEwen, James Hunter, Geo. Alexander, Wm. T. Elsing, Thomas G. Wall, Horace G. Miller, and Elders William Onderdonk and Alexander Wilson.

The following were also excused for a part of Wednesday afternoon, Rev. Messrs. Anson P. Atterbury and Nicholas Bjerring and Elder A. R. Ledoux.

The following protest, of which notice was given at the last session of the Court, was then presented by A. P. Ketcham, and signed by A. P. Ketcham, Wm. G. T. Shedd, Geo. L. Shearer, Robert Russell Booth, Israel H. Northrup, Charles S. Robinson, Henry B. Elliott, Thomas Douglas, Hugh Pritchard, Samuel Bowden, W. B. Floyd, A. W. Sproull, Conrad Doench, H. G. Miller, Robert Houston, James Hall, Abbott L. R. Waite, Thomas Anderson, Wm. R. Worrall, Edward P. Payson.

PROTEST.

The undersigned, members of the Presbytery of New York, present at the judicial proceedings held on the fifth and sixth days of December, 1892, in the case of the Presbyterian Church in the United States of America against the Rev. Charles A. Briggs, D. D., and not approving of the proceedings in said case as hereinafter recited, do in compliance with section 104 of the Book of Dicipline, respectfully protest against the injurious and erroneous acts and proceedings hereinafter described.

The attention of the judicatory has been called to the fact that the stenographic report of the proceedings of this body upon December 5, 1892, includes about twenty pages of stenographer's notes beginning at the last line of page 448, erased page No. 461, to a point be- 418 low the middle of page 468, erased page No. 484, which contain words and matter which were not spoken upon the floor of the Presbytery, and, as it is stated by the stenographer, were inserted into the stenographic report, upon the request or suggestion of Professor Briggs, with the approval of the Moderator. This insertion of about twenty pages of new matter, which purports to be evidence in the case, now before the Presbytery, was made by the stenographer in the interval between two sessions of the judicatory, and after it had been announced to the house that both of the parties had fully presented their evidence and after the argument in behalf of the Prosecuting Committee had been begun. The fact that it was proposed to insert in the stenographer's minutes said twenty pages of notes, purporting to be evidence in the case, was not passed upon or authorized by the judicatory or mentioned upon the floor, or in any way called to the attention of the house until towards the close of the next day's session. (Stenographer's Report, p. 572.)

The attention of the judicatory has also been called to 419 the fact, that in addition to the twenty pages of stenographer's notes, containing new matter purporting to be evidence in this case inserted in the stenographer's report as above described, that it appears, by page 578 of the stenographer's report of the proceedings of December 6, 1892, that there had been inserted at page 468 of the official stenographic report of the proceedings of this body, held on Monday, December 5, 1892, fifteen additional printed sheets, which fifteen additional printed sheets are said to contain words and matter which were not spoken upon the floor of the Presbytery, and were introduced by the stenographer into the official stenographic report of the proceedings, as the minutes of December 6, 1892 (page 578), show, upon the request or suggestion of Prof. Briggs, and by direction of the Moderator.

This insertion of fifteen additional printed sheets of new matter which purports to be evidence in the case now before this Presbytery was made by the stenographer after it had been announced to the house that both of the parties had fully presented their evidence and after the argument in behalf of the Prosecuting Committee had been begun.

The fact that it was proposed to insert in the stenographer's minutes the said fifteen additional printed sheets, purporting to be evidence in the case, was not passed upon or authorized by the judicatory as such.

The Prosecuting Committee having called attention to these unauthorized additions to the stenographer's record, above referred to, and having taken exception thereto, they asked that the said twenty pages of stenographer's notes and the said fifteen additional printed sheets, purporting to be evidence in the judicial case, so introduced into the official stenographic record, should be stricken therefrom, and that the accused should not be permitted to refer to or use the contents of said twenty pages of stenographer's notes or of the said fifteen additional printed sheets, or any of the extracts, documents or books in either of them contained, recited or referred to, as evidence upon the trial, or in any manner whatever before this judicatory, and a motion having been duly made and seconded, that the judicatory should comply with the request of the Prosecuting Committee and strike out all such matter from the stenographic report, said motion was declared by the Moderator to be out of order and was not put to the house; subsequently, on motion made and seconded, the record upon the official minutes of Presbytery of the request of the Prosecuting Committee to strike out said twenty pages of stenographer's notes and said fifteen additional printed sheets, was stricken from the minutes of Presbytery, and exception was taken thereto by the Prosecuting Committee.

We respectfully protest against the above-described proceedings and action of the judicatory for the following reasons:

First. The stenographic report of the proceedings of a Judicatory should give an exact report of all that is said upon the floor, and nothing more. By the proceedings protested against there has been added to the stenographer's record much new matter, which should not have been inserted there.

Second. As the new matter thus introduced and improperly inserted in the stenographer's record, purports to be evidence in the case, it is misleading, erroneous and irregular and may greatly hamper, embarrass and possibly vitiate the entire judicial proceedings.

Third. Orderly procedure and obligation to set forth upon the record the exact facts in a judicial proceeding, require that no pains should be spared to secure the accuracy and integrity of the official stenographic report of the proceedings.

Fourth. By the proceedings and action now protested against, the entire record of this important judicial case may be rendered invalid and ineffectual, thus bringing discredit upon our system and working irreparable damage to one or other of the parties, to the cause of truth and the exercise of a wise and just discipline.

Signed as above.
New York, December 8, 1892.

It was then resolved that a committee be appointed to prepare an answer to the above protest to be entered on the record.

Whereupon the following were appointed such a committee: Rev. Messrs. Francis Brown and Duncan J. McMillan, with Elder Cleveland H. Dodge.

After the reading and approving of the minutes as far as written, Presbytery took a recess till to-morrow at 2 P. M.

S. D. ALEXANDER,
Stated Clerk.

NEW YORK, 14th December, 1892.
424   BRIGGS CASE.

SCOTCH CHURCH, TUESDAY, DEC. 14, 2 P. M.

Presbytery met after recess and was opened with prayer.
Present : Ministers—John C. Bliss, Mod.; Geo. Alexander, Saml. D. Alexander, Antonio Arreghi, Anson P. Atterbury, W. Wallace Atterbury, Frederick G. Beebe, Geo. W. F. Birch, Robert R. Booth, Saml. Bowden, Thomas S. Bradner, Charles A. Briggs, Francis Brown, Walter D. Buchanan, James Chambers, Edward L. Clark, John B. Devins, Ira S. Dodd, D. Stuart Dodge, Conrad Doench, William Durant, Thomas Douglas, Howard Duffield, John H. Edwards, Frank F. Ellinwood, Henry B. Elliot, Wm. T. E. Elsing, Charles P. Fagnani, Henry M. Field, Walter B. Floyd, Jesse F. Forbes, Herbert Ford, Charles R. Gillett, Henri Grandlienard, James Hall, A. Woodruff Halsey, Wm. R. Harshaw, Thomas S. Hastings, Edward W. Hitchcock, James H. Hoadley, James Hunter, Saml. M. Jackson, A. D. Lawrence Jewett, Joseph R. Kerr, Albert B. King, A. Dunlap King, Joseph J. Lampe, Milton S. Littlefield, John C. Lowrie, Daniel E. Lorenz, Wm. M. Martin, Charles P.
425 Mallery, Francis H. Marling, Henry T. McEwen, James H. Ilvaine, Alex. H. McKinney, Alexr. McLean, Duncan J. McMillan, Horace G. Miller, Geo. J. Mingins, Wm. L. Moore, James C. Nightingale, Geo. Nixon, Israel H. Northrup, Daniel H. Overton, Levi H. Parsons, James G. Patterson, John R. Patterson, Edward P. Payson, Vincent Pisek, Hugh Pritchard, James S. Ramsey, Daniel Redmon, Charles S. Robinson, Stealy B. Rossiter, Albert G. Ruliffson, Wm. A. Rice, Robert F. Sample, Joseph Sanderson, Joseph A. Saxton, Philip Schaff, J. Balcom Shaw, George L. Shearer, Wm. G. T. Shedd, Andrew Shiland, Wilton M. Smith, Wm. C. Stitt, Charles A. Stoddard, J. Ford Sutton, Alex. W. Sproull, Geo.

L. Spining, Charles L. Thompson, John J. Thompson, Henry M. Tyndall, Henry Van Dyke, Marvin R. Vincent, Thomas G. Wall, Abbott L. R. Waite, W. Scott Watson, Geo. S. Webster, Erskine N. White, Livingston Willard, David G. Wylie.

Elders—Moses P. Brown, Adams Memorial; James Tompkins, Bethany; Alex. P. Ketcham, Calvary; Wm. Mickens, Central; Andrew Robinson, Christ; James McDowell, East Harlem; H. Edwards Rowland, Fifth Avenue; Eugene McJimpsey, First; John McWilliam, Fourth; Geo. E. Sterry, Fourth Avenue; Saml. Reeve, Fourteenth Street; Saml. H. Willard, Harlem; Joseph Moorhead, Knox; Charles H. Woodbury, Madison Square; Robert Johnson, First Morrisania; Thomas Anderson, New York; G. C. King, North; Henry Q. Hawley, Park; James E. Ware, Phillips; Geo. C. Lay, Puritans; Cleveland H. Dodge, Riverdale; Wm. M. Onderdonk, Rutgers, R.; Robert Houston, Scotch; James Anderson, Seventh; Wm. R. Worrall, Thirteenth Street; C. E. Garey, Tremont; Thomas Bond, University Place; Robert Gentle, Union Tabernacle; Wm. A. Wheelock, Washington Heights; Robert Jaffray, West; C. P. Leggett, West End; Richd. Drummond, Westminster.

After the roll call Dr. Briggs continued his argument. At twenty minutes of four o'clock an intermission of ten minutes was taken, after which Dr. Briggs continued his argument until recess.

It was resolved that Dr. Briggs have leave to present to the Court a part of his argument in print without reading, and that this part go into the official report of the stenographer.

The Prosecuting Committee excepted and asks to have its exception noted upon the record to the action of the Presbytery in resolving that Dr. Briggs have leave to present to the Court a part of his argument in print without reading, and that this fact go into the official report of the stenographer.

Whereupon Dr. Sutton gave notice of protest against this action.

After the reading and approval of the minutes as far as written, and prayer, Presbytery took a recess.

S. D. ALEXANDER,
Stated Clerk.

NEW YORK, 15TH DECEMBER, 1892.

BRIGGS CASE.

SCOTCH CHURCH, 2 P. M.

After recess Presbytery met and was opened with prayer.

Present: Ministers—John C. Bliss, Mod.; Geo. Alexander, Saml. D. Alexander, Antonio Arreghi, Anson P. Atterbury, W. Wallace Atterbury, Frederick G. Beebe, Geo. W. F. Birch, Nicholas Bjerring, Robert R. Booth, Saml. Bowden, Thomas S. Bradner, Charles A. Briggs, Francis Brown, Walter D. Buchanan, James Chambers, Edward L. Clark, John B. Devins, Ira S. Dodd, D. Stuart Dodge, Conrad Doench, Wm. Durant, Thomas Douglas, Howard Duffield, John H. Edwards, Frank F. Ellinwood, Henry B. Elliot, Wm. T. Elsing, Charles P. Fagnani, Henry M. Field, Walter B. Floyd, Jesse F. Forbes, Herbert Ford, Charles R. Gillett, Henri L. Grandlienard, James Hall, A. Woodruff Halsey, Wm. R. Harshaw, Thomas S. Hastings, Edward W. Hitchcock, James H. Hoadley, James Hunter, Saml. M. Jackson, A. D. Lawrence Jewett, Joseph H. Kerr, Albert B. King, A. Dunlop King, Joseph J. Lampe, Theodore Leonhard, Milton S. Littlefield, John C. Lowrie, Daniel E. Lorenz, Wm. M. Martin, Ch. P. Mallery, Francis H. Marling, Henry T. McEwen, James H. McIlvaine, Alex. H. McKinney, Alex. McLean, Duncan McMillan, Horace G. Miller, Geo. J. Mingins, Wm. L. Moore, James C. Nightingale, Geo. Nixon, Israel H. Northrup, Daniel H. Overton, Levi H. Parsons, James G. Patterson, John R. Paxton, Edward P. Payson, Geo. S. Payson, Vincent Pisek, Hugh Pritchard, James S. Ramsay, Daniel Redmon, Charles S.

Robinson, Stealy B. Rossiter, Albert G. Ruliffson, Wm. A. Rice, Robert F. Sample, Joseph Sanderson, Joseph A. Saxton, Philip Schaff, J. Balcom Shaw, Geo. L. Shearer, Wm. G. T. Shedd, Andrew Shiland, Wilton M. Smith, Wm. C. Stitt, Charles A. Stoddard, J. Ford Sutton, Alex. W. Sproull, Geo. L. Spining, Charles L. Thompson, John J. Thompson, Henry M. Tyndall, Henry Van Dyke, Marvin R. Vincent, Fred. E. Voegelin, Thomas G. Wall, Abbott L. R. Waite, W. Scott Watson, Geo. S. Webster, Erskine N. White, Livingston Willard, David G. Wylie.

Elders—Moses P. Brown, Adams Memorial; James Tompkins, Bethany; Albert R. Ledoux, Brick; Alexander P. Ketcham, Calvary; William Mickens, Central; Andrew Robinson, Christ; James McDowell, East Harlem; H. Edwards Rowland, Fifth Avenue; Eugene McJimpsey, First; John McWilliam, Fourth; Geo. E. Sterry, Fourth Avenue; Saml. Reeve, Fourteenth Street; Saml. H. Willard, Harlem; Joseph Moorhead, Knox; Charles H. Woodbury, Madison Square; Robert Johnson, First Morrisania; Thomas Anderson, New York; G. C. King, North; Henry Q. Hawley, Park; James E. Ware, Phillips; Geo. C. Lay, Puritans; Cleveland H. Dodge, Riverdale; Wm. M. Onderdonk, Rutgers, R.; Robert Houston, Knox; James Anderson, Seventh; Wm. R. Worrall, Thirteenth Street; C. E. Garey, Tremont; Thomas Bond, University Place; Robert Gentle, Union Tabernacle; Wm. A. Wheelock, Washington Heights; Robert Jaffray, West; C. P. Leggett, West End; Richard Drummond, Westminster, etc.

After the calling of the roll Dr. Briggs continued his argument.

At twenty minutes to four an intermission of a few minutes was taken, after which Dr. Briggs handed to the members of the Court in print a portion of that part of his argument referred to in the resolution of yesterday. He then continued his argument until the hour of recess.

Under the rule, and with unanimous consent, the following ministers were excused from Monday's session:

C. L. Thompson, Henry T. McEwen, Wm. Durant, Erskine N. White, Frank F. Ellinwood and Milton S. Littlefield.

After reading and approving the minutes so far as written, Presbytery took a recess until to-morrow at 2 P. M.

Concluded with prayer.

S. D. ALEXANDER,
Stated Clerk.

432 NEW YORK, 19TH DECEMBER, 1892.

SCOTCH CHURCH, DECEMBER 19, 2 P. M.

Presbytery met after recess and was opened with prayer.

Present: Ministers—John C. Bliss, Moderator; Geo. Alexander, Saml. D. Alexander, Antonio Arreghi, Anson P. Atterbury, W. Wallace Atterbury, Frederick G. Beebe, Geo. W. F. Birch, Nicholas Bjerring, Robert R. Booth, Saml. Bowden, Thos. S. Bradner, Chas. A. Briggs, Francis Brown, Walter D. Buchanan, James Chambers, Edward L. Clark, John B. Devins, Ira S. Dodd, D. Stuart Dodge, Conrad Doench, Thomas Douglas, Howard Duffield, John H. Edwards, Frank F. Ellinwood, Henry B. Elliot, Wm. T. Elsing, Charles P. Fagnani, Henry M. Field, Walter B. Floyd, Jesse F. Forbes, Herbert Ford, Charles R. Gillett, Henri Grandlienard, James Hall, A. W. Halsey, Wm. R. Harshaw, Thomas S. Hastings, Edward W. Hitchcock, James H. Hoadley, James Hunter, Saml. M. Jackson, A. D. Lawrence Jewett, Jos. R. Kerr, Albert B. King, A. Dunlop King, Joseph J. Lampe, Theodore Leonhard, Milton S. Littlefield, John C. Lowrie, Daniel E. Lorenz, Wm. M. Martin, Charles P. Mallery, Francis H. Marling, Henry T. McEwen, Alex. McLean, Duncan J. McMillan, Horace G. Miller, Geo. J. 433 Mingins, James C. Nightingale, Geo. Nixon, Israel H. Northrup, Daniel H. Overton, Levi H. Parsons, James G. Patterson, Edward P. Payson, Geo. S. Payson, Vincent Pisek, Hugh Pritchard, James S. Ramsay, Daniel Redmon, Charles S. Robinson, Stealy B. Rossiter, Albert G. Ruliffson, Wm. A. Rice, Robert F. Sample, Jos. Sanderson, Jos. A. Saxton, Philip Schaff, J. Balcom Shaw, Geo. L. Shearer, Andrew Shiland, Wilton M. Smith, Wm. C. Stitt, Charles A. Stoddard, J. Ford Sutton, Alex. W. Sproull, Geo. L. Spining, Ch. L. Thompson, John J. Thompson, Henry M. Tyndall, Henry Van Dyke, Marvin R. Vincent, Frederick E. Voegelin, Thos. G. Wall, Abbott L. R. Waite, W. Scott Watson, Geo. S. Webster, Erskine N. White, Livingston Willard, David G. Wylie.

Elders—Moses P. Brown, Adams Memorial; James Tompkins, Bethany; Albert R. Ledoux, Brick; Alex. P. Ketcham, Calvary; Wm. Mickens, Central; Andrew Robinson, Christ; James McDowell, East Harlem; H. Edwards Rowland, Fifth Avenue; Eugene McJimpsey, First; John McWilliam, Fourth; Geo. E. Sterry, Fourth Avenue; Saml. Reeve, Fourteenth Street; Saml. H. Willard, Harlem; Joseph Moorhead, Knox; Charles H. Woodbury, Madison Square; Robert Johnson, First Morrisania; G. C. King, North; Henry Q. Hawley, Park; James E. Ware, Phillips; Geo. C. Lay, Puritans; Cleveland H. Dodge, Riverdale; Wm. M. Onderdonk, Rutgers, R.; Robert Houston, Scotch; James Anderson, Seventh; Wm. R. Worrall, Thirteenth Street; C. E. Garey, Tremont; Thomas Bond, University Place; Robert Gentle, Union Tabernacle; Wm. A. Wheelock, Washington Heights; Robert Jaffray, West; C. P. Leggett, West End; Richard Drummond, Westminster.

After the calling of the roll Dr. Briggs continued his argument.

At a quarter to four a brief intermission was taken, when Dr. Briggs concluded his argument.

Dr. Briggs raised the following question, viz.: that according to the Book of Discipline the Prosecution have no right to rebuttal.

On this question Dr. Briggs asked for a ruling.

The hour of adjournment having arrived, it was resolved at this point that the time be extended fifteen minutes. After hearing from the parties the Moderator ruled:

1. That the usage in such cases is against the point which is raised.

2. That usage is based upon the law of the Church, governing complaints and appeals, which distinctly give us this order of the opening, and the closing being on the part of those who present their case, the greater including the less.

3. That the parties cannot have been said to have been heard until the Prosecution has had a full opportunity to present its whole case. It has only presented a part of that case so far. It has taken a very small portion of time compared with that accorded to the defendant.

436 You have heard the defendant patiently and fully, as you should have done, and now, in the view of the Moderator, it is only fair, it is only in accordance with our usage and with the principles of the Book, that the Prosecution should be heard fully, but not presenting new matter.

An appeal from the decision of the Moderator was then taken; whereupon the Moderator's decision was by vote of the house sustained.

Under the rules Rev. Messrs. Jos: R. Kerr and Shearer were, by unanimous consent, excused for to-morrow.

After reading and approving the minutes, as far as written, and prayer, Presbytery took a recess until tomorrow, at 2 P. M.

S. D. ALEXANDER,
Stated Clerk.

437   NEW YORK, 20th December, 1892.

SCOTCH CHURCH, TUESDAY, DEC. 20TH, 2 P. M.

Presbytery met after recess and was opened with prayer.

Present: Ministers—John C. Bliss, Mod.; Geo. Alexander, Saml. D. Alexander, Antonio Arreghi, Anson P. Atterbury, W. Wallace Atterbury, Fred. G. Beebe, Nicholas Bjerring, Robert R. Booth, Saml. Bowden, T. S.

Bradner, Charles A. Briggs, Geo. W. F. Birch, Francis Brown, Walter D. Buchanan, James Chambers, Edward L. Clark, Ira S. Dodd, D. Stuart Dodge, Conrad Doench, Wm. Durant, Thos. Douglas, Howard Duffield, John H. Edwards, Frank F. Ellinwood, Henry B. Elliot, Wm. T. Elsing, Charles P. Fagnani, Henry M. Field, Walter B. Floyd, Jesse F. Forbes, Herbert Ford, Charles R. Gillett, Henri Grandlienard, James Hall, A. Woodruff Halsey, Wm. R. Harshaw, Thos. S. Hastings, Edward W. Hitchcock, James H. Hoadley, James Hunter, Saml. M. Jackson, A. D. Lawrence Jewett, Joseph R. Kerr, Albert B. King, A. Dunlop King, Joseph J. Lampe, Theodore Leonhard, Milton S. Littlefield, John C. Lowrie, Daniel E. Lorenz, Wm. M. Martin, Charles P. Mallery, Francis H. Marling, Henry T. McEwen, James H. McIlvaine, Alex. H. McKinney, Alex. McLean, Duncan J. McMillan, Horace G. Miller, Geo. J. Mingins, Wm. L. Moore, James C. Nightingale, Geo. Nixon, Israel H. Northrup, Dan. H. Overton, Levi H. Parsons, James G. Patterson, John R. Paxton, Edward P. Payson, Geo. S. Payson, Vincent 438 Pisek, Hugh Pritchard, James S. Ramsay, Daniel Redmon, Charles S. Robinson, Stealy B. Rossiter, Albert G. Ruliffson, Wm. A. Rice, Robert F. Sample, Joseph Sanderson, Joseph A. Saxton, Philip Schaff, J. B. Shaw, Geo. L. Shearer, Andrew Shiland, Wilton M. Smith, Wm. C. Stitt, Charles A. Stoddard, J. Ford Sutton, Alex. W. Sproull, Geo. L. Spining, Ch. L. Thompson, John J. Thompson, Henry M. Tyndall, Henry Van Dyke, Marvin R. Vincent, Fred. E. Voegelin, Thomas G. Wall, Abbott L. R. Waite, W. Scott Watson, Geo. S. Webster, E. N. White, Livingston Willard, David G. Wylie.

Elders—Moses P. Brown, Adams Memorial; James Tompkins, Bethany; Albert R. Ledoux, Brick; Alex. P. Ketcham, Calvary; Wm. Mickens, Central; Andrew Robinson, Christ; James McDowell, East Harlem; H Edwards Rowland, Fifth Avenue; Eugene McJimpsey First; John McWilliam, Fourth; Geo. E. Sterry, University Place; Saml. Reeve, Fourteenth Street; Saml. H. 439 Willard, Harlem; Joseph Moorhead, Knox; Ch. H.

Woodbury, Madison Square; Robert Johnson, Morrisania First; Thomas Anderson, New York; G. C. King, North; Henry Q. Hawley, Park; James E. Ware, Phillips; Geo. C. Lay, Puritans; Cleveland H. Dodge, Riverdale; Wm. M. Onderdonk, Rutgers; Robert Houston, Scotch; James Anderson, Seventh; Wm. R. Worrall, Thirteenth Street; C. E. Garey, Tremont; Thomas Bond, University Place; Robert Gentle, Union Tabernacle; Wm. A. Wheelock, Washington Heights; Robert Jaffray, West; C. P. Leggett, West End; Richard Drummond, Westminster.

After the calling of the roll the Committee appointed to bring in an answer to the protest made December 13, 1892, presented the following answer, viz.: The Presbytery desires to record the following answer in accordance with Section 106 of the Book of Discipline, to the protest signed by A. P. Ketcham, W. G. T. Shedd, Geo. L. Shearer and others against action of this Judicatory relating to the record of evidence in the case of the Rev. Charles A. Briggs, D. D.

I. The Presbytery calls attention to the fact that though the protest is declared to be made against "injurious and erroneous acts and proceedings," it cites but one act against which protest is lawful. Section 104 of the Book of Discipline gives to members of a minority the right to protest. A minority exists only when some question has been decided by a majority vote. The only such action related in the protest is the vote of the Presbytery to strike out the record of a request made by the Prosecution. Against this action only, among the proceedings set forth in the protest, is the protest lawful. But it is noteworthy that, of the four reasons assigned by the protestants, not one relates to the question whether the Presbytery erred in striking out the record of this request.

The reasons therefore do not sustain the protest, and it might be enough to record the fact as a sufficient legal answer to the protest. But inasmuch as the protest calls in question certain other proceedings, on alleged grounds of justice and error, the Presbytery deems it wise and proper, notwithstanding this technical defect, to cover in its answer all the matters embraced in the protest.

II. The Presbytery finds the relation of facts in the protest to be incomplete, inaccurate and misleading in several particulars, and desires to supplement and correct it, as follows:

(*a*) The matter now appearing on pp. 448–468 of the stenographer's official notes and in the printed sheets inserted at p. 468 of the said notes, and referred to in the protest, was all brought to the notice of the Presbytery, was placed in the hands of each member of the Presbytery and of the Prosecution in printed form, was offered by the defendant as evidence, and was sufficiently described and identified by him.

(*b*) The defendant was prepared and ready to read the evidence if the Presbytery so desired, and omitted the reading of it solely to save the time of the Presbytery, already severely taxed.

(*c*) In this, the defendant evidently acted in good faith, and with the simple desire to meet the convenience of the Presbytery, and the Presbytery so understood and acquiesced without a word of dissent.

(*d*) After the defendant had offered all his evidence, including the evidence which has been made the occasion of protest, the Presbytery voted "that the documentary evidence which has been offered by the defendant be considered competent." (Minutes of Presbytery, December 5, 1892, p. 384.)

(*e*) The contents of the pages indicated, in the stenographer's report, are therefore not "new matter which purports to be evidence," as the protest terms them, nor were they introduced after the time for the lawful introduction of evidence was past, but they are a part of the evidence introduced by the defendant lawfully and at the proper time.

(*f*) Assuming it to be true that the matter on pages 448–468 of the stenographer's report was there recorded by the authority of the Moderator, it is evident that the authority of the Moderator, in this, gave effect to the will of the Presbytery indicated by its acquiescence and consent aforesaid.

(*g*) In addition to his general powers as representative of the Presbytery, the Moderator had the special powers vested in him as Chairman and representative of the Committee appointed November 28, 1892, "to supervise the official stenographer's report of the proceedings." (Minutes of November 28, 1892, p. 347.)

(*h*) There is no evidence in the stenographer's notes or elsewhere, that the contents of pp. 448-468, of said notes or any part of them, were "inserted" in any other sense than would properly apply to all the stenographer's materials, including his short-hand notes and such written or printed documents as are placed in his hands, which are put in the type-written form "in the interval between two sessions of the judicatory."

444 (*i*) The fifteen sheets of printed matter referred to in the protest were introduced by the direction of the Moderator in open Presbytery, and with the full accord of Presbytery; the Moderator making his decision distinctly, stating it repeatedly, and calling attention to the fact that his decision was subject to an appeal to the house, if any one should appeal; and neither the Prosecution nor any one of the protestants, nor any other member of the judicatory, made a motion, or showed a desire to take such an appeal. (Minutes of Dec. 6, 1892, pp. 389, 390; Stenographer's Report, pp. 577, 578.)

(*j*) He previously decided that evidence need not be read to the Presbytery in order to be competent evidence (Minutes Nov. 30, 1892, pp. 362, 370; stenographer's report, pp. 297, 314, 364), and the action concerning the evidence now under consideration accorded with that decision.

(*k*) The Presbytery calls attention to the statement of the protest that "a motion having been duly made and seconded, that the judicatory should comply with the request of the Prosecuting Committee and strike out all such matter from the stenographer's report, such motion was declared out of order by the Moderator, and was not put to the house," as an erroneous statement, in that, it appears from the stenographer's notes, no such motion 445 was made. The only motion offered in behalf of the Prosecution in this matter was the motion to have their request entered on the minutes; an amendment was offered to the effect that their request be excluded from the minutes, and the motion passed in the amended form. (Stenographic report, pp. 582, 591, 662, 681, 684, 696, especially pp. 664, 671 and 672.)

III. The reasons assigned in the protest are, as already indicated, totally irrelevant, since they have no connection with the only part of the proceedings referred to against which protest is lawful, viz.: the decision of Presbytery to exclude from the record a request made by the Prosecution. But they embody criticisms of action taken by the Moderator and the Presbytery which the Presbytery is unwilling to pass by without notice.

(*a*) The first "reason" is, in the judgment of the Presbytery, an invalid criticism, because, while the stenographer's report of the proceedings should be an exact 446 record, that report may and properly should include whatever is received and taken as read and spoken, and so given the effect of read or spoken words. The evidence under consideration was, to save valuable time, offered without reading and taken as read.

(*b*) The second "reason" is, in the judgment of the Presbytery, an invalid criticism, because no "new matter" was introduced into the stenographer's notes, because the matter referred to had been brought before the Presbytery, and was properly introduced, and because said matter is actually evidence in the case, admitted by the Presbytery as competent. The Presbytery is therefore unable to see how there can be therein anything "misleading, erroneous and irregular," or anything "that may greatly hamper, embarrass and possibly vitiate the entire judicial proceedings."

(c) The third "reason" is, in the judgment of the Presbytery, an invalid criticism, because the accuracy and integrity of the official stenographic report of the proceedings were in fact secured by the incorporation of the said matter in the said report, and would not have been secured otherwise.

447 (d) The fourth "reason" is, in the judgment of the Presbytery, an invalid criticism, because the Presbytery is unable to see how "the entire records of this important case may be rendered invalid and ineffectual," by the action criticised, unless the incorporation in the record of all the evidence which the judicatory has admitted as competent, instead of the admission of a part, should have the effect of making the record "invalid and ineffectual," which seems absurd.

IV. Although a protest, with relevant reasons, against the action of the Presbytery in excluding the record of the request of the Prosecution from the minutes of Presbytery, would be technically in order, it seems surprising that any should suppose the record of the request to be admissible.

(a) No action on the request was taken, or even proposed, and the minutes do not include a record of action not taken.

448 (b) The request was to the effect that the said twenty pages of the stenographer's notes and the said fifteen additional printed sheets should be stricken from the official stenographic record, "and that the accused should not be permitted to refer to or use the contents of said twenty pages of stenographer's notes, or of the said fifteen additional printed sheets, or any of the extracts, documents or books in either of them contained, recited or referred to, as evidence upon the trial, or in any manner whatever, before this judicatory." Notwithstanding the facts that the Presbytery had by vote declared this with the other evidence offered by the defendant to be competent evidence, and that it was actually a part of the lawful evidence presented by the defendant, and that the Moderator had explicitly so recognized it and secured

its embodiment in the official stenographic record as aforesaid, and that no appeal had been taken from the decision of the Moderator that it should be embodied therein, and that for these reasons the Prosecution had no right to make the request, and that the Moderator had ruled that the request was not in order, and matters declared to be not in order have no place on the official record of proceedings.

(c) The attempt to secure the record of the said request under the guise of the record of an exception, which exception the prosecution were entitled, if they thought best, to take to any part of the proceedings that they disapproved was improper and out of order.

V. Inasmuch as,

(a) The failure to include in the official stenographer's report a part of the evidence which had been offered by the defendant, taken as read by the acquiescence and consent of the judicatory, and by vote accepted as competent, would have been an irregular act, and one of singular injustice to the defendant; and (b) the inclusion of the said evidence in the said report involved no wrong, hardship or injustice to the prosecution, and the prosecution therefore had no just ground for desiring that it be not included, or for seeking to deprive the defendant of his right to use it for the purposes of his defense before the judicatory, and (c) the action and the decisions of the Moderator, in reference to this matter, and the acquiescence of the Presbytery therein, appear to have been equitable and right, and (d) the exclusion of the request of the prosecution from the minutes, by vote of the Presbytery, was in accordance with precedent and the requirements of the case.

Therefore, in view of all the foregoing considerations, the Presbytery is unable to see any justification for the protest, or any proper ground for the criticisms contained therein.

The following persons were excused under the rule and by unanimous consent, for being absent yesterday: Rev. Messrs. S. B. Rossiter, W. L. Moore, W. C. Stitt, J. H.

McIlvaine, A. H. McKinney, with Thomas Anderson. For to-day the following were thus excused: J. R. Paxton, W. W. Atterbury, with Elders A. P. Ketcham and Samuel Reeve. For to-morrow C. S. Robinson and N. Bjerring.

The Rev. Joseph J. Lampe, of the Prosecuting Committee, was then heard. At twenty-five minutes of four a brief intermission was taken, when Dr. Lampe continued his argument till recess.

The Committee of Arrangements presented suggestions for taking the vote. The report, was, on motion, laid on the table until to-morrow.

The minutes were read and approved as far as written. Presbytery now took a recess. Concluded with prayer.

S. D. ALEXANDER,
Stated Clerk.

451 NEW YORK, 21ST DECEMBER, 1892.

SCOTCH CHURCH, 2 P. M.

Presbytery met and was opened with prayer.

Present: Ministers—John C. Bliss, Moderator; Geo. Alexander, Saml. D. Alexander, Antonio Arreghi, Anson P. Atterbury, W. Wallace Atterbury, Fred. G. Beebe, Geo. W. F. Birch, Nicholas Bjerring, Robt. R. Booth, Saml. Bowden, Thos. S. Bradner, Charles A. Briggs, Francis Brown, Walter D. Buchanan, James Chambers, Edward L. Clark, Ira S. Dodd, D. Stuart Dodge, Conrad Doench, William Durant, Thos. Douglas, Howard Duffield, John H. Edwards, Henry B. Elliot, Wm. T. Elsing, Charles P. Fagnani, Henry M. Field, Walter B. Floyd, Jesse F. Forbes, Herbert Ford, Charles R. Gillett, Henri Grandlienard, James Hall, A. W. Halsey, Wm. R. Harshaw, Thomas S. Hastings, Edward W. Hitchcock, James H. Hoadley, James Hunter, Saml. M. Jackson, A. D. L. Jewett, Jos. R. Kerr, Albert B. King, A. Dunlop King, Jos. J. Lampe, Theo. Leonhard, Milton S. Littlefield, John C. Lowrie, Daniel E. Lorenz, Wm. M. Martin,
452 Charles P. Mallery, Francis H. Marling, Henry T. Mc-

Ewen, James H. McIlvaine, A. H. McKinney, Alex. McLean, Duncan J. McMillan, Horace G. Miller, Geo. J. Mingins, Wm. L. Moore, J. C. Nightingale, Geo. Nixon, I. H. Northrup, Dan. H. Overton, Levi H. Parsons, James G. Patterson, Edward P. Payson, Geo. S. Payson, Vincent Pisek, Hugh Pritchard, James S. Ramsay, Daniel Redmon, Charles S. Robinson, Stealy B. Rossiter, A. G. Ruliffson, Wm. A. Rice, Robt. F. Sample, Jos. Sanderson, Jos. A. Saxton, Philip Schaff, J. Balcom Shaw, Geo. L. Shearer, Andrew Shiland, Wilton M. Smith, Wm. C. Stitt, Ch. A. Stoddard, J. Ford Sutton, Alex. W. Sproull, Geo. L. Spining, C. L. Thompson, John J. Thompson, Henry M. Tyndall, Henry Van Dyke, Marvin R. Vincent, Fred. E. Voegelin, Thomas G. Wall, A. L. R. Waite, W. Scott Watson, Geo. S. Webster, E. N. White, L. Willard, David G. Wylie.

Elders—James Tompkins, Bethany; Albert R. Ledoux, Brick; A. P. Ketcham, Calvary; Wm. Mickens, Central; James McDowell, East Harlem; H. Edwards Rowland, Fifth Avenue; Eugene McJimpsey, First; John McWilliam, Fourth; Geo. E. Sterry, Fourth Avenue; Saml. H. Willard, Harlem; Saml. Reeve, Fourteenth Street; Joseph Moorhead, Knox; Chas. H. Woodbury, Madison Square; Robert Johnson, Morrisania First; Thomas Anderson, New York; G. C. King, North; Henry Q. Hawley, Park; James E. Ware, Phillips; Geo. C. Lay, Puritans; Cleveland H. Dodge, Riverdale; Wm. M. Onderdonk, Rutgers; Robert Houston, Scotch; James Anderson, Seventh; Wm. R. Worrall, Thirteenth Street; C. E. Garey, Tremont; Thomas Bond, University Place; Robert Gentle, Union Tabernacle; Wm. A. Wheelock, Washington Heights; Robert Jaffray, West; C. P. Leggett, West End; Richard Drummond, Westminster.

After the calling of the roll, Dr. Briggs took exception to the proceedings of yesterday, as follows:

I beg leave to take exception to that part of the proceedings of the Presbytery, of yesterday, recorded in the stenographical report, which permitted the Rev. Dr. Lampe, arguing on behalf of the Prosecution, under

the cloak of a rebuttal, to introduce new evidence and new matter, and, in large measure, to reargue the Amended Charges and Specifications apart from and without regard to the argument of the accused ; in that (1) he introduced new evidence without the permission of Presbytery, and without notification to the accused, as follows: Henry B. Smith's Introduction to Christian Theology ; Henry B. Smith's Sermon on Inspiration ; Presbyterian and Reformed Review, 1892 ; Article in the Congregationalist, February 21, 1889 ; John Ball's Catechism ; The Bible Doctrine of Inspiration ; Farrar's Life of St. Paul ; Homiletical Review, May, 1891 ; Westcott's Introduction to the Gospels ; D'Aubigne's History of the
455 Reformation ; Life of Calvin, chap. IV. ; and also a considerable number of extracts from the works of Luther and Calvin. (2) In that he introduced new matter, as, for example, an argument on the metaphysical categories from the usage of Aristotle and Kant ; an argument from the use of the Old Testament by Christ and his Apostles ; an argument from the dynamic theory of inspiration ; an argument from the stress laid upon single words of the Old Testament by New Testament writers. (3) In that he argued in more than three-fourths of his argument against the statements of the Inaugural Address, the response to the Original Charges, the lectures on the Bible, the Church and the Reason, and the other writings of the accused, and in not more than one-fourth of it was it an effort in rebuttal of the argument of the accused, viz.: Stenographical Report (*a*) pp. 1120–1126, as far as "I is of the utmost importance," (*b*) p. 1131, beginning with "Dr. Briggs' Argument," as far as "It is not our faith," 1133 ; (*c*) p. 1136, as far as "through the Word of God," p. 1137 ; (*d*) the reference to Isaiah viii., 20, on p. 1141 ;
456 (*e*) and to I. John v., 10, on pp. 1144–1145 ; (*f*) pp. 1147–1152, as far as "We are not raising the question" ; (*g*) a brief allusion to my interpretation of the Confession of Faith, I., 1, on p. 1163 ; (*h*) a brief reference to passages cited by me from Luther, on p. 1181; (*i*) and to passages cited by me from Calvin, pp. 1185–1186 ; and of these, (*c*),

(*d*) and (*i*) may have been written in view of the evidence adduced in the Bible, the Church, and the Reason, before the delivery of the argument for the defense.

Dr. Lampe, of the Prosecuting Committee, now continued his argument.

At twenty-five minutes of four an intermission of a few minutes was taken, when Dr. Lampe continued until recess.

Under the rule and by unanimous consent the following were excused for a part of to-day's session: Rev. W. W. Atterbury and Elders J. E. Ware and Andrew Robinson. The Rev. A. W. Halsey was also excused for a part of to-morrow.

After reading and approving the minutes as far as written, Presbytery took a recess.

Concluded with prayer.

S. D. ALEXANDER,
Stated Clerk.

NEW YORK, 22ND DECEMBER, 1892.

SCOTCH CHURCH, 2 P. M.

Presbytery met after recess and was opened with prayer.

Present: Ministers—John C. Bliss, Mod'r.; Geo. Alexander, Saml. D. Alexander, Antonio Arreghi, Anson P. Atterbury, W. Wallace Atterbury, Fred. G. Beebe, Nicholas Bjerring, Robert R. Booth, Saml. Bowden, Thomas S. Bradner, Francis Brown, Walter D. Buchanan, James Chambers, Edward L. Clark, John B. Devins, Ira S. Dodd, D. Stuart Dodge, Conrad Doench, Wm. Durant, Thomas Douglas, Howard Duffield, John H. Edwards, Frank F. Ellinwood, Henry B. Elliot, Wm. T. Elsing, Charles P. Fagnani, Henry M. Field, Walter B. Floyd, Jesse F. Forbes, Herbert Ford, Ch. R. Gillett, Henri L. Grandlienard, James Hall, A. Woodruff Halsey, Wm. R. Harshaw, Thos. S. Hastings, Edward W. Hitchcock, James H. Hoadley, James Hunter, Saml. M. Jackson,

A. D. Lawrence Jewett, Joseph R. Kerr, Albert B. King,
458 A. Dunlop King, Joseph J. Lampe, Theo. Leonhard,
Milton S. Littlefield, John C. Lowrie, Daniel E. Lorenz,
Wm. M. Martin, Charles P. Mallery, Francis H. Marling,
Henry T. McEwen, James H. McIlvaine, Alexander H.
McKinney, Alex. McLean, Duncan McMillan, Horace G.
Miller, Geo. J. Mingins, Wm. L. Moore, James C.
Nightingale, Geo. Nixon, Israel H. Northrup, Daniel H.
Overton, Levi H. Parsons, James G. Patterson, Ed. P.
Payson, Geo. S. Payson, Vincent Pisek, Hugh Pritchard,
J. S. Ramsay, Daniel Redmon, Ch. S. Robinson, Stealy
B. Rossiter, Albert G. Ruliffson, Wm. A. Rice, Joseph
Sanderson, Jos. A. Saxton, Philip Schaff, J. Balcom
Shaw, Geo. L. Shearer, Andrew Shiland, W. M. Smith,
Wm. C. Stitt, Ch. A. Stoddard, J. F. Sutton, Alex. W.
Sproull, Geo. L. Spining, Charles L. Thompson, John J.
Thompson, Henry M. Tyndall, Henry Van Dyke, Marvin
R. Vincent, Fred. E. Voegelin, Thomas G. Wall, Abbott
L. R. Waite, W. Scott Watson, Geo. S. Webster, Erskine
N. White, Livingston Willard, David G. Wylie.

459 Elders—James Tompkins, Bethany; Albert R. Ledoux,
Brick; Alex. P. Ketcham, Calvary; Wm. Mickens, Central; Andrew Robinson, Christ; James McDowell, East
Harlem; H. Edwards Rowland, Fifth Avenue; Eugene
McJimpsey, First; John McWilliam, Fourth; Geo. E.
Sterry, Fourth Avenue; Saml. Reeve, Fourteenth Street;
Saml. H. Willard, Harlem; Jos. Moorhead, Knox; Ch.
H. Woodbury, Madison Square; Robert Johnson, First
Morrisania; Thomas Anderson, New York; G. C. King,
North; Henry Q. Hawley, Park; James E. Ware,
Phillips; Geo. C. Lay, Puritans; Cleveland H. Dodge,
Riverdale; Wm. M. Onderdonk, Rutgers; Robert Hous-
460 ton, Scotch; James Anderson, Seventh; C. E. Garey,
Tremont; Wm. R. Worrall, Thirteenth Street; Thomas
Bond, University Place; Robert Gentle, Union Tabernacle; Wm. A. Wheelock, Washington Heights; Robert
Jaffray, West; C. P. Leggett, West End; Richard Drummond, Westminster.

After the calling of the roll Dr. Briggs took exception to a portion of the proceedings of yesterday, as follows, viz.:

I beg leave to take exception to that part of the proceedings of yesterday recorded in the stenographical report, which permitted the Rev. Dr. Lampe, arguing in behalf of the Prosecution, under the cloak of a rebuttal, to introduce new evidence, and new matter, and in large measure to reargue the Amended Charges and Specifications, apart from and without regard to the argument of the accused ; in that (1) he introduced *new evidence* without the permission of Presbytery and without notification to the accused, as follows :

John Goodwin's Divine Authority of the Scriptures, Capel's Remains, Matthew Poole's Commentary, Baxter's Reasons of the Christian Religion, Chillingworth's Works, Vol. 1 ; Henry Hammond's Paraphrases, Lightfoot's Difficulties of Scripture, Timothy Dwight's Sermons, Jonathan Dickinson's Sermons, Samuel Davies's Sermons, Jonathan Edwards's Works, S. S. Smith's Principles of Natural and Revealed Religion, Sprague's Annals, McWhorter's Sermons, Witherspoon's Works, Ashbel Green's Lectures on the Shorter Catechism, Archibald Alexander's Canon, Gardiner's Spring's Bible not of Man, Albert Barnes's Commentaries, Skinner's Discussions in Theology, Augustine's Letters, Bibliotheca Sacra, 1892, Liddon's Divinity of our Lord.

(2) In that he introduced new matter, as for example : An argument on verbal inspiration and dictation ; an argument against an errant Bible ; an argument against a statement of the Response ; an argument against rationalistic critics ; an argument from predictive prophecy ; an argument against the theory of accommodation ; an argument against the errancy of Jesus.

(3) In that he argued in more than two-thirds of his argument against the statements of the Inaugural Address, the Response to the Original Charges, the lectures on the Bible, the Church and the Reason, and the other writings

of the accused, and in not more than one-third of it can be recognized as an effort in rebuttal of the argument of the accused, and in this part the argument can be considered as rebuttal only in so far as the argument for the defense included certain portions of "the Bible, the Church, and the Reason," and all of this, with the exception of the two lines, " This is substantially the view of Dr. Briggs, as shown by the documents put in your hands by him" (p. 1241, stenographer's report); and possibly of these also was probably composed before the delivery of the argument for the defense, for there is no other reference to that argument in the argument of Dr. Lampe of yesterday.

463 At the suggestion of Dr. Briggs it was resolved that Dr. Lampe have power to incorporate in the stenographer's notes his printed argument as presented to the house, including the portions not spoken to the Court, for the purpose of saving time.

Dr. Lampe concluded his argument.

Under the rule and by unanimous consent Dr. Jewett was excused for absence from the session of Wednesday.

Elder A. P. Ketcham was also excused from attendance at the session of Thursday.

It was resolved that the Presbytery now give the defendant an opportunity to reply. Dr. Briggs was then heard.

After an intermission of ten minutes the Moderator decided that the hearing of the parties is now closed.

464 The Prosecuting Committee excepts, and asks to have entered on the record an exception to the decision of the Moderator, after hearing Dr. Briggs, and without hearing the Prosecuting Committee in reply thereto, that the hearing of the parties is closed.

The Committee of Arrangements made the following report, which was on motion adopted.

1. That when the parties have been heard the Presbytery adjourn to the Lecture Room.

2. That the Stated Clerk be requested to submit to the Court a list of the ministers and elders entitled to vote.

3. That tickets of admission be issued to members of the Court.

It was resolved that all the names that are in question be referred to the Committee on Leave of Absence, and that they report to the Court on reassembling. The names in question presented were the Rev. Messrs. John R. Paxton, Nathaniel W. Conkling, Wm. G. T. Shedd, Charles H. Parkhurst, Frank F. Ellinwood and Charles H. Tyndall and Elder Moses P. Brown.

The time was extended for half an hour.

For the orderly conduct of the Court in taking the vote, a paper was presented, and on motion laid on the table until the next meeting of the Court.

It was now resolved to take a recess until next Wednesday, at 2 P. M.

After reading and approving the minutes as far as written, and prayer, Presbytery took recess.

S. D. ALEXANDER,
Stated Clerk.

LECTURE ROOM,

SCOTCH CHURCH, DECEMBER 28, 2 P. M.

Presbytery met and was opened with prayer.

Present: Ministers—John C. Bliss, Moderator; Geo. Alexander, Samuel D. Alexander, Antonio Arreghi, Anson P. Atterbury, W. Wallace Atterbury, Fred. G. Beebe, Robert R. Booth, Thomas S. Bradner, Charles A. Briggs, Francis Brown, Walter D. Buchanan, James Chambers, Edward L. Clark, John B. Devins, Ira S. Dodd, D. Stuart Dodge, Conrad Doench, Wm. Durant, Thos. Douglas, Howard Duffield, John H. Edwards, Henry B. Elliot, Wm. T. Elsing, Charles P. Fagnani, Henry M. Field, Walter B. Floyd, Jesse F. Forbes, Herbert Ford, Charles R. Gillett, Henri L. Grandlienard, A. Woodruff Halsey, Wm. R. Harshaw, Thomas S. Hastings, Edward W. Hitchcock, James H. Hoadley, James Hunter, A. D. L. Jewett, Joseph R. Kerr, Albert B. King, A. Dunlop King, Theodore Leonhard, Milton S. Littlefield, John C.

Lowrie, D. E. Lorenz, Wm. M. Martin, Charles P. Mallery, Francis H. Marling, Henry T. McEwen, James H. McIlvaine, A. H. McKinney, Alexander McLean, Duncan J. McMillan, Horace G. Miller, Wm. L. Moore, James C. Nightingale, Geo. Nixon, Israel H. Northrup, Levi H. Parsons, James G. Patterson, Edward P. Payson, George S. Payson, Vincent Pisek, Hugh Pritchard, James S. Ramsay, Daniel Redmon, Charles S. Robinson, Stealy B. Rossiter, Albert G. Ruliffson, Wm. A. Rice, Joseph Sanderson, Joseph A. Saxton, Philip Schaff, J. Balcom Shaw, Geo. L. Shearer, Andrew Shiland, Wilton M. Smith, William C. Stitt, Charles A. Stoddard, J. Ford
467 Sutton, Alexander W. Sproull, Geo. L. Spining, Charles L. Thompson, John J. Thompson, Henry Van Dyke, Marvin R. Vincent, Frederick E. Voegelin, Thomas G. Wall, Abbott L. R. Waite, W. Scott Watson, Geo. S. Webster, Erskine N. White, Livingston Willard, David G. Wylie.

Elders—James Tompkins, Bethany; Albert R. Ledoux, Brick; Alex. P. Ketcham, Calvary; Wm. Mickens, Central; Andrew Robinson, Christ; James McDowell, East Harlem; H. Edwards Rowland, Fifth Avenue; Eugene McJimpsey, First; John McWilliam, Fourth; Geo. S. Sterry, Fourth Avenue; Saml. L. Reeve, Fourteenth Street; Saml. H. Willard, Harlem; Jos. Moorhead, Knox; Ch. H. Woodbury, Madison Square; Robert Johnson, First Morrisania; Thomas Anderson, New York; G. C. King, North; Henry Q. Hawley, Park; James E. Ware, Phil-
468 lips; Geo. C. Lay, Puritans; Cleveland H. Dodge, Riverdale; Wm. M. Onderdonk, Rutgers R.; Robert Houston, Scotch; James Anderson, Seventh; Wm. R. Worrall, Thirteenth Street; C. E. Garey, Tremont; Thomas Bond, University Place; Robert Gentle, Union Tabernacle; Wm. A. Wheelock, Washington Heights; Robert Jaffray, West; C. P. Leggett, West End; Richard Drummond, Westminster.

After the calling of the roll, Dr. Briggs presented the following exception:

I beg leave to take exception to that part of the proceedings of the Presbytery of Thursday last, recorded in the stenographical report, which permitted the Rev. Dr. Lampe, arguing in behalf of the Prosecution, under the cloak of a rebuttal, to introduce new evidence and new matter, and in large measure to reargue the Amended Charges and Specifications apart from and without regard to the argument of the accused; in that (1) Dr. Lampe introduced new evidence without the permission of Presbytery and without notification to the accused, as follows:

The Andover Review, vol. xiii.; Pepys' Diary; F. Hall's English Adjectives; F. Hall's Modern English.

(2) In that Dr. Lampe introduced new matter, e. g., an argument from the assumption that the ministry of the word will not continue in the next world, and an argument from the assumed instantaneous sanctification of believers at the second advent.

(3) In that Dr. Lampe argued for the most part against statements of the Inaugural Address, the response to the Original Charges, the Article of Redemption after Death in the Magazine of Christian Literature; many of which, such as those referring to race redemption, the moral character of Abraham, and the doctrine of election, were not included in the Amended Charges; and the argument of Dr. Lampe was not in any respect a rebuttal of the argument of the accused, of which argument the argument of Dr. Lampe on the Sixth Charge seems entirely unconscious.

(4) In that Dr. Lampe argued on the Seventh Charge of the Amended Charges which the Presbytery directed the Prosecution to remove from the list of Charges.

(5) In that Dr. Lampe argued that the accused was "under the influence of a philosophical principle of Naturalism," a matter not included in the Charges.

The Committee on Leave of Absence reported as directed at the last meeting, whereupon Dr. Ellinwood, by consent of the parties and the house, was allowed to sit in the Court.

The following resolutions were adopted for the taking of the vote :

Order of Procedure:

471 I. When the Court has gone into private session, members who desire shall have three minutes in which to express their opinion on the case, the roll shall be called in alphabetical order, and members not desiring to speak shall not have the privilege of giving their time to others.

2. When the opinions have been given the vote on the Charges and Specifications shall be taken without debate, in the following order: (1) The vote on each Charge and its Specification shall be at one roll call ; (2) Each member shall vote (1) on the Specifications, and (2) on the Charge in its several items, the vote on each being "sustained" or "not sustained."

3. Following the vote a Committee of three shall be appointed by the Moderator to bring in the result of the vote and the judgment of the judicatory.

An intermission of ten minutes was now taken.

After intermission it was resolved that in case the vote
472 is not concluded on Thursday the Court must convene on Friday afternoon.

The following resolution was presented and a motion to lay it on the table was lost by a vote of 52 to 67, viz. :

The Court deems it proper to declare that a vote by any member of this Court not to sustain the charges preferred against Rev. Charles A. Briggs, D. D., does not denote approval of his theological or critical views or of the manner in which they have been advanced, but only a judgment that the specific charges have not been established.

After discussion it was resolved that the resolution be laid on the table until after the vote has been taken.

It was resolved that we now take a recess, to meet tomorrow in the Church at 2 P. M. The minutes were read and approved as far as written.

Concluded with prayer.

S. D. ALEXANDER,
Stated Clerk.

NEW YORK, 29TH DECEMBER, 1892.

SCOTCH CHURCH, THURSDAY, DEC. 29, 2 P. M.

Presbytery met and was opened with prayer.
Present: Ministers—John C. Bliss, D. D., Moderator; Geo. Alexander, Samuel D. Alexander, Antonio Arreghi, Anson P. Atterbury, W. Wallace Atterbury, Frederick G. Beebe, Nicholas Bjerring, Robert R. Booth, Samuel Bowden, Thomas S. Bradner, Francis Brown, Walter D. Buchanan, James Chambers, Edward L. Clark, John B. Devins, Ira S. Dodd, D. Stuart Dodge, Conrad Doench, Wm. Durant, Thomas Douglas, Howard Duffield, John H. Edwards, Henry B. Elliot, Frank F. Ellinwood, Wm. T. Elsing, Charles P. Fagnani, Henry M. Field, Walter B. Floyd, Jesse F. Forbes, Herbert Ford, Charles R. Gillett, Henri L. Grandlienard, James Hall, A. W. Halsey, Wm. R. Harshaw, Thos. S. Hastings, Edward W. Hitchcock, James H. Hoadley, James Hunter, Samuel M. Jackson, A. D. L. Jewett, Joseph R. Kerr, Albert B. King, A. Dunlop King, Theodore Leonhard, Milton S. Littlefield, John C. Lowrie, Daniel E. Lorenz, Wm. M. Martin, Charles P. Mallery, Francis H. Marling, Henry T. McEwen, James H. McIlvaine, Alexander H. McKinney, Alexander McLean, Duncan McMillan, Horace G. Miller, Geo. J. Mingins, Wm. L. Moore, James C. Nightingale, Geo. Nixon, Israel H. Northrup, Daniel H. Overton, Levi H. Parsons, James G. Patterson, Edward P. Payson, Geo. S. Payson, Vincent Pisek, Hugh Pritchard, James S. Ramsay, Daniel Redmon, Charles S. Robinson, Stealy B. Rossiter, Albert G. Ruliffson, Wm. A. Rice, Joseph Sanderson, Jos. A. Saxton, Philip Schaff, J. Balcom Shaw, Geo. L. Shearer, Andrew Shiland, Wilton M. Smith, Wm. C. Stitt, Charles A. Stoddard, J. F. Sutton, Alexander W. Sproull, Geo. L. Spining, Charles L. Thompson, John J. Thompson, Henry M. Tyndall, Henry VanDyke, Marvin R. Vincent, Fred. E. Voegelin, Thomas G. Wall, A. L. R. Waite, W. Scott Watson, Geo. S. Webster, E. N. White, Livingston Willard, David G. Wylie.

Elders—James Tompkins, Bethany; Alex. P. Ketcham, Calvary; Albert R. Ledoux, Brick; Wm. Mickens, Central; Andrew Robinson, Christ; James McDowell, East
475 Harlem; H. Edwards Rowland, Fifth Avenue; Eugene McJimpsey, First; John McWilliam, Fourth; Geo. E. Sterry, Fourth Avenue; Samuel H. Willard, Harlem; Jos. Moorhead, Knox; Charles H. Woodbury, Madison Square; Robert Johnson, First Morrisania; Thos. Anderson, New York; G. C. King, North; Henry Q. Hawley, Park; James E. Ware, Phillips; Geo. C. Lay, Puritans; Cleveland H. Dodge, Riverdale; Wm. Onderdonk, Rutgers, R.; Robert Houston, Scotch; James Anderson, Seventh; Wm. P. Worrall, Thirteenth Street; C. E. Garey, Tremont; Thomas Bond, University Place; Robert Gentle, Union Tabernacle; Wm. A. Wheelock, Washington Heights; Robert Jaffray, West; C. P. Leggett, West End; Richard Drummond, Westminster.

476 After the calling of the roll Dr. Briggs presented the following exception:

Inasmuch as the Presbytery gave Dr. Lampe " power to incorporate in the stenographer's minutes the argument in printed form as presented, including the portion omitted in reading," I beg leave to take exception to that part of the proceedings of Presbytery which permitted Dr. Lampe, arguing in behalf of the Prosecution, under the cloak of a rebuttal, to introduce new evidence as follows:

Alexander, on Isaiah; Rawlinson, in Pulpit Commentary; Ray, Introduction in Bible Commentary; Manly's Bible Doctrine of Inspiration, Hebraica, October, 1888; Prof. John Kennedy, A Popular Argument for the Unity of Isaiah, 1891; Prof. John Forbes, The Servant of the Lord, in Isaiah xl., lxvi., 1890; Rector F. Watson, The Law and the Prophets, Hulsean Lecture for 1882; Prof. Stanley, Leathes, The Law in the Prophets, 1891; Very Rev. R. Payne Smith, The Mosaic Authorship and Credibility of the Pentateuch, 1869; James Sime,

F. R. S. E., The Kingdom of all Israel, 1883; Prof. Robert Watts, The Newer Criticism, etc., 1882; Principal Rainy, The Bible and Criticism, 1878; Bishop A. C. Hervey, The Books of Chronicles in Relation to the Pentateuch, etc., 1892; Bishop C. J. Ellicot, Christus Comprobator, 1892; Rev. Henry Hayman, D. D., "Prophetic Testimony to the Pentateuch," Bib. Sac., 1892; Pastor, Tr. Roos, Die Geschichtlinckett des Pentateuchs, 1883; Adolph Zahn, Das Deuteronomium, 1890; Eduard Böhl, Zum Gassetz und Zum Zeugniss, 1883; Pastor G. Schumann, Die Wellhausenische Pentateuchthe, 1892; R. S. Poole, "Date of the Pentateuch, Theory and Facts," Cont. Review, 1887; Conder, "Ancient Men and Modern Critics," Cont. Review, 1887; Edersheim, Prophecy and History in Relation to the Messiah, Warburten Lectures, 1880-1884; Waller, "Is Genesis a Compilation?" Theological Monthly, 1891; Pastor Naumann, "Das Erste Buch der Bible," 1890; Prof. William H. Green, Moses and the Pentateuch Vindicated; Prof. E. Cone Bissell, The Pentateuch; Vos, Mosaic Origin of the Pentateuch Codes, 1886; Stebbins, A Study of the Pentateuch, 1881; S. C. Bartlett, Sources of History in the Pentateuch, Stone Lectures, 1882; Rabbi I. M. Wise, Pronaos to Holy Writ, 1891; Lias, "Wellhausen on the Pentateuch," in the Theological Review.

At the request of the Stated Clerk the Rev. Thomas G. Wall was appointed to him in taking the vote.

After the calling of the roll Dr. Sutton moved that the members of the Faculty and the Trustees of Union Theological Seminary, who may be members of the Court, and the Librarian of the Seminary, and such other members who, as editors and publishers, have recorded their views on this case before this Court was convened, be deemed incompetent to sit and vote in this case because on the ground of personal interest in the result.

The Moderator decided the motion to be out of order.

Dr. Sutton appealed from the decision. The Moderator was sustained.

142

The calling of the roll was now begun for an expression of the members of the Court, under the three-minute rule adopted at the last session.

At five minutes to five o'clock it was resolved to take a recess until to-morrow at 2 P. M.

After reading and approving the minutes as far as written, Presbytery took a recess.

Concluded with prayer.

S. D. ALEXANDER,
Stated Clerk.

NEW YORK, 30TH DECEMBER, 1892.

SCOTCH CHURCH, FRIDAY, DEC. 30, 2 P. M.

479 Presbytery met and was opened with prayer.

Present: Ministers—John C. Bliss, Moderator; George Alexander, Samuel D. Alexander, Antonio Arreghi, Anson P. Atterbury, W. Wallace Atterbury, Frederick G. Beebe, Robert R. Booth, Samuel Bowden, Thomas S. Bradner, Francis Brown, Walter D. Buchanan, James Chambers, Edward L. Clark, John B. Devins, Ira S. Dodd, D. Stuart Dodge, Conrad Doench, Wm. Durant, Thomas Douglas, Howard Duffield, John H. Edwards, Henry B. Elliot, Wm. T. Elsing, Charles P. Fagnani, Henry M. Field, Walter B. Floyd, Jesse F. Forbes, Herbert Ford, Charles R. Gillett, Henri Grandlienard, James Hall, A. Woodruff Halsey, Wm. R. Harshaw, Thos. S. Hastings, Edward W. Hitchcock, James H. Hoadley, James Hunter, Samuel M. Jackson, A. D. L. Jewett, Joseph R. Kerr, Albert B. King, Alexander D. King, Theodore Leonhard, Milton S. Littlefield, John C. Lowrie, Daniel E. Lorenz, Wm. M. Martin, Charles P. Mallery, Francis H. Marling, Henry T. McEwen, James H. McIlvaine, Alexander H. McKinney, Alexander McLean, Duncan J. McMillan, Horace G. Miller, Geo. J. Mingins, Wm. L. Moore, James
480 C. Nightingale, Geo. Nixon, Israel H. Northrup, Daniel H. Overton, Levi H. Parsons, James G. Patterson, Edward P. Payson, George S. Payson, Vincent Pisek, Hugh Pritchard, James S. Ramsay, Daniel Redmon,

Charles S. Robinson, Stealy B. Rossiter, Albert G. Ruliffson, Wm. A. Rice, Joseph Sanderson, Joseph A. Saxton, Philip Schaff, J. Balcom Shaw, Geo. L. Shearer, Andrew Shiland, Wilton M. Smith, William C. Stitt, Ch. A. Stoddard, J. Ford Sutton, Alex. W. Sproull, Geo. L. Spining, Charles L. Thompson, John J. Thompson, Henry M. Tyndall, Henry VanDyke, Marvin R. Vincent, Frederick E. Voegelin, Thomas G. Wall, Abbott L. R. Waite, W. Scott Watson, Geo. S. Webster, Erskine N. White, Livingston Willard, David G. Wylie.

Elders—James Tompkins, Bethany; Albert R. Ledoux, Brick; Alex. P. Ketcham, Calvary; Wm. Mickens, Central; Andrew Robinson, Christ; James McDowell, East Harlem; H. Edwards Rowland, Fifth Avenue; Eugene McJimpsey, First; John McWilliam, Fourth; Geo. E. Sterry, Fourth Avenue; Saml. Reeve, Fourteenth Street; Saml. H. Willard, Harlem; Joseph Moorhead, Knox; Charles H. Woodbury, Madison Square; Robert Johnson, First Morrisania; Thos. Anderson, New York; G. C. King, North; Henry Q. Hawley, Park; James E. Ware, Phillips; Geo. C. Lay, Puritans; Cleveland H. Dodge, Riverdale; Wm. M. Onderdonk, Rutgers, R.; Robert Houston, Scotch; James Anderson, Seventh; Wm. R. Worrall, Thirteenth Street; C. E. Garey, Tremont; Thomas Bond, University Place; Robert Gentle, Union Tabernacle; Wm. A. Wheelock, Washington Heights; Robert Jaffray, West; C. P. Leggett, West End; Richd. Drummond, Westminster.

The roll was now taken up where it was left at the close of the last meeting, and the expression of the opinions of the members under the rule was concluded.

Whereupon the Court proceeded to take the vote under the rule adopted.

A few moments before five o'clock it was resolved that the session be prolonged until the vote was completed.

After which the Rev. Messrs. Geo. Alexander and Henry Van Dyke, with Elder Robert Jaffray, were appointed a committee to bring in the result of the vote, and the judgment of the judicatory.

The final vote by ayes and noes on page 485.

The following resolution was adopted :

Resolved, that the members of this Court desire to place on record its high appreciation of the fidelity and ability with which the Moderator, the Rev. John C. Bliss, D. D., has presided over its deliberations in the judicial case now brought to a close. His helpful and uplifting prayers, his impartial rulings, and the calm Christian spirit maintained by him at all times, have been invaluable in aiding to preserve the fitting attitude of the Court to secure a dispassionate decision.

The Court also thanks the Committee of Arrangements and the authorities of the Scotch Church for the excellent facilities afforded for the trial.

The Moderator made an appropriate reply.

The resolution in reference to those who should vote "not sustain," and which was laid on the table until the vote should be taken, was now taken up and referred to the Committee appointed to bring in the vote and judgment of the Court.

It was resolved that when we take a recess we do so to meet in this house on Monday, January 9th, at 2 P. M.

After reading and approving the minutes as far as written, Presbytery took a recess.

Concluded with prayer.

S. D. ALEXANDER,
Stated Clerk.

VOTE FOR SUSTAINING OR NOT SUSTAINING THE CHARGES.

Ministers.		I. Sp. 1	Sp. 2	Charge A	B	II. Sp. 1	Sp. 2	Charge A	B	Sp. 1	III. Charge A	B	C	Sp. 1	IV. Sp. 2	Charge A	B	V. Sp. 1	Sp. 2	Charge A	B	VI. Sp. 1	Ch.
Alexander, Geo..........	Not sust.........	1	1	1	1	1	1	1	1	1	1	1	1	1	1	1	1	1	1	1	1	1	1
	Sust..........																						
Alexander, S. D..........	Not sust.........	1	1	1	1	1	1	1	1	1	1	1	1	1	1	1	1	1	1	1	1	1	1
	Sust..........																						
Arreghi, Antonio.........	Not sust.........	1	1	1	1	1	1	1	1	1	1	1	1	1	1	1	1	1	1	1	1	1	1
	Sust..........																						
Atterbury, A. P..........	Not sust.........	1	1	1	1	1	1	1	1	1	1	1	1	1	1	1	1	1	1	1	1	1	1
	Sust..........																						
Atterbury, W. W........	Not sust.........	1	1	1	1	1	1	1	1	1	1	1	1	1	1	1	1	1	1	1	1	1	1
	Sust..........																						
Beebe, T. G..............	Not sust.........	1	1	1	1	1	1	1	1	1	1	1	1	1	1	1	1	1	1	1	1	1	1
	Sust..........																						
Bowden, Saml............	Not sust.........	1	1	1	1	1	1	1	1	1	1	1	1	1	1	1	1	1	1	1	1	1	1
	Sust..........																						

146

MINISTERS.		I.				II.				III.				IV.			V.			VI.	
		Sp. 1	Sp. 2	Charge A.	B.	Sp. 1	Sp. 2	Charge A.	B.	Sp.	Charge A.	B.	C.	Sp.	Charge A.	B.	Sp.	Charge A.	B.	Sp.	Ch.
Bradner, T. S.	Not sust.	1	1	1	1	1	1	1	1	1	1	1	1	1	1	1	1	1	1	1	1
	Sust.	1	1	1	1	1	1	1	1	1	1	1	1	1	1	1	1	1	1	1	1
Brown, Francis	Not sust.	1	1	1	1	1	1	1	1	1	1	1	1	1	1	1	1	1	1	1	1
	Sust.	1	1	1	1	1	1	1	1	1	1	1	1	1	1	1	1	1	1	1	1
Buchanan, W. D.	Not sust.	1	1	1	1	1	1	1	1	1	1	1	1	1	1	1	1	1	1	1	1
	Sust.	1	1	1	1	1	1	1	1	1	1	1	1	1	1	1	1	1	1	1	1
Chambers, James	Not sust.	1	1	1	1	1	1	1	1	1	1	1	1	1	1	1	1	1	1	1	1
	Sust.	1	1	1	1	1	1	1	1	1	1	1	1	1	1	1	1	1	1	1	1
Clark, E. L.	Not sust.	1	1	1	1	1	1	1	1	1	1	1	1	1	1	1	1	1	1	1	1
	Sust.	1	1	1	1	1	1	1	1	1	1	1	1	1	1	1	1	1	1	1	1
Devins, J. B.	Not sust.	1	1	1	1	1	1	1	1	1	1	1	1	1	1	1	1	1	1	1	1
	Sust.	1	1	1	1	1	1	1	1	1	1	1	1	1	1	1	1	1	1	1	1
Dodd, I. S.	Not sust.	1	1	1	1	1	1	1	1	1	1	1	1	1	1	1	1	1	1	1	1
	Sust.	1	1	1	1	1	1	1	1	1	1	1	1	1	1	1	1	1	1	1	1

MINISTERS.		I.				II.				III.			IV.			V.			VI.	
		Sp.		Charge		Sp.		Charge	Sp.		Charge		Sp.	Charge		Sp.	Charge		Sp.	Ch.
		1	2	A.	B.	1	2	A.	B.	1	A.	B.	C.	Sp.	A.	B.	Sp.	A.	B.	
Dodge, D. Stuart	Not sust.	1	1	1	1	1	1	1	1	1	1	1	1	1	1	1	1	1	1	1
	Sust.	1	1	1	1	1	1	1	1	1	1	1	1	1	1	1	1	1	1	1
Doench, C.	Not sust.	1	1	1	1	1	1	1	1	1	1	1	1	1	1	1	1	1	1	1
	Sust.	1	1	1	1	1	1	1	1	1	1	1	1	1	1	1	1	1	1	1
Durant, W.	Not sust.	1	1	1	1	1	1	1	1	1	1	1	1	1	1	1	1	1	1	1
	Sust.	1	1	1	1	1	1	1	1	1	1	1	1	1	1	1	1	1	1	1
Douglass, T.	Not sust.	1	1	1	1	1	1	1	1	1	1	1	1	1	1	1	1	1	1	1
	Sust.	1	1	1	1	1	1	1	1	1	1	1	1	1	1	1	1	1	1	1
Duffield, H.	Not sust.	1	1	1	1	1	1	1	1	1	1	1	1	1	1	1	1	1	1	1
	Sust.	1	1	1	1	1	1	1	1	1	1	1	1	1	1	1	1	1	1	1
Edwards, J. H.	Not sust.	1	1	1	1	1	1	1	1	1	1	1	1	1	1	1	1	1	1	1
	Sust.	1	1	1	1	1	1	1	1	1	1	1	1	1	1	1	1	1	1	1
Elliott, H. B.	Not sust.	1	1	1	1	1	1	1	1	1	1	1	1	1	1	1	1	1	1	1
	Sust.	1	1	1	1	1	1	1	1	1	1	1	1	1	1	1	1	1	1	1

MINISTERS.	I.					II.					III.			IV.			V.			VI.	
	Sp.		Charge			Sp.		Charge			Sp.	Charge		Sp.	Charge		Sp.	Charge		Sp.	Ch.
	1	2	A	B		1	2	A	B		1	A	B	C	1	A	B	1	A	B		
Elsing, W. T. {Not sust. / Sust.	1 1	1 1	1 1	1 1		1 1	1 1	1 1	1 1		1 1	1 1	1 1	1 1	1 1	1 1	1 1	1 1	1 1	1 1	1 1	1 1
Fagnani, C. P. {Not sust. / Sust.	1 1	1 1	1 1	1 1		1 1	1 1	1 1	1 1		1 1	1 1	1 1	1 1	1 1	1 1	1 1	1 1	1 1	1 1	1 1	1 1
Field, H. M. {Not sust. / Sust.	1 1	1 1	1 1	1 1		1 1	1 1	1 1	1 1		1 1	1 1	1 1	1 1	1 1	1 1	1 1	1 1	1 1	1 1	1 1	1 1
Floyd, W. B. {Not sust. / Sust.	1 1	1 1	1 1	1 1		1 1	1 1	1 1	1 1		1 1	1 1	1 1	1 1	1 1	1 1	1 1	1 1	1 1	1 1	1 1	1 1
Forbes, Jesse F. {Not sust. / Sust.	1 1	1 1	1 1	1 1		1 1	1 1	1 1	1 1		1 1	1 1	1 1	1 1	1 1	1 1	1 1	1 1	1 1	1 1	1 1	1 1
Ford, H. {Not sust. / Sust.	1 1	1 1	1 1	1 1		1 1	1 1	1 1	1 1		1 1	1 1	1 1	1 1	1 1	1 1	1 1	1 1	1 1	1 1	1 1	1 1
Gillett, O. R. {Not sust. / Sust.	1 1	1 1	1 1	1 1		1 1	1 1	1 1	1 1		1 1	1 1	1 1	1 1	1 1	1 1	1 1	1 1	1 1	1 1	1 1	1 1

MINISTERS.		I.				II.				III.			IV.		V.		VI.	
		Sp.		Charge		Sp.		Charge	Sp.	Charge		Sp.	Charge	Sp.	Charge	Sp.	Ch.
		1	2	A.	B.	1	2	A.	B.	1	A.	B.	C.	A.	B.	A.	B.	
Grandlienard, H. L.	Not sust.	1	1	1	1	1	1	1	1	1	1	1	1	1	1	1	1	1
	Sust.	1	1	1	1	1	1	1	1	1	1	1	1	1	1	1	1	1
Hall, James	Not sust.	1	1	1	1	1	1	1	1	1	1	1	1	1	1	1	1	1
	Sust.	1	1	1	1	1	1	1	1	1	1	1	1	1	1	1	1	1
Halsey, A. W.	Not sust.	1	1	1	1	1	1	1	1	1	1	1	1	1	1	1	1	1
	Sust.	1	1	1	1	1	1	1	1	1	1	1	1	1	1	1	1	1
Harshaw, W. R.	Not sust.	1	1	1	1	1	1	1	1	1	1	1	1	1	1	1	1	1
	Sust.	1	1	1	1	1	1	1	1	1	1	1	1	1	1	1	1	1
Hastings, T. S.	Not sust.	1	1	1	1	1	1	1	1	1	1	1	1	1	1	1	1	1
	Sust.	1	1	1	1	1	1	1	1	1	1	1	1	1	1	1	1	1
Hitchcock, E. W.	Not sust.	1	1	1	1	1	1	1	1	1	1	1	1	1	1	1	1	1
	Sust.	1	1	1	1	1	1	1	1	1	1	1	1	1	1	1	1	1
Hoadley, J. H	Not sust.	1	1	1	1	1	1	1	1	1	1	1	1	1	1	1	1	1
	Sust.	1	1	1	1	1	1	1	1	1	1	1	1	1	1	1	1	1

150

MINISTERS.		I.				II.				III.			IV.			V.			VI.	
		Sp. 1	Sp. 2	Charge A.	Charge B.	Sp. 1	Sp. 2	Charge A.	Charge B.	Sp. 1	Charge A.	B. C.	Sp. Charge	A.	B.	Sp. Charge	A.	B.	Sp. Ch.	
Hunter, J............	{ Not sust....	1	1	1	1	1	1	1	1	1	1	1	1	1	1	1	1	1	1	1
	Sust.........	1	1	1	1	1	1	1	1	1	1	1	1	1	1	1	1	1	1	1
Jackson, S. M.......	{ Not sust....	1	1	1	1	1	1	1	1	1	1	1	1	1	1	1	1	1	1	1
	Sust.........	1	1	1	1	1	1	1	1	1	1	1	1	1	1	1	1	1	1	1
Jewett, A. D. L......	{ Not sust....	1	1	1	1	1	1	1	1	1	1	1	1	1	1	1	1	1	1	1
	Sust.........	1	1	1	1	1	1	1	1	1	1	1	1	1	1	1	1	1	1	1
Kerr, Jos. R.........	{ Not sust....	1	1	1	1	1	1	1	1	1	1	1	1	1	1	1	1	1	1	1
	Sust.........	1	1	1	1	1	1	1	1	1	1	1	1	1	1	1	1	1	1	1
King, Albert B......	{ Not sust....	0	0	0	0	0	0	0	0	1	1	1	1	0	0	0	0	0	1	1
	Sust.........	1	1	1	1	1	1	1	1	1	1	1	1	1	1	1	1	1	1	1
King, A. D..........	{ Not sust....	1	1	1	1	1	1	1	1	1	1	1	1	0	0	0	0	0	1	1
	Sust.........	1	1	1	1	1	1	1	1	1	1	1	1	1	1	1	1	1	1	1
Leonhard, Theo......	{ Not sust....	1	1	1	1	1	1	1	1	1	1	1	1	1	1	1	1	1	1	1
	Sust.........	1	1	1	1	1	1	1	1	1	1	1	1	1	1	1	1	1	1	1

MINISTERS.		I.				II.				III.			IV.			V.			VI.	
		Sp.		Charge		Sp.		Charge	Sp.	Charge			Sp.	Charge		Sp.	Charge		Sp.	Ch.
		1	2	A.	B.	1	2	A.	B.	1	A.	B.	C.		A.	B.		A.	B.	
Littlefield, M. S.	{ Not sust.	1	1	1	1	1	1	1	1	1	1	1	1	1	1	1	1	1	1	1
	Sust.	1	1	1	1	1	1	1	1	1	1	1	1	1	1	1	1	1	1	1
Lowrie, J. O.	{ Not sust.	1	1	1	1	1	1	1	1	1	1	1	1	1	1	1	1	1	1	1
	Sust.	1	1	1	1	1	1	1	1	1	1	1	1	1	1	1	1	1	1	1
Lorenz, D. E.	{ Not sust.	1	1	1	1	1	1	1	1	1	1	1	1	1	1	1	1	1	1	1
	Sust.	1	1	1	1	1	1	1	1	1	1	1	1	1	1	1	1	1	1	1
Martin, W. M.	{ Not sust.	1	1	1	1	1	1	1	1	1	1	1	1	1	1	1	1	1	1	1
	Sust.	1	1	1	1	1	1	1	1	1	1	1	1	1	1	1	1	1	1	1
Mallery, C. P.	{ Not sust.	1	1	1	1	1	1	1	1	1	1	1	1	1	1	1	1	1	1	1
	Sust.	1	1	1	1	1	1	1	1	1	1	1	1	1	1	1	1	1	1	1
Marling, F. H.	{ Not sust.	1	1	1	1	1	1	1	1	1	1	1	1	1	1	1	1	1	1	1
	Sust.	1	1	1	1	1	1	1	1	1	1	1	1	1	1	1	1	1	1	1
McEwen, H. T.	{ Not sust.	1	1	1	1	1	1	1	1	1	1	1	1	1	1	1	1	1	1	1
	Sust.	1	1	1	1	1	1	1	1	1	1	1	1	1	1	1	1	1	1	1

152

MINISTERS.		I.			II.			III.			IV.		V.		VI.	
		Sp. 1	Sp. Charge 2	A.|B.	Sp. 1	Sp. Charge 2	A.|B.	Sp. 1	Charge	A.|B.|C.	Sp. Charge	A.|B.	Sp. Charge	A.|B.	Sp.	Ch.
McIlvaine, J. H.	{ Not sust.	1	1	1	1	1	1	1	1	1	1	1	1	1	1	1
	Sust.	1	1	1	1	1	1	1	1	1	1	1	1	1	1	1
McKinney, Alex.	{ Not sust.	1	1	1	1	1	1	1	1	1	1	1	1	1	1	1
	Sust.	1	1	1	1	1	1	1	1	1	1	1	1	1	1	1
McLean, Alex.	{ Not sust.	1	1	1	1	1	1	1	1	1	1	1	1	1	1	1
	Sust.	1	1	1	1	1	1	1	1	1	1	1	1	1	1	1
McMillan, D. J.	{ Not sust.	1	1	1	1	1	1	1	1	1	1	1	1	1	1	1
	Sust.	1	1	1	1	1	1	1	1	1	1	1	1	1	1	1
Miller, H. G.	{ Not sust.	1	1	1	1	1	1	1	1	1	1	1	1	1	1	1
	Sust.	1	1	1	1	1	1	1	1	1	1	1	1	1	1	1
Mingins, G. J.	{ Not sust.	1	1	1	1	1	1	1	1	1	1	1	1	1	1	1
	Sust.	1	1	1	1	1	1	1	1	1	1	1	1	1	1	1
Moore, W. L.	{ Not sust.	1	1	1	1	1	1	1	1	1	1	1	1	1	1	1
	Sust.	1	1	1	1	1	1	1	1	1	1	1	1	1	1	1

	I.				II.				III.				IV.			V.			VI.	
	Sp.	Sp.	Charge		Sp.	Sp.	Charge	Sp.		Charge		Sp.	Sp.	Charge	Sp.	Sp.	Charge	Sp.	Sp.	Ch.
MINISTERS.	1	2	A.	B.	1	2	A.	B.	1	A.	B.	C.		A.	B.		A.	B.		
Nightingale, J. C. {Not sust. / Sust.	1 1	1 1	1 1	1 1	1 1	1 1	1 1	1 1	1 1	1 1	1 1	1 1	1 1	1 1	1 1	1 1	1 1	1 1	1 1	1 1	1 1
Nixon, Geo. {Not sust. / Sust.	1 1	1 1	1 1	1 1	1 1	1 1	1 1	1 1	1 1	1 1	1 1	1 1	1 1	1 1	1 1	1 1	1 1	1 1	1 1	1 1	1 1
Northrup, I. H. {Not sust. / Sust.	1 1	1 1	1 1	1 1	1 1	1 1	1 1	1 1	1 1	1 1	1 1	1 1	1 1	1 1	1 1	1 1	1 1	1 1	1 1	1 1	1 1
Overton, D. H. {Not sust. / Sust.	1 1	1 1	1 1	1 1	1 1	1 1	1 1	1 1	1 1	1 1	1 1	1 1	1 1	1 1	1 1	1 1	1 1	1 1	1 1	1 1	1 1
Parsons, L. H. {Not sust. / Sust.	1 1	1 1	1 1	1 1	1 1	1 1	1 1	1 1	1 1	1 1	1 1	1 1	1 1	1 1	1 1	1 1	1 1	1 1	1 1	1 1	1 1
Patterson, J. C. {Not sust. / Sust.	1 1	1 1	1 1	1 1	1 1	1 1	1 1	1 1	1 1	1 1	1 1	1 1	1 1	1 1	1 1	1 1	1 1	1 1	1 1	1 1	1 1
Payson, E. P. {Not sust. / Sust.	1 1	1 1	1 1	1 1	1 1	1 1	1 1	1 1	1 1	1 1	1 1	1 1	1 1	1 1	1 1	1 1	1 1	1 1	1 1	1 1	1 1

	I.				II.				III.			IV.			V.			VI.	
Ministers	Sp. 1	Sp. 2	Charge A.	Charge B.	Sp. 1	Sp. 2	Charge A.	Charge B.	Charge A.	Charge B.	Charge C.	Sp.	Charge A.	Charge B.	Sp.	Charge A.	Charge B.	Sp.	Ch.
Payson, G. S. { Not sust.	1	1	1	1	1	1	1	1	1	1	1	1	1	1	1	1	1	1	1
{ Sust.	1	1	1	1	1	1	1	1	1	1	1	1	1	1	1	1	1	1	1
Pisek, V. { Not sust.	1	1	1	1	1	1	1	1	1	1	1	1	1	1	1	1	1	1	1
{ Sust.	1	1	1	1	1	1	1	1	1	1	1	1	1	1	1	1	1	1	1
Pritchard, Hugh { Not sust.	1	1	1	1	1	1	1	1	1	1	1	1	1	1	1	1	1	1	1
{ Sust.	1	1	1	1	1	1	1	1	1	1	1	1	1	1	1	1	1	1	1
Ramsay, J. S. { Not sust.	1	1	1	1	1	1	1	1	1	1	1	1	1	1	1	1	1	1	1
{ Sust.	1	1	1	1	1	1	1	1	1	1	1	1	1	1	1	1	1	1	1
Redmon, D. { Not sust.	1	1	1	1	1	1	1	1	1	1	1	1	1	1	1	1	1	1	1
{ Sust.	1	1	1	1	1	1	1	1	1	1	1	1	1	1	1	1	1	1	1
Robinson, C. H. { Not sust.	1	1	1	1	1	1	1	1	1	1	1	0	0	0	0	0	0	1	1
{ Sust.	1	1	1	1	1	1	1	1	1	1	1	1	1	1	1	1	1	1	1
Rossiter, S. B. { Not sust.	1	1	1	1	1	1	1	1	1	1	1	1	1	1	1	1	1	1	1
{ Sust.	1	1	1	1	1	1	1	1	1	1	1	1	1	1	1	1	1	1	1

155

Ministers		I.				II.				III.			IV.			V.			VI.	
		Sp.		Charge		Sp.		Charge		Charge			Sp.	Charge		Sp.	Charge		Sp.	Ch.
		1	2	A.	B.	1	2	A.	B.	A.	B.	C.		A.	B.		A.	B.		
Ruliffson, A. G.	Not sust.	1	1	1	1	1	1	1	1	1	1	1	1	1	1	1	1	1	1	1
	Sust.	1	1	1	1	1	1	1	1	1	1	1	1	1	1	1	1	1	1	1
Rice, W. A.	Not sust.	1	1	1	1	1	1	1	1	1	1	1	1	1	1	1	1	1	1	1
	Sust.	1	1	1	1	1	1	1	1	1	1	1	1	1	1	1	1	1	1	1
Sanderson, Jos.	Not sust.	1	1	1	1	1	1	1	1	1	1	1	1	1	1	1	1	1	1	1
	Sust.	1	1	1	1	1	1	1	1	1	1	1	1	1	1	1	1	1	1	1
Saxton, J. A.	Not sust.	1	1	1	1	1	1	1	1	1	1	1	1	1	1	1	1	1	1	1
	Sust.	1	1	1	1	1	1	1	1	1	1	1	1	1	1	1	1	1	1	1
Schaff, P.	Not sust.	1	1	1	1	1	1	1	1	1	1	1	1	1	1	1	1	1	1	1
	Sust.	1	1	1	1	1	1	1	1	1	1	1	1	1	1	1	1	1	1	1
Shaw, W. B.	Not sust.	1	1	1	1	1	1	1	1	1	1	1	1	1	1	1	1	1	1	1
	Sust.	1	1	1	1	1	1	1	1	1	1	1	1	1	1	1	1	1	1	1
Shearer, Geo. L.	Not sust.	1	1	1	1	1	1	1	1	1	1	1	1	1	1	1	1	1	1	1
	Sust.	1	1	1	1	1	1	1	1	1	1	1	1	1	1	1	1	1	1	1

156

MINISTERS.		I.				II.				III.			IV.			V.			VI.	
		Sp.		Sp. Charge		Sp.	Sp. Charge		Sp.	Charge		Sp. Charge		Sp. Charge		Sp.	Ch.
		1	2	A.	B.	1	2	A.	B.	1	A.	B.	C.	A.	B.	A.	B.	
Shiland, A.	{ Not sust.	1	1	1	1	1	1	1	1	1	1	1	1	1	1	1	1	1
	Sust.	1	1	1	1	1	1	1	1	1	1	1	1	1	1	1	1	1
Smith, W. M.	{ Not sust.	1	1	1	1	1	1	1	1	1	1	1	1	1	1	1	1	1
	Sust.	1	1	1	1	1	1	1	1	1	1	1	1	1	1	1	1	1
Stitt, W. C.	{ Not sust.	1	1	1	1	1	1	1	1	1	1	1	1	1	1	1	1	1
	Sust.	1	1	1	1	1	1	1	1	1	1	1	1	1	1	1	1	1
Stoddard, C. A.	{ Not sust.	1	1	1	1	1	1	1	1	1	1	1	1	1	1	1	1	1
	Sust.	1	1	1	1	1	1	1	1	1	1	1	1	1	1	1	1	1
Sutton, J. F.	{ Not sust.	1	1	1	1	1	1	1	1	1	1	1	1	1	1	1	1	1
	Sust.	1	1	1	1	1	1	1	1	1	1	1	1	1	1	1	1	1
Sproull, A. W.	{ Not sust.	1	1	1	1	1	1	1	1	1	1	1	1	1	1	1	1	1
	Sust.	1	1	1	1	1	1	1	1	1	1	1	1	1	1	1	1	1
Spining, G. L.	{ Not sust.	1	1	1	1	1	1	1	1	1	1	1	1	1	1	1	1	1
	Sust.	1	1	1	1	1	1	1	1	1	1	1	1	1	1	1	1	1

	I.				II.				III.			IV.			V.			VI.	
MINISTERS.	Sp.		Charge		Sp.		Charge	Sp.	Charge			Sp.	Charge		Sp.	Charge		Sp.	Ch.
	1	2	A	B	1	2	A	B	1	A	B	C		A	B		A	B		
Thompson, C. L. {Not sust. / Sust.	1	1	1	1	1	1	1	1	1	1	1	1	1	1	1	1	1	1	1	1
Thompson, J. J. {Not sust. / Sust.	1	1	1	1	1	1	1	1	1	1	1	1	1	1	1	1	o	o	1	1
Tyndall, H. M. {Not sust. / Sust.	1	1	1	1	1	1	1	1	1	1	1	1	1	1	1	1	1	1	1	1
Van Dyke, H. {Not sust. / Sust.	1	1	1	1	1	1	1	1	1	1	1	1	1	1	1	1	1	1	1	1
Vincent, M. R. {Not sust. / Sust.	1	1	1	1	1	1	1	1	1	1	1	1	1	1	1	1	1	1	1	1
Voegelin, F. E. {Not sust. / Sust.	1	1	1	1	1	1	1	1	1	1	1	1	1	1	1	1	1	1	1	1
Wall, T. G. {Not sust. / Sust.	1	1	1	1	1	1	1	1	1	1	1	1	1	1	1	1	1	1	1	1

158

Ministers.		I.				II.				III.				IV.			V.			VI.	
		Sp. 1	Sp. 2	Charge A	B	Sp. 1	Sp. 2	Charge A	B	Sp.	Charge A	B	C	Sp.	Charge A	B	Sp.	Charge A	B	Sp.	Ch.
Waite, A. L. R.	Not sust.	1	1	1	1	1	1	1	1	1	1	1	1	1	1	1	1	0	0	1	1
	Sust.	1	1	1	1	1	1	1	1	1	1	1	1	1	1	1		0			
Watson, W. S.	Not sust.	1	1	1	1	1	1	1	1	1	1	1	1	1	1	1	1	1	1	1	1
	Sust.	1	1	1	1	1	1	1	1	1	1	1	1	1	1	1		1			
Webster, G. S.	Not sust.	1	1	1	1	1	1	1	1	1	1	1	1	1	1	1	1	1	1	1	1
	Sust.	1	1	1	1	1	1	1	1	1	1	1	1	1	1	1		1			
White, E. N.	Not sust.	1	1	1	1	1	1	1	1	1	1	1	1	1	1	1	1	1	1	1	1
	Sust.	1	1	1	1	1	1	1	1	1	1	1	1	1	1	1		1			
Willard, L.	Not sust.	1	1	1	1																
	Sust.	1	1	1																	
Wylie, H. G.	Not sust.	1	1	1	1	1	1	1	1	1	1	1	1	1	1	1	1	1	1	1	1
	Sust.	1	1	1	1	1	1	1	1	1	1	1	1	1	1	1		1			

159

ELDERS.		I. Sp. Sp.	I. Charge A. B.			II. Sp. 1	II. Sp. 2	II. Charge A.	II. Charge B.	II. Sp. 1	III. Charge A.	III. Charge B.	III. Charge C.	IV. Sp.	IV. Charge A.	IV. Charge B.	V. Sp.	V. Charge A.	V. Charge B.	VI. Sp.	VI. Ch.
		1	2	A.	B.																
Bethany	Tompkins, Jas	{ Not sust																			
	Sust	1	1	1	1	1	1	1	1	1	1	1	1	1	1	1	1	1	1	1	1
Brick	Ledoux, Albert R	{ Not sust																			
	Sust	1	1	1	1	1	1	1	1	1	1	1	1	1	1	1	1	1	1	1	1
Calvary	Ketcham, A. P	{ Not sust	1		1		1		1		1		1				1		1			
	Sust	1	1	1	1	1	1	1	1	1	1	1	1	1	1	1	1	1	1	1	1
Central	Mickens, Wm	{ Not sust																			
	Sust	1	1	1	1	1	1	1	1	1	1	1	1	1	1	1	1	1	1	1	1
Christ	Robinson, Andrew	{ Not sust																			
	Sust	1	1	1	1	1	1	1	1	1	1	1	1	1	1	1	1	1	1	1	1
E. Harlem	McDowell, Jr	{ Not sust																			
	Sust	1	1	1	1	1	1	1	1	1	1	1	1	1	1	1	1	1	1	1	1
5th Avenue	Rowland H. Edwards	{ Not sust																			
	Sust	1	1	1	1	1	1	1	1	1	1	1	1	1	1	1	1	1	1	1	1

160

ELDERS.		I. Sp.		I. Charge		II. Sp.		II. Charge Sp.			III. Charge			IV. Sp.	IV. Charge		V. Sp.	V. Charge		VI. Sp.	VI. Ch.
		1	2	A.	B.	1	2	A.	B.	1	A.	B.	C.		A.	B.		A.	B.		
First.......McJimpsey, E.......	Not sust.....	1	1	1	1	1	1	1	1	1	1	1	1	1	1	1	0	0	0	1	1
	Sust.....	1	1	1	1	1	1	1	1	1	1	1	1	1	1	1	0	0	0	1	1
Fourth......McWilliams, Jno...	Not sust......	1	1	1	1	1	1	1	1	1	1	1	1	1	1	1	1	1	1	1	1
	Sust.....	1	1	1	1	1	1	1	1	1	1	1	1	1	1	1	1	1	1	1	1
Fourth Ave..Sterry, Geo. E.....	Not sust.....	1	1	1	1	1	1	1	1	1	1	1	1	1	1	1	1	1	1	1	1
	Sust.....	1	1	1	1	1	1	1	1	1	1	1	1	1	1	1	1	1	1	1	1
14th Street..Reeve, Samuel H....	Not sust.....	1	1	1	1	1	1	1	1	1	1	1	1	1	1	1	1	1	1	1	1
	Sust.....	1	1	1	1	1	1	1	1	1	1	1	1	1	1	1	1	1	1	1	1
Harlem......Williard, Samuel H..	Not sust.....	1	1	1	1	1	1	1	1	1	1	1	1	1	1	1	1	1	1	1	1
	Sust.....	1	1	1	1	1	1	1	1	1	1	1	1	1	1	1	1	1	1	1	1
Knox.......Moorhead, Jos.......	Not sust.....	1	1	1	1	1	1	1	1	1	1	1	1	1	1	1	1	1	1	1	1
	Sust.....	1	1	1	1	1	1	1	1	1	1	1	1	1	1	1	1	1	1	1	1
Madison Sq..Woodbury, Chas. H..	Not sust.....	1	1	1	1	1	1	1	1	1	1	1	1	1	1	1	1	1	1	1	1
	Sust.....	1	1	1	1	1	1	1	1	1	1	1	1	1	1	1	1	1	1	1	1

ELDERS.		I.				II.				III.				IV.			V.			VI.	
		Sp. Sp.	Charge		Sp.	Sp.	Charge		Sp.	Charge			Sp.	Charge		Sp.	Charge		Sp.	Ch.
		1	2	A.	B.	1	2	A.	B.	1	A.	B.	C.		A.	B.		A.	B.		
Morrisania 1st. Johnson, Robt	Not sust.																			0	0
	Sust.	1	1	1	1	1	1	1	1	1	1	1	1	1	1	1	1	1	1	1	1
New York.....Anderson, Thos.	Not sust.	1	1	1	1	1	1	1	1	1	1	1	1	1	1	1	1	1	1	1	1
	Sust.	1	1	1	1	1	1	1	1	1	1	1	1	1	1	1	1	1	1	1	1
North.........King, G. C........	Not sust.	1	1	1	1	1	1	1	1	1	1	1	1	1	1	1	1	1	1	1	1
	Sust.	1	1	1	1	1	1	1	1	1	1	1	1	1	1	1	1	1	1	1	1
Park.... ....Hawley, Henry Q.	Not sust.	1	1	1	1	1	1	1	1	1	1	1	1	1	1	1	1	1	1	1	1
	Sust.	1	1	1	1	1	1	1	1	1	1	1	1	1	1	1	1	1	1	1	1
Phillips.. ....Ware, Jos. E.......	Not sust.	1	1	1	1	1	1	1	1	1	1	1	1	1	1	1	1	1	1	1	1
	Sust.	1	1	1	1	1	1	1	1	1	1	1	1	1	1	1	1	1	1	1	1
Puritans......Lay, Geo. C	Not sust.	1	1	1	1	1	1	1	1	1	1	1	1	1	1	1	1	1	1	1	1
	Sust.	1	1	1	1	1	1	1	1	1	1	1	1	1	1	1	1	1	1	1	1
Riverdale......Dodge, C. H.....	Not sust.	1	1	1	1	1	1	1	1	1	1	1	1	1	1	1	1	1	1	1	1
	Sust.	1	1	1	1	1	1	1	1	1	1	1	1	1	1	1	1	1	1	1	1

	I.				II.				III.				IV.			V.			VI.	
	Sp.		Charge		Sp.		Charge		Sp.	Charge			Sp.	Charge		Sp.	Charge		Sp.	Ch.
Elders.	1	2	A.	B.	1	2	A.	B.	1	A.	B.	C.		A.	B.		A.	B.		
Rutgers......Onderdonk, W. H.. { Not sust...... { Sust.............	1 1	1 1	1 1	1 1	1 1	1 1	1 1	1 1	1 1	1 1	1 1	1 1	1 1	1 1	1 1	1 1	1 1	1 1	1 1	1 1
Scotch......Houston, Robt...... { Not sust...... { Sust.............	1 1	1 1	1 1	1 1	1 1	1 1	1 1	1 1	1 1	1 1	1 1	1 1	1 1	1 1	1 1	1 1	1 1	1 1	1 1	1 1
Seventh......Anderson, Jas...... { Not sust...... { Sust.............	1 1	1 1	1 1	1 1	1 1	1 1	1 1	1 1	1 1	1 1	1 1	1 1	1 1	1 1	1 1	1 1	1 1	1 1	1 1	1 1
13th St......Worrall, Wm. R... { Not sust...... { Sust.............	1 1	1 1	1 1	1 1	1 1	1 1	1 1	1 1	1 1	1 1	1 1	1 1	1 1	1 1	1 1	1 1	1 1	1 1	1 1	1 1
Tremont......Garry, C. E......... { Not sust...... { Sust.............	1 1	1 1	1 1	1 1	1 1	1 1	1 1	1 1	1 1	1 1	1 1	1 1	1 1	1 1	1 1	o o	o o	1 1	1 1	1 1
University Pl.Bond, Thos......... { Not sust...... { Sust.............	1 1	1 1	1 1	1 1	1 1	1 1	1 1	1 1	1 1	1 1	1 1	1 1	1 1	1 1	1 1	1 1	1 1	1 1	1 1	1 1
Union Tab....Gentle, Robt......... { Not sust...... { Sust.............	1 1	1 1	1 1	1 1	1 1	1 1	1 1	1 1	1 1	1 1	1 1	1 1	1 1	1 1	1 1	1 1	1 1	1 1	1 1	1 1

163

ELDERS.		I.				II.				III.			IV.			V.			VI.	
		p.	Sp.	Charge		Sp.	Sp.	Charge		Sp.	Charge		Sp.	Charge		Sp.	Charge		Sp.	Ch.
		1	2	A.	B.	1	2	A.	B.	1	A.|B.|C.			A.|B.		A.|B.		
Wash. Hghts..Wheelock, W. A.	Not sust.	1	1	1	1	1	1	1	1	1	1	1	1	1	1	1	1	1	1	1
	Sust.	1	1	1	1	1	1	1	1	1	1	1	1	1	1	1	1	1	1	1
West ....Jaffray, Robt.	Not sust.	1	1	1	1	1	1	1	1	1	1	1	1	1	1	1	1	1	1	1
	Sust.	1	1	1	1	1	1	1	1	1	1	1	1	1	1	1	1	1	1	1
West End ....Leggett, C. P.	Not sust.	1	1	1	1	1	1	1	1	1	1	1	1	1	1	1	1	1	1	1
	Sust.	1	1	1	1	1	1	1	1	1	1	1	1	1	1	1	1	1	1	1
Westminster..Drummond, R.	Not sust.	1	1	1	1	1	1	1	1	1	1	1	1	1	1	1	1	1	1	1
	Sust.	1	1	1	1	1	1	1	1	1	1	1	1	1	1	1	1	1	1	1

NEW YORK, 9th January, 1893.

494 LECTURE ROOM, SCOTCH CHURCH, 2 P. M.

Presbytery met after recess, and was opened with prayer.
Present: Ministers—J. C. Bliss, Moderator, Geo. Alexander, Samuel D. Alexander, Antonio Arreghi, Anson P. Atterbury, W. Wallace Atterbury, Frederick G. Beebe, Robert R. Booth, Samuel Bowden, Thomas S. Bradner, Francis Brown, Walter B. Buchanan, James Chambers, Edward L. Clark, John B. Devins, Ira S. Dodd, D. S. Dodge, Conrad Doench, Wm. Durant, Thos. Douglas, Howard Duffield, John H. Edwards, Henry B. Elliot, Wm. T. Elsing, Ch. P. Fagnani, Henry M. Field, Walter B. Floyd, Jesse F. Forbes, Herbert Ford, Charles R. Gillett, Henri Grandlienard, James Hall, Wm. R. Harshaw, Thomas S. Hastings, Ed. W. Hitchcock, James H. Hoadley, James Hunter, Samuel M. Jackson, A. D. L. Jewett, Joseph R. Kerr, Albert B. King, A. Dunlop King, Theodore Leonhard, Milton S. Littlefield, John C. Lowrie, Daniel E. Lorenz, Wm. M. Martin, Ch. P. Mallery, Francis H. Marling, Henry T. McEwen, James H. McIlvaine, Alex. H. McKinney, Alex. McLean, Duncan J. McMillan, Horace G. Miller, Geo. J. Mingins, W. L. Moore, James C. Nightingale, Geo. Nixon, Israel H. Northrup,
495 D. H. Overton, Levi H. Parsons, James G. Patterson, Ed. P. Payson, Daniel Redmon, Ch. S. Robinson, Stealy B. Rossiter, Wm. A. Rice, Albert G. Ruliffson, Joseph Sanderson, Jos. A. Saxton, Philip Schaff, Geo. L. Shearer, Andrew Shiland, Wilton M. Smith, Ch. A. Stoddard, J. Ford Sutton, Alex. W. Sproull, Geo. L. Spining, John J. Thompson, Henry M. Tyndall, Henry Van Dyke, Fred. E. Voegelin, Thomas G. Wall, Geo. S. Webster, Erskine N. White, David G. Wylie.

Elders—James Tompkins, Albert R. Ledoux, A. P. Ketcham, Wm. Mickens, Andr. Robinson, James McDowell, John McWilliam, G. E. Sterry, Saml. Reeve, Saml. H. Willard, Jos. Moorhead, Charles H. Woodbury, Rob-

ert Johnson, Thomas Anderson, Henry Q. Hawley, James
E. Ware, Geo. C. Lay, Cleveland H. Dodge, Robert
Houston, James Anderson, Wm. R. Worrall, C. E. Garey,
Thomas Bond, Robert Gentle, Wm. A. Wheelock, Robert Jaffray, C. P. Leggett.

After the roll call was completed the following protest was presented:

PROTEST.

The undersigned hereby presents for record his protest against the action of the Moderator, on the 30th day of December, 1892, in "The Presbyterian Church in the United States of America against the Rev. Charles A. Briggs, D. D.," as follows:

Whereas, our Revised Book of Discipline, Chapter 4, Section 28, states that "No member of a judicatory, who has not been present during the whole of the trial, shall be allowed to vote on any question arising therein, except by unanimous consent of the judicatory."

And whereas, Rev. Geo. J. Mingins, having been absent during six days of aforesaid trial, and not having been excused, by "unanimous consent of the judicatory," for three of those days;

And whereas, Rev. Edward P. Payson objects to the said absentee being allowed to vote on the final issue of the case; the Moderator, nevertheless, ruled that his vote should be admitted, contrary to the rules of the Church and the interests of justice; therefore, against this action of the Moderator, the undersigned respectfully enters his protest, which protest is emphasized by the following considerations, viz.:

(1) The gravity of this protest is increased by the fact that the protestant had on two previous occasions (Dec. 5th and Dec. 21st) objected to the vote of Mr. Mingins, on account of absence from the trial, but his first objection had been quietly ignored, and his second thwarted by the Moderator.

(2) The gravity of this protest is further increased by the fact, that during the protestant's statement of his

objection and the reasons therefor, on Dec. 30th the Moderator allowed strong and continuous hissing by the opposition, without a word or sign of remonstrance on his part; all of which tended to the detriment of justice and the deep disgrace of the judicatory.

(3) The gravity of this protest is still further increased by the fact, that by his ruling the Moderator persistently retained his seat in the Court for Mr. Mingins, although absent from the trial during six days, four of which were spent in lecture tours, while he promptly unseated Rev. Dr. W. G. T. Shedd for but four days' absence from the trial, and that on account of illness, for each and all of which reasons, the undersigned hereby respectfully presents for record his emphatic protest, as above stated.

(Signed)   EDWARD P. PAYSON.

The Rev. Messrs. John H. Edwards and James C. Nightingale were appointed to bring in an answer to the protest.

They subsequently reported the following :
Your Committee deem it sufficient to state that the absence of Rev. Mr. Mingins was excused by the Court, and his name kept accordingly upon the roll. The Rev. Dr. Shedd and others lost their membership in the Court and their places upon the roll, under the rules adopted by the Court. (1) "That the excuse of absence shall relate to a positive and important duty ; (2) That it shall not involve absence during two consecutive sessions."

In the judgment of your Committee the Court is satisfied with the conduct of the Moderator in the matter referred to by the protestant.

(Signed)   JOHN H. EDWARDS.
                    JAMES C. NIGHTINGALE.

The Committee appointed to bring in the result of the vote and the judgment of the judicatory, presented the following report. The report was accepted.

The case of the Presbyterian Church in the United States of America against the Reverend Charles A.

Briggs, D. D., having been dismissed by the Presbytery of New York on November 4, 1891, was remanded by the General Assembly of 1892 to the same Presbytery with instruction that "it be brought to issue and tried on the merits thereof as speedily as possible."

In obedience to this mandate the Presbytery of New York has tried the case. It has listened to the evidence and argument of the Committee of Prosecution acting in fidelity to the duty committed to them. It has heard the defense and evidence of the Rev. Charles A. Briggs, D. D., presented in accordance with the rights secured to every minister of the Church.

The Presbytery has kept in mind these established principles of our polity, "That no man can rightly be convicted of heresy by inference or implication," that in the interpretation of ambiguous expression "candor requires that a Court should favor the accused by putting upon his words the more favorable rather than the less favorable construction," and that "there are truths and forms with respect to which men of good character may differ." Giving due consideration to the defendant's explanations of the language used in his Inaugural Address, accepting his frank and full disclaimer of the interpretation which has been put upon some of its phrases and illustrations, crediting his affirmations of loyalty to the Standards of the Church and to the Holy Scriptures as the only infallible rule of faith and practice, the Presbytery does not find that he has transgressed the limits of liberty allowed under our Constitution to scholarship and opinion.

Therefore, without expressing approval of the critical or theological views embodied in the Inaugural Address, or the manner in which they have been expressed and illustrated, the Presbytery pronounces the Rev. Charles A. Briggs, D. D., fully acquitted of the offences alleged against him, the several Charges and Specifications accepted for probation having been "not sustained" by the following vote:

			SUSTAINED.			NOT SUSTAINED.		
			MINISTERS.	ELDERS.	TOTAL.	MINISTERS.	ELDERS.	TOTAL.
I.	1 Specification,		41	17	58	55	15	70
	2 "		42	17	59	54	15	69
	Charge	a	42	17	59	54	15	69
		b	42	17	59	54	15	69
II.	1 Specification		39	16	55	56	16	72
	2 "		39	16	55	56	16	72
	Charge	a	39	16	55	56	16	72
		b	39	16	55	56	16	72
III.	Specification,		44	17	61	52	15	67
	Charge	a	44	17	61	52	15	67
		b	42	17	59	54	15	69
		c	44	17	61	52	15	67
IV.	Specification,		39	15	54	55	17	72
	Charge	a	39	15	54	55	17	72
		b	39	15	54	55	17	72
V.	Specification,		35	14	49	57	16	73
	Charge	a	35	14	49	57	16	73
		b	35	14	49	57	16	73
VI.	Specification,		41	16	57	55	14	69
	Charge,		41	16	57	55	14	69

Accordingly the Presbytery, making full recognition of the ability, sincerity and patience with which the Committee of Prosecution have performed the onerous duty assigned them, does now, to the extent of its Constitutional power, relieve said Committee from further responsibility in connection with this case. In so doing the Presbytery is not undertaking to decide how far that Committee is subject to the authority of the body appointing it, but intends by this action to express an earnest conviction that the grave issues involved in this case will be more wisely and justly determined by calm investigation and fraternal discussion than by judicial arraignment and process.

In view of the present disquietude in the Presbyterian Church, and of the obligation resting upon all Christians to walk in charity and to have tender concern for the consciences of their brethren, the Presbytery earnestly counsels its members to avoid, on the one hand, hasty or over-confident statement of private opinion on points concerning which profound and reverent students of God's word are not yet agreed, and, on the other hand, suspicions and charges of false teaching which are not clearly capable of proof.

Moreover, the Presbytery advises and exhorts all subject to its authority to regard the many and great things in which we agree rather than the few and minor things in which we differ, and turning from the paths of controversy, to devote their energies to the great and urgent work of the Church, which is the proclamation of the Gospel and the edifying of the Body of Christ. 504

(Signed) GEORGE ALEXANDER,
HENRY VAN DYKE,
ROBERT JAFFRAY.

After discussion Presbytery took an intermission of fifteen minutes, at 3 P. M.

During this interval Presbytery met in regular session.

It was resolved that 40 per cent. be added to the annual assessment of the churches, to meet the extraordinary expenses incurred in the trial of Dr. Briggs. 505

At 3.15 Presbytery resumed its sitting in a judicial capacity.

Presbytery now continued the discussion of the report begun before the intermission; after which a motion to lay the second part of the report on the table was lost by a vote of 47 to 58. The report was then adopted in its several parts, and then it was adopted as a whole by a majority vote, and the Moderator declared that this be the judgment of the Court, and that it be entered accordingly.

506 The thanks of the body was extended to the Committee having in charge the supervision of the stenographer's report.

On motion, Presbytery now sat with open doors, when the Prosecuting Committee presented the following exception :

As the Prosecuting Committee find many omissions from, additions to, and mistakes and errors, in the copy of the stenographic report of the judicial proceedings in this case, as furnished by the stenographer, and as the Prosecuting Committee has not had access to the so-called official stenographic report as corrected and amended by the Committee of which the Moderator is Chairman, nor opportunity to compare the copy furnished to them by the stenographer with the so-called official stenographic

507 report, the Prosecuting Committee therefore excepts and asks to have entered upon the record its exception to the so-called official stenographic report being considered or accepted as a part of the record in this case, or as an accurate, full and complete stenographic report of the proceedings in this case before the Presbytery of New York, which would entitle it to be used upon the hearing of the appeal in this case in a higher Court.

The following persons presented their respectful dissent from the action of the Court on the first part of the Committee's report, viz. :

William R. Worrall, Saml. Bowden, Edward P. Payson, George Nixon, Andrew Shiland, Abbott L. R. Waite, Levi H. Parsons, Alex. W. Sproull, James C. Nightingale.

The Moderator then read the judgment of the Court, whereupon the Prosecuting Committee presented the following exception :

The Prosecuting Committee excepts and asks to have entered upon the record its exception to the final judgment in this case as now read, and to each and every part thereof.

After reading and approving the minutes the Court adjourned. 508
Concluded with prayer and the Apostolical benediction.

S. D. ALEXANDER,
Stated Clerk.

PRESBYTERY OF NEW YORK,

153 EAST 78TH STREET, NEW YORK.

MAY 8th, 1893.

I have examined the above print, pages 37 (page 43 of this volume) to 165 (page 171 of this volume), inclusive, being a copy of all of the proceedings had in the Presbytery of New York in the case of the Presbyterian Church in the United States of America *versus* Rev. Charles A. Briggs, D. D., from the 13th day of June, 1892, when the mandate of the General Assembly in said case was received by the said Presbytery, up to and including the 9th day of January, 1893, when the final judgment in said case was entered, as recorded in Volume 14 of the Records of the Presbytery of New York, and I hereby authenticate the same as in entire agreement with the records of this Presbytery.

S. D. ALEXANDER,
Stated Clerk.

V.

APPELLANT'S OPENING ARGUMENT IN FAVOR OF THE
ENTERTAINMENT OF THE APPEAL, PRESENTED BY THE
REV. GEORGE W. F. BIRCH, D. D., CHAIRMAN OF
THE PROSECUTING COMMITTEE.

Mr. Moderator, Fathers and Brethren.

Your Appellant is that original party which was, in accordance with Section 11 of the Book of Discipline and Section V. of Chapter XII. of the Form of Government, declared by this Supreme Judicatory, at its meeting in 1892, to be the Committee of Prosecution in the case of the Presbyterian Church in the United States of America against the Rev. Charles A. Briggs, D. D.*

It is proposed in opening this case, for the sake of saving the time of the Court, and because of the legal, moral and ecclesiastical status, which the Appeal read in the hearing of the Assembly gives your Appellant, to present a brief abstract of the argument prepared by the speaker to be used on the present occasion.

The past history of this case deepens my impression of the truth uttered by the speaker at the last Assembly,

---
* Minutes, General Assembly, 1892, pages 90 and 119.

that the members of the Committee of Prosecution "appear before you for the reason that impelled Paul and Barnabas to lay their cause before the first council of the Christian Church at Jerusalem. They were there because the Church at Antioch could not settle the question which made its membership like the troubled sea."*

A comparison of the action of the Apostolic Council, with respect to the appeal of Paul and Barnabas, with the action of the General Assembly of 1892, with respect to the appeal of the Committee of Prosecution, is exceedingly suggestive.

The Apostolic Council entertained the appeal of Paul and Barnabas and issued it by sustaining it and by sending down a decree to the Church at Antioch which defined the limits of the Christian liberty of those Gentiles who might be admitted to Church membership.

The General Assembly of 1892 entertained the appeal of the Committee of Prosecution; issued the said appeal by sustaining it, and by sending down a decree to the Presbytery of New York defining the limits of its liberty with respect to this case.

The decree of the Apostolic Council to the Church at Antioch reads as follows:

ACTS XV.

" 23 And they wrote *letters* by them after this manner : The apostles and elders and brethren *send* greeting unto

---
* Acts xv.

the brethren which are of the Gentiles in Antioch and Syria and Cilicia :

24 For as much as we have heard, that certain which went out from us have troubled you with words, subverting your souls, saying, *Ye must* be circumcised, and keep the law; to whom we gave no *such* commandment :

25 It seemed good unto us, being assembled with one accord, to send chosen men unto you with our beloved Barnabas and Paul,

26 Men that have hazarded their lives for the name of our Lord Jesus Christ.

27 We have sent therefore Judas and Silas, who shall also tell *you* the same things by mouth.

28 For it seemed good to the Holy Ghost, and to us, to lay upon you no greater burden than these necessary things ;

29 That ye abstain from meats offered to idols, and from blood, and from things strangled, and from fornication : from which if ye keep yourselves, ye shall do well. Fare ye well."

The decree of the General Assembly of 1892 to the Presbytery of New York reads as follows :

| "THE PRESBYTERIAN CHURCH IN THE UNITED STATES OF AMERICA vs. REV. CHARLES A. BRIGGS, D. D. | *Appeal from the judgment of the Presbytery of New York, dismissing the case.* |

"The General Assembly having, on the 28th day of May, 1892, duly sustained all the specifications of error alleged and set forth in the appeal and specifications in this case,

"It is now, May 30, 1892, ordered, that the judgment of the Presbytery of New York, entered November 4, 1891, dismissing the case of the Presbyterian Church in the United States of America against Rev. Charles A. Briggs, D. D., be, and the same is hereby, reversed. And the case is remanded to the Presbytery of New York for a new trial, with directions to the said Presbytery to proceed to pass upon and determine the sufficiency of the charges and specifications in form and legal effect, and to permit the Prosecuting Committee to amend the specifications or charges, not changing the general nature of the same, if, in the furtherance of justice, it be necessary to amend, so that the case may be brought to issue and tried on the merits thereof as speedily as may be practicable.

"And it is further ordered, that the Stated Clerk of the General Assembly return the record, and certify the proceedings had thereon, with the necessary papers relating thereto, to the Presbytery of New York."

The decree of the Apostolic Council was at once the warrant of the freedom of the Gentile Christians from the rite of circumcision—the letter of the law of Moses—and the direction which regulated that liberty by the meaning and spirit of that letter.

The decree of the General Assembly ordered the Presbytery of New York to try this case on its merits, and gave it liberty to amend the indictment in accordance with the general nature of the same. So that the Presbytery was free only to examine the charges, weigh the testimony for and against them, and then to decide to sustain or not to sustain.

The decree of the Apostolic Council was obeyed by the Gentile Christians, and its revelation of their Christian liberty made them rejoice over the consolation of its exhortation.

The decree of the General Assembly was not obeyed by the New York Presbytery, as it transcended its own proper function as a trial court by recording its unwillingness to express its approval of the critical or theological views which were the basis of the charges and specifications, which charges and specifications it declared to be sufficient in form and legal effect. The Presbytery acquitted the defendant on the ground that although he might deny that Moses wrote the law which the Gentile Christians of Antioch observed; although there were cases where Church and Reason could do what the Bible could not do (enable a man to find God), yet that such statements did not transgress the limits of liberty allowed under the constitution of the Presbyterian Church to scholarship and opinion.

The decree of the Apostolic Council taught the Gentile Christians of Antioch that purity was the absolute condition of peace. So that when the question was between purity and loss of concord, the former was to be preferred to the latter.

That the appeal of the Committee of Prosecution is warranted by the example of Paul is evident from the following comment on the Antiochan controversy, so much the more significant in the present case, since it is from Lange on Acts, page 278, issued under the editorial supervision of Professor Schaff of the Union Theological Seminary. "Paul did not feel at liberty to connive at error by silence or to yield. Peace is a blessing of very great value, and unity in the church is an important end. Yet it would be unwise to seek or to maintain peace *at any price*, and to regard unity as absolutely and unconditionally the sovereign good. Truth is higher than all things else. The pure word of the grace of God in Christ alone must be maintained or recovered even with the loss of concord. This is the course which the Apostles and the Reformers of the Church, in their day, invariably pursued."

The decree of the General Assembly taught the Presbytery of New York the same thing. But the final judgment of the inferior court was an unscriptural, unconstitutional and disloyal effort to reach peace by a compromise with and a toleration of error.

This venerable court needs no additional information with reference to the persistent effort continued from the beginning of this process until the present, to question the standing of the Committee of Prosecution in spite of the six distinct instances in which the Presbytery by vote and act determined its character as an original party, and in spite of the confirmation of this determination by the Assembly of 1892, both in its majority and minority.*

* Record of the Case, May, 1892, pages 58, 59, 68, 145. Printed Document, May, 1893, pages 73, 162. Minutes General Assembly, 1892, page 90.

We are here to invoke this Supreme Court to put an end to the dissension and disputation which the New York Presbytery vainly endeavored to silence, first by the dismissal of the case against Dr. Briggs on November 4th, 1891, and, second, by the acquittal of Dr. Briggs, on January 9th, 1893, qualifying both the said dismissal and the said acquittal by the positive disclaimer of any approval of the controverted statements of the Inaugural Address, as to critical or theological views, and manner of expression.

But the familiar question arises: Why pass by the Synod? We make but a single remark concerning this exceptional course. In a pamphlet copyrighted by the Appellee, entitled "The Case against Professor Briggs," there is a record of a truth which he told the Assembly at Portland, when he said "The presumption is always against exceptions," * Dr. Briggs availed himself of that presumption in two speeches before the Assembly, which cover eighty pages of the pamphlet referred to. After listening to the speeches the General Assembly decided that the *presumption* in the matter of the Appeal of the Prosecuting Committee from the action of the New York Presbytery in the Case of Professor Briggs, was not against the exceptions.

Hence several of the Presbyteries, and some individuals who think that we can *go slow* only by going wrong, seem to have forgotten that, just now, the Synod of New York is the resort of those who want the Church to contradict

---
* Case against Professor Briggs, page 81.

the fact that the judicial decisions of the General Assembly are final and obligatory in all controversies respecting doctrine and discipline.

These considerations, along with the three reasons set forth in the Appeal,* are certainly sufficient to establish the essential, the utter unconstitutionality of any disposition of this case which would force it down to the Synod of New York.

The form in which the final judgment of the Presbytery was returned, gives the impression that the alleged errors of Professor Briggs were unimportant and that no essential doctrines had been contradicted. In fact there has been a tendency to minimize the full force of the indictment. The errors charged are fundamental. The question is not simply whether the inspired Word is free from error. That question is referred to, in but one of the charges. The charges relate :

(1) To the question as to the supreme and only authority in matters of faith and practice. The fountain of divine authority—is it threefold or one?

(2) To the question as to the inerrancy or truthfulness of the inspired Word of God.

(3) To the historical validity of the Old Testament.

(4) To the question as to the fulfillment of Messianic prediction—a question of supreme importance in its bearing upon the view which is taken (*a*) of the truthfulness of Scripture, and (*b*) of the truthfulness of God.

---
* Printed Document, May, 1893, page 17.

(5) Lastly the doctrine of redemption, concerning which it has been alleged that Professor Briggs' teachings have been especially erroneous and hurtful, but which could be only partially tried in the lower court as will be seen by reference to specification second under both the first and second grounds of appeal.

The *Christian Intelligencer* of January 18th, 1893, contains the following communication from a theological professor of the Reformed Church :

" In the comments in the last number of the *Intelligencer* upon the Briggs' trial, one point of vast importance was overlooked. The decision of the Presbytery in effect amounted to this :

" 1. It may be taught in the seminaries, schools, pulpits, Sunday-schools, families, and publications of all kinds, that a person may deny that Jesus Christ is the Son of God, that the Word was made flesh, that He made atonement for our sins, that there is no other name whereby we can be saved, and other essential doctrines of Christianity, and yet find God and be saved ; Martineau being the proof.

" 2. That the Church of Rome is a fountain of authority, and able to give certainty to a doubting soul; Cardinal Newman being the proof.

" 3. That the Bible (not translations nor copied manuscripts), the Book as received by all, contains errors, and that not a few, but as the defendant in the trial said, ' I can give an indefinite number of instances, both in the Old Testament and the New.' (More than one hundred of these have been already found by infidels and answered by Christians.)

"4. That Christ in asserting that Moses gave us the law (thora), and that we have the writings of Moses, and that the Apostles, in stating certain passages to be utterances of Isaiah, were mistaken.

"Now, Mr. Editor, all this has not been done in a corner. The Presbytery was not a private debating society. The question and the answer are before the whole world. It matters very little whether the members of the Presbytery approve or disapprove of the above-stated doctrines; one thing they do, united, shield locked with shield, they stand before the community to protect those who teach them."

"S. M. WOODBRIDGE."
"New Brunswick, Jan. 13, 1893."

Another statement is as follows :

The final judgment of the Presbytery is an attack upon

(1) The fundamental proposition that guarantees to us the whole divine authority and reliability of the entire Bible. An attack is made upon its inerrant, unerring inspiration.

(2) The fundamental proposition that underlies the absolute necessity of sending the Gospel to the heathen, to turn them from darkness to light, and from the power of Satan unto God, viz.: "There is none other name under heaven given among men whereby we must be saved." Acts 4 : 12.

(3) The fundamental proposition that if Moses did not write of Christ, the Jew, is, by the very words of Christ, absolved from believing on Him. "For had ye believed Moses, ye would have believed Me, *for he wrote of Me.* But if ye believe not his writings, how shall ye believe My words?" John 5 : 46–47.

(4) The fundamental proposition that Jesus Christ, in His prophetic office as a Teacher of the Truth, is inerrant and infallible in all that He says, when citing as witnesses to His Messianic claims Moses and the Prophets.

(5) The fundamental proposition that the souls of all who die in the Lord are "blessed from henceforth," and are among "the spirits of just men made perfect." Rev. 14 : 13 and Heb. 12 : 23.

Here is a series of errors covering the whole fundamental structure of our faith. It is not a local issue like the settlement of difficulties in a single congregation, or of two or more congregations. It is a question purely doctrinal, and therefore of universal importance so far as Presbyterianism is concerned. It can be finally settled by no presbytery, by no synod. It requires the decision of the Presbyterian Church in its highest court.

Your Appellant is persuaded that this Court is not blind to the great magnitude of "*conclusions*" such as these —to the real vital issues involved in this case; to critical and theological views which are the outflow of that negative criticism which, under the name of christian scholarship, threatens to sweep away the one foundation on which we have built our Christian homes and institutions, thus putting both our Christian faith and heritage in peril.

But we are told that an appeal from a verdict of acquittal is out of order, and, therefore, that your Appellant should be thrown out of Court, as if each presbytery were independent of every other presbytery, as if our General Assembly did not possess the power of deciding in all controversies respecting doctrine and discipline,* as if in our Presbyterian system the whole Church were not greater than any of its parts.† The sitting of this venerable Court to-day in this city, as the capital of the nation, is due to the fact that treasure and blood were spent to establish the truth that such a doctrine in our political system was nothing else than treason against the government. So does this Court know that he who teaches that the power of the General Assembly, representing the whole Church, can be nullified by the will of a single presbytery lifts the banner of treason against the Presbyterian Church.

It rather puzzles the ordinary mind to find the Presbytery of New York pronouncing a verdict of full acquittal, and at the same time emphasizing the lower Court's failure to express approval of the critical and theological views of the Appellee, and hinting that the present disquietude in the Presbyterian Church is due to his hasty and over-confident statement of private opinion. Hence, from the standpoint of the inferior Court, the verdict is against the evidence. The Presbytery so qualifies its finding that the full acquittal is tantamount to a conviction. The lower judicatory seems to have mistaken "the grave issues involved in the case" and "the present disquietude of the Presbyterian Church" for certainty of evidence *against* the Appellee.

The final judgment is an attempt to apply the Craighead case of the Assembly of 1824 to this procedure, by

---
* Form of Government, Chapter XII., Section V.
† Form of Government, Chapter X., Section I.

making it the precedent of action.* When the inferior Court affirms that no man can be convicted of heresy by inference or implication, it means that such is still the case though the inference be necessary—though the implication be undoubted.

In this connection it is proper to remark :

(1) That the Craighead case and the case against Professor Briggs are not analogous on the points at issue.

(2) The position that a man cannot be convicted of heresy upon an inference, even though it be a necessary inference, is a false one, and that was not the principle upon which the General Assembly of 1824 based its decision in the Craighead case. The Apostle Paul condemned the heretical Jews of his time by clear logical inference scores of times.† What reader of the Bible is not familiar with the *therefore* and *wherefore*, and *so that* with which he introduces the word of condemnation?

(3) The use of the Craighead case in this matter is an EVASION of the FACTS, and what lawyers would call confession and avoidance—a subterfuge on the part of the inferior court to evade its clear duty.

The Appellee stands before the world doing his work as a Presbyterian Minister, as a representative of the Presbyterian Church, in the department of theological instruction. Now the deliverances of the General Assemblies of 1882, 1883, 1888, 1889 and 1892 (Dr. Briggs himself voting for that of 1882), the disapproval of his

* Minutes, General Assembly, 1824, page 122.
† Romans II : 17–29–X : 1–3.

appointment by the Assembly of 1891, the entertainment and sustaining by the Assembly of 1892 of the appeal of the Committee of Prosecution, the qualified language of the final judgment of the New York Presbytery, the fact that of those who have supported Dr. Briggs, whether from pulpit, press, or seminary, not one in one hundred, as I estimate it, will subscribe to the doctrine of the Inaugural Address, all prove that the Appellee does not properly represent the fundamental theological opinions of the Presbyterian Church.

Dr. Briggs, the Appellee, as a professor in the Union Theological Seminary, is a representative of the Presbyterian Church in the United States of America, in the department of theological instruction by virtue (1) of the fact that he is a minister of said Church, and (2) of his scholarship and of his qualifications as a teacher of Biblical Theology.

But the ministry and membership of the Presbyterian Church, thus represented by Dr. Briggs, include those who in his opinion are intellectually inferior to himself. And this very case proves that there are crises in which that ministry and membership have a right to know how he means to act, and what opinions on all things which concern his public duty he intends should guide his conduct. If any of these opinions are unacceptable to the great majority of the members of the Presbyterian Church, it is for Dr. Briggs to satisfy that majority that he nevertheless deserves to be their representative ; and if they are wise, they will overlook, in favor of his general value, many and great differences between his opinions and their own.

There are some differences, however, which cannot be overlooked. Whoever of the ministry or membership of the Presbyterian Church feels the amount of interest in the relation of his denomination to the Church of our Lord Jesus Christ which befits a Presbyterian, has *some* convictions on the doctrines of grace which are his lifeblood; which the strength of his belief in their truth, and the importance he attaches to them, forbid him to make the subject of compromise or postpone to the judgment of any one, however great his learning. Such convictions (the points of direct attack by Dr. Briggs in the Inaugural Address), possess the heart, soul, strength, and mind of the large proportion of the ministry, ruling eldership, and private membership of the Presbyterian Church in the United States of America. No body of people can be well represented in opposition to their primary notions of right. A correct estimate of the relation of a representative to his constituency does not require the latter to consent to be represented by one who intends to represent them (in this case to teach and to preach), in opposition to their fundamental convictions. If the constituency avail themselves of the representative capacities, of useful service in other respects, when the points on which he is vitally at issue with them are not likely to be mooted, they are justified in dismissing him at the first moment when a question arises involving said points.*

* Mill, on Representative Government, Chapter XII.

Such is the philosophy of the relation of Dr. Briggs, as a representative in the department of theological instruction and opinion of the Presbyterian Church in the United States of America, to the said Presbyterian Church. And that philosophy teaches by example in the history of the "Case against Professor Briggs," as set forth in this Argument.

This, then, is the case which your Appellant, the Committee of Prosecution, has brought before the General Assembly for final settlement. If the remedy which we seek on behalf of the Church is extraordinary, it is because the case is extraordinary.

It has sometimes been assumed that the persistence of the prosecution in the case of Professor Briggs is an exhibition of willful disregard of the peace of the church; of a litigious and disturbing spirit; and it has been maintained that the American Presbyterian Church is justified in tolerating what in other churches is called Broad Church principles, in defiance of the teaching of Holy Scripture and our Standards. I cannot close without referring to these assumptions. In trials for alleged offences against the standards of doctrine, against what are believed to be essential doctrine, it is impossible that any local court, however learned and however careful, should determine the issue for the whole Church. With all respect to the accused in this case, I am ready to say that his personal interest in the case is as nothing in comparison to the interests of the Church, in whose name he has been teaching.

The Presbytery of New York has decided that a Presbyterian minister may lawfully teach doctrines alleged to be contra-scriptural and contra-confessional which Professor Briggs admits he has taught. The question is : Will the Church consent to regard that judgment as final, and, by refusing the right of direct appeal, to the Prosecution, permit the Presbytery of New York to determine *ex-cathedra* what is really Presbyterian doctrine? The questions involved have to be answered by the whole Church. It is not the prerogative of the Prosecuting Committee, of Professor Briggs, nor of the Presbytery of New York, nor of the Synod of New York, to determine finally what is right in this matter. It is a question which is to be answered not for ourselves alone, but for all American Presbyterians both now and for some years to come.

If this Prosecuting Commitee had failed to call attention to the irregularities of the trial below, and the mistakes in the decision, they would deserve censure at the hands of this great representative body. The Prosecuting Committee might have escaped much of the sometimes harsh criticism which has been directed at them from certain quarters, but they would have done a wrong to the Church. They might not have been called litigious or disturbers of the peace and work of the Church, but they might have deserved the accusation of being recreant to their obvious duty, and unwilling to vindicate the Presbyterian claim to bear witness to the truth.

Hence, as the spokesman of hundreds of thousands

of Presbyterians, both at home and over the wide world, in the name of law and order, in the name of denominational loyalty and denominational honesty, in the name of Scripture precept and Bible example—aye in the name of the historic, orthodox, evangelical, constitutional, missionary, Presbyterian Branch of the Church of our Lord Jesus Christ I beseech this venerable court to bless the Church and the world, by exercising its authority in a crisis so momentous, as to make every plea for a delay of judgment entirely out of order.

Thus your honorable body will protect our communion from what one of your number has called "the peril of a broadness that would empty our souls of conviction and our lives of victory."*

---
* Rev. Herrick Johnson, D. D., in his opening address, McCormick Theological Seminary, Sept. 1893.

VI.

ARGUMENT OF MR. MCCOOK, A MEMBER OF THE PROSECUTING COMMITTEE, IN FAVOR OF ENTERTAINING THE APPEAL.

MODERATOR, FATHERS AND BRETHREN :

All the preliminary questions involved in this case were fully discussed and determined by the General Assembly of 1892.

Among the questions thus determined are the following:

1. That the appeal was taken by the Presbyterian Church in the United States of America, as an original party.

2. That the original party is represented by the Prosecuting Committee.

3. That such committee is a Prosecuting Committee appointed under Section 11 of the Book of Discipline.

4. The original party, by its Prosecuting Committee, has the right in this case, to take such an appeal from the Presbytery directly to the General Assembly.

5. That such an appeal is regular and in order.

Under a strict interpretation of the Constitution and the precedents established by the General Assembly, as the Supreme Court of our Church, these and some other questions passed upon by the last Assembly are *res adjudicata* and should not be again discussed.

The law of the Presbyterian Church is, that it is not competent for one General Assembly to *revise* or *review any proceedings* of a previous Assembly taken *in a judicial case.* (See Appeal of Lowry, Minutes, 1824, page 115, Case of Worrell, Minutes, 1864, page 398.)

I must take a few minutes of your valuable time, to deal with the technical points raised by the Appellee.

The Appellee's argument that the Appellant must prove himself an aggrieved party, though brilliant in detail and interesting in method, was wholly irrelevant, as he himself frankly stated at the outset. In the new Book of Discipline, he tells us, the term "original party" replaces that of "aggrieved party" in the old Book. It is fair to presume that this change was made designedly, but in any event the revised Book says nothing of the "aggrieved party." Section 94 of the new Book gives the right of appeal to "either of the original parties," and gives it as an unquestioned constitutional right.

The Appellee enunciated a strange principle when he informed us that a decision in a judicial case is not a decision as to doctrine. He intimated that litigation does not lead to final interpretation of law. Granting that this court cannot give a final interpretation, nothing could be easier or simpler than for this Assembly, in its legislative capacity, by deliverance, to affirm the decision made by the Assembly as a Court. But the general statement is erroneous. The Supreme Court of the United States, by the Constitution, is made the final interpreter of the Constitution. Cases are constantly carried thither to secure a definitive and final interpretation. The General Assembly is made the final interpreter of our Constitution. It has almost invariably refused to decide principles, *in thesi*, requiring a concrete case upon which to render a decision. True, the General Assembly, like the United States Supreme Court, may err; but its decision, like that of the United States Supreme Court, is final, is law, and must be submitted to.

The Appellee said that the decision of the New York Presbytery does not bind the Church. True; but if ignored it will bind the Church, for it permits the doctrines alleged to be heretical, to be preached within the bounds of that Presbytery without rebuke. We are not Congregationalists; we are Presbyterians. The New York Presbytery is not like the Manhattan Congregational Association; it is a part of the one great Church, whose representatives are assembled here. Its decisions, touching doctrine, affect the whole Church from the Atlantic to the Pacific.

The ingenious argument of the Appellee respecting the use of the terms "decision" and "final judgment" in the title of the appeal has very little to do with the case. In so far as the term "final judgment" is concerned, it matters not whether it be confined to the mere assertion of acquittal, or be extended, as the Presbytery evidently intended, and as the Committee of Prosecution thinks it should be, to cover the whole judgment rendered and recorded as the judgment of the New York Presbytery on January 9, 1893. In this discussion by the Appellee, Section 95 of the Book of Discipline was not read to you. That section gives, among other grounds of appeal, the following: "Hastening to a *decision* before the testimony is fully taken, and mistake or injustice in the *decision*." All that portion of the appeal against which the Appellee protested so earnestly is relevant. While the appeal itself, as you will see from page 4 of the printed document placed in your hands, is from the final judgment only, yet according to Section 95, all errors, all actions in any portion of the proceedings from their inception, to the record of the final judgment, are proper grounds for appeal. By reference to the printed record, pages 160 and 163, you will see that the entire report of "the Committee appointed to bring in the result of the vote and the judgment of the Judicatory" was accepted, adopted in its several parts, then as a whole, and that on the 9th day of January, 1893, the report was declared to be the judgment of the court, and was entered accordingly.

After glancing at the minutes of the meeting of the Presbytery of New York, held on December 30, 1892 (printed document, pages 137-8, pages 143-4 of this volume), a meeting from which, under the provisions of Section 23 of the Book of Discipline, the parties and all other persons not members of the body were excluded, you will see that the acts there recorded do not fix the time, from which the ten days for giving notice of appeal under Section 96 runs. The minutes do not indicate that the result of the vote was made known; it is not recorded as a part of the proceedings of the meeting. A committee was appointed to bring in the result of the vote and the judgment of the Judicatory. The parties were again admitted to the Judicatory on January 9th, after the report of the Committee had been read, accepted, adopted, and entered upon the minutes as the final judgment of the Judicatory (printed document, pages 160, 163, 164, pages 166, 169, 170, of this volume). The parties were then readmitted to the court, and the final judgment, as entered, was made known to them.

Section 96 of the Book of Discipline provides that "Written notice of appeal, with specifications of the errors alleged, shall be given within ten days after the judgment has been rendered." Within ten days after the judgment was entered in this case and made known to the parties, written notice of appeal was given.

In view of these facts, I ask, is it frank, is it fair, is it candid to suggest that this appeal was not taken in due time? However, this quibble, raised by the Appellee, is not relevant or material now, for both the majority and minority of the Judicial Committee have reported the appeal to be in order, and this Assembly has already—

"*Resolved*, That the General Assembly finds that due notice of the appeal in this case has been given, and that the appeal and specifications of the errors alleged have been filed *in due time* and *that the appeal is in order* in accordance with the provisions of the Book of Discipline."

I should not have taken a second of your time with these details, but I felt it was necessary to show how irrelevant to the question now before the house, was the long discussion of preliminary points, with which the Appellee favored us during the afternoon session of yesterday, all of which points have been definitely settled in this case by this or the last Assembly. Most, if not all, of these preliminary questions discussed by the Appellee yesterday are now *res adjudicata in this case*, and should not engage your attention for a moment.

But as the Appellee in this case, has persistently urged the contrary view, in all the Courts of our Church, out of abundant caution and so that no duty towards the Church at large, which the Prosecuting Committee represents, may be neglected or overlooked, the following considerations are presented.

PRELIMINARY SUGGESTIONS.

The Judicial Committee and the minority thereof, having reported that the Appeal of the Presbyterian Church in the United States of America, Appellant, against the Rev. Charles A. Briggs, D. D., Appellee, is in order, the only question now before the Assembly, sitting as a Court, is whether the Appeal shall be entertained.

This is a technical legal question which the members of the Assembly must determine by bringing their intelligence and common sense to bear, in the interpretation of a few clearly expressed sections of the Book of Discipline and of the Form of Government of the Church.

These sections now to be referred to, do not contain words of double meaning, nor do they leave any one who studies them, in uncertainty as to what was meant by the persons who drafted the sections referred to, or by those who voted to make them a part of the Constitution of the Presbyterian Church in the United States of America.

Every Minister and Elder, a member of this Assembly, at the time of his ordination, solemnly asserted that he approved of the Government and Discipline of the Presbyterian Church in the United States.

The time has come, when, as Commissioners representing your respective Presbyteries, you are brought face to face with a great crisis in the affairs of our Church. And it behooves each one to give full weight and consideration to the obligation assumed, when that ordination vow was taken, and without fear or favor, to see to it that his duty in this behalf is fully performed.

The proceedings now to be taken in this case must be conducted under the provisions of two or three sections of the Form of Government, and a few sections of the Book of Discipline.

THE BOOK OF DISCIPLINE.

This Book of Discipline has been part of the Constitution of the Presbyterian Church for nearly ten years, and is the controlling statute which determines what is constitutional and what is or is not lawful, in the procedure with which we are now to deal. This Book of Discipline was not adopted by the Presbyterian Church to cover this case, or any particular case, but its provisions are to be applied in exact equity and fairness to all cases where the power of discipline may be invoked, to secure the results which the 2d Section of the Book of Discipline so well describes as follows: "2. The ends of Discipline are the maintenance of the "truth, the vindication of the authority and honor of "Christ, the removal of offences, the promotion of the "purity and edification of the Church, and the spirit- "ual good of offenders."

ATTEMPTS TO DISCREDIT THE BOOK.

It has been popular of late, in certain quarters, to cast reflections upon this Book of Discipline and to discredit it. Whether its provisions have been wisely or unwisely adopted we need not now discuss. It is the law of the Church, which must control in all matters of discipline. Even if some of its provisions should seem unwise, to those who are not likely to be satisfied with the results which naturally follow from a clear, definite and logical enforcement of the same, yet it is a part of the Constitution of our Church. Those who still honor and respect that Constitution, and their obligation to it, assumed when they took their ordination vow, will, I am sure, give their voices and votes in favor of a proper enforcement of its provisions.

THE OLD BOOK AND PRECEDENTS THEREUNDER ARE
NO LONGER AUTHORITATIVE.

It should be understood from the first, that the provisions of the old Book of Discipline, in so far as they have not been re-enacted in the new Book, and the precedents based thereon, have at this time, no force or effect whatever as law or precedents in the Courts of our Church.

PLAN AND PURPOSE OF THE REVISED BOOK.

The intention of the committee, which so deliberately and skillfully drafted the present Book of Discipline, is perfectly evident to those who study its provisions, carefully and without prejudice. That committee began its labors in 1878, and continued the study and work of preparation until the Assembly of 1884. The idea of the Committee was to make the enforcement of discipline effective, and at the same time, by the provisions of the Book, to discourage unnecessary or litigious proceedings. The plan evidently was to do away with the undesirable and often irresponsible charges which arose under the Common Fame clause of the old Book.

As former trials had in more than one instance aroused strong personal feeling among members of the same Presbytery, it was determined, if possible, to prevent the recurrence in the future of such a condition of affairs.

To remove the personal element as far as possible, it was provided by Sections 6 and 10 of the Book of Discipline that when a judicatory finds it necessary for the ends of discipline to investigate an alleged offence and when the prosecution is initiated by a judicatory, as in this case, the proceedings shall be instituted in the name of the Presbyterian Church in the United States of America and that the Church at large *shall be* the prosecutor and an original party.

To place the proceedings on the highest possible plane, the plan of the Book was to make all of the members of the judicatory sitting as a Court, Judges, in the highest and best meaning of that term. They were not to be advocates or partisans. Provision was also made in Section 11 that when the prosecution is initiated by a judicatory, a committee, known as the Prosecuting Committee, shall be appointed to conduct the prosecution in all its stages, in whatever judicatory, until the final issue be reached. The members of such a committee, when appointed, are, by that act, removed from the body of the Court, as Judges. Like the minister or elder who may prepare or exhibit the cause of the accused, they are not permitted to sit in judgment in the case.

The intention of these provisions of the Book of Discipline was evidently to place the members of a judicatory sitting as a Court, in a purely judicial attitude, and to preclude any one who might exhibit prejudice or undue zeal, because of his activity in conducting the prosecution, from participating in any way in the decisions of the Court.

THE PROVISIONS OF THE BOOK SAFEGUARD AND PROTECT ALL INTERESTS.

The result of this is that the interests of every minister, officer and member of the Church, subject to discipline under the provisions of the Book, are protected in the most careful way, and proceedings are not so likely to be instituted by individual prosecutors as under the old Book. If, however, proceedings are instituted by a judicatory, and it finds, after an examination by a special committee, that it is necessary for the ends of discipline to investigate the alleged offence, every possible safeguard and protection has been thrown about the interests of the parties concerned.

The Book of Discipline of the Presbyterian Church is a part of its Constitution. All ministers and officers of the Church, by their ordination vows have approved of and accepted it as such and have committed themselves to its support and enforcement. When we know what the provisions of the Book are and apply them to the facts of a particular case, every member of this Assembly should be able to reach a wise and just conclusion, and to determine what his duty is under the circumstances.

The Book of Discipline, Sec. 94, provides as follows:

"An Appeal is the removal of a judicial case, by a "written representation, from an inferior to a superior "judicatory; and may be taken, by either of the "original parties, from the final judgment of the "lower judicatory. These parties shall be called "Appellant and Appellee."

No question has been raised or can be raised as to the fact that the judgment entered in this matter by the Presbytery of New York, on January 9, 1893, and now appealed from, is the final judgment of the lower judicatory in this case. This having been determined, and the fact is, I believe, unquestioned, the only other important point in this section, requiring attention at this time, is whether the appeal has been taken by either of the original parties.

ORIGINAL PARTIES.

To learn who are the original parties we must turn to Section 10 of the Book of Discipline, which is as follows: "10. When the prosecution is initiated by a "judicatory, the Presbyterian Church in the United "States of America shall be the prosecutor, and an "original party; in all other cases, the individual pros-"ecutor shall be an original party."

Such an investigation was made in this case by a special committee. It made a full examination and report, which was discussed in Presbytery. The recommendations of the committee were adopted, and a judicial investigation was ordered, before the Prosecuting Committee had been appointed. There is no question as to who is the original party. This section (10) makes it mandatory that the Presbyterian Church in the United States of America *shall be* the prosecutor and an original party.

PROSECUTING COMMITTEES.

Within the bounds of a Presbytery which is sitting in a judicial capacity, the Church at large can act only through a committee or as represented by a committee. This fact was taken into account in preparing the Book of Discipline, and provision was made therefor, in Section 11, as follows:

"When the prosecution is initiated by a judicatory, "it shall appoint one or more of its own members a "Committee to conduct the prosecution in all its "stages in whatever judicatory, until the final issue be "reached; *provided*, that any appellate judicatory "before which the case is pending shall, if desired "by the prosecuting committee, appoint one or more "of its own members to assist in the prosecution, "upon the nomination of the prosecuting committee."

The provisions of this section are also mandatory. It does not say that the judicatory may in its discretion, or if necessary appoint, but it is emphatic and declares that it *shall* appoint a committee to conduct the prosecution, in *all* its stages, in *whatever* judicatory, *until* the final issue be reached.

Notice, here, that this is not a temporary committee, to be quickly created and quickly discharged. Such a committee is, in no sense, a "Judicial Committee" to digest and arrange papers, etc., such as is provided for by Rule XLI. of the General Rules for Judicatories, the members of which may sit and vote in the case in which they act. The prosecuting committee provided for by Section 11 of the Book of Discipline cannot be appointed until the prosecution has been initiated by a judicatory. And this, as provided in Section 6, must be after the judicatory has found it necessary for the ends of discipline to investigate the alleged offence.

STATUS OF THE PROSECUTING COMMITTEE.

Throughout the conduct of this case the position of the Prosecuting Committee has been attacked. Although the status of the Committee was fully and finally determined by the last General Assembly, this question has been again raised by the Appellee, in his argument in opposition to the entertainment of the Appeal.

Under these circumstances it becomes important that the members of this Assembly should have a complete understanding of what the Presbytery of New York, the Synod of New York and the General Assembly have done with reference to the status of the Prosecuting Committee as representing the Presbyterian Church in the United States of America, the Appellant in this case. The following are the facts:

ACTION OF NEW YORK PRESBYTERY AS TO THE PROSECUTING COMMITTEE.

At a meeting of the Presbytery of New York in April, 1891, a committee was appointed to consider the Inaugural Address of the Appellee in its relation to the Confession of Faith. This Committee, in its report, recommended "that the Presbytery enter at once upon the judicial investigation of the case," and the Presbytery having adopted the recommendation, the report was adopted. That was the inception of the case. The Prosecuting Committee, of which the Rev. G. W. F. Birch, D. D., is Chairman, was appointed at the meeting of the Presbytery of New York held in May, 1891, "to arrange and prepare the necessary proceedings appropriate in the case of Dr. Briggs." The intent of the Presbytery in appointing the Committee was to make it such a Committee as is contemplated by

Section 11 of the Book of Discipline—namely, a Prosecuting Committee.

An appeal was made to you this morning by the Appellee, on the ground that he had not been courteously or fairly dealt with by this Committee. This Committee has no explanation or apology to make for anything that it has done, as it believes, under the instruction and provision of the Constitution of the Presbyterian Church in the United States of America, and in protecting the interests of that Church against what is believed to be fundamental error. Although we have been so often criticised, in the public press and elsewhere, I wish to call the attention of this Assembly to the fact, that never, except upon the floor of the Courts of this Church, so far as I know, has any member of this Committee given public expression to his views or ideas. We have held that we represented the Presbyterian Church in the United States of America, as a whole, and if it appeared to be for the interest of any one to criticise or blame us, that we would have to take the blame, until the final issue is reached, and the Presbyterian Church determines whether we have or have not done our duty. But the suggestion was made by him that courtesy had not been extended to the Appellee in this matter. It is only right and fair that you should know (everybody in the Presbytery of New York knows it, for the letter I am about to read has been read in the hearing of that Presbytery), that before a single step was taken by the Committee appointed by the Presbytery to consider the Inaugural Address, the Chairman of that Committee wrote to the Rev. Dr. Briggs, suggesting that meetings of the Committee would be held at a certain time and place, and asking that Dr. Briggs would join them, for conference, before any action was taken. I will now read to you, without comment, the answer received by the Committee to their invitation, and then I shall let the matter pass.

"120 West 93d Street,
"NEW YORK, April 24, 1891.
"The REV. G. W. F. BIRCH, D. D.
"My dear Sir:
"In response to your letter of April 23d, "inviting me to be present at the next meeting of a "committee, of which you are Chairman, I beg leave "to say: (1) The state of my health will not admit of "my compliance with your invitation, and (2) If I "were in good health, I would still be obliged to "decline, for the reason that it would seem that your "committee were appointed to consider my 'Inaugural "Address,' and not to consider any explanations of it "I might be willing to make.

"Yours respectfully,

"C. A. BRIGGS."

The Presbytery of New York has regarded the said Committee, at all times, as a Prosecuting Committee, appointed in accordance with Section 11 of the Book of Discipline, as is evidenced by the following action and extracts from its records.

The Presbytery accepted and adopted the charges and specifications prepared by the Committee and entered upon the trial, with this Committee acting as a Committee of Prosecution, and the Appellee himself agreed in open session of the Presbytery, on October 6, 1891, that he would so proceed to trial, and that arrangement is recorded at page 479 of Volume 13 of the Records of the Presbytery of New York, as follows:

"By agreement between Dr. Briggs and the *Prosecuting Committee* * it was resolved that the 4th day of November, 1891, at 10 A. M., be fixed as the day on which the citation is returnable and that the citation

---
* The italics throughout, unless otherwise indicated, are mine.—
J. J. McC.

be issued for that date, in accordance with Section 19 of the Book of Discipline."

The following is an extract from the citation served upon Dr. Briggs by the Moderator, in the presence of the Presbytery of New York, on September 6, 1891 :

"CITATION.

"You are hereby furnished with a copy of the charges and specifications presented to the Presbytery on the 5th day of October, 1891, by the *Committee of Prosecution* appointed by the Presbytery of New York at its meeting in May last, which report, with its accompanying recommendations, were accepted and adopted by this Presbytery on the said 5th day of October, 1891.

"(Signed) JOHN C. BLISS, Moderator."

The certificate accompanying the charges and specifications served upon Dr. Briggs by the Moderator, in the presence of the Presbytery, on October 6, 1891, is as follows:

"I hereby certify that the foregoing is an authentic copy of the charges and specifications against Prof. Charles A. Briggs, which *the Presbytery of New York has ordered shall be prosecuted.*

"(Signed) JOHN C. BLISS, Moderator."

"October 6, 1891."

The following quotations are from Volume 13 of the Records of the Presbytery of New York, and fully indicate the status of the Prosecuting Committee and the purpose and intent of the Presbytery in appointing the same.

Page 434. " The time having come in the order of business to receive the report of the *Committee of Prosecution* in the case of the Rev. Charles A. Briggs, Rev. George Alexander asked leave to introduce," etc., and he introduced a paper.

Also on page 434. "Objection was made on the ground that Dr. Birch, *as Chairman of the Committee of Prosecution*, had the floor, and that the motion to suspend the order of the day could not be introduced."

Page 435. "The *Committee of Prosecution* in the case of Dr. Briggs, *appointed in compliance with Section* 11 *of the Book of Discipline*, at the meeting of Presbytery in May last, reported as follows":

The following is an extract from the paper proposed by the Rev. George Alexander, D. D., as a substitute for the recommendation contained in the report of the Prosecuting Committee:

Page 463. "Whereas, the Presbytery of New York, at its meeting in May last, on account of utterances contained in an inaugural address delivered January 20th, 1891, *appointed a committee to formulate charges* against the author of that address, the Rev. Charles A. Briggs, D. D."

Page 463. The report made by the Prosecuting Committee containing the charges and specifications "was accepted by the Presbytery."

Page 470. The recommendation in the report of the Prosecuting Committee in the matter of Dr. Briggs was adopted.

During the proceedings of the Presbytery of New York, on November 4th, 1891, when the case was dismissed, the minutes, Vol. 14, page 90, show that the following action was taken:

"At this point (after the reading of Dr. Briggs' Response), the question as to the status of the Prosecuting Committee was raised. The Moderator decided that the Committee was properly a Committee of Prosecution in view of the previous action of Presbytery as recorded, and represented the Presbyterian Church in the United States of America, and was in the house as an original party in the case, under provision of Section 10 of the Book of Discipline, and is now virtually independent of Presbytery."

"An appeal was taken from the decision of the Moderator. The question was divided. The Moderator was sustained in the point that the Committee was in the house as a properly appointed Committee of Prosecution. The Moderator was also sustained in the point that the Committee as representing the Presbyterian Church in the United States of America was an original party in the Complaint."

This action of the Judicatory in sustaining the Moderator upon the appeal from his decision as to the status of the Prosecuting Committee is itself conclusive evidence of the intent of the Presbytery in appointing and recognizing the Prosecuting Committee as such.

The above ruling of the Moderator of the Presbytery of New York as to the status of the Prosecuting Committee, which was appealed from and sustained by the Presbytery, was undoubtedly in accordance with the provisions of the Book of Discipline, under which the Presbytery was then acting as a judicatory.

APPROVAL BY THE SYNOD OF NEW YORK OF THE PRESBYTERY'S RECORDS.

An examination of Volume 13 of the Records of the Presbytery of New York, covering all the proceedings above referred to, except the last, shows at page 483 that the Synod of New York during its session held at Watertown, New York, on October, 22 1891, examined and approved of the said record. The said Synod has therefore approved of the appointment of this Committee and of its action as a Committee of Prosecution up to October 22, 1891. The period covers the appointment of the Prosecuting Committee, the adoption of its report, including the charges and specifications, the service of citation by the Moderator upon Dr. Briggs, and his agreement with the Prosecuting Committee in open Presbytery as to the day upon which the citation was to be returnable.

RELATION OF A PROSECUTING COMMITTEE TO THE CHURCH AT LARGE.

The mere assignment or appointment of certain members of the Presbytery to act as a Prosecuting Committee, when once made, under Section 11 of the Book of Discipline, gives that Committee a relation to the Church at large. It acts on behalf of the Presbyterian Church in the United States of America. It represents the entire Church, and, as such, is an original party. In its representative capacity it is the prosecutor and cannot be disturbed by the Presbytery.

If this were not so, the Church at large could not take and perfect an appeal, although it is one of the original parties. Yet all proceedings initiated by a judicatory, as in this case, *must be* instituted in the name of the Church, in compliance with Section 10 of the Book of Discipline.

Whenever a judicial process is initiated by the judicatory, special conditions arise. The Presbytery is placed in extraordinary and exceptional relations to the Church at large, in that the Presbyterian Church becomes a prosecutor at its bar; for such exceptional relations, exceptional provisions are needed, and they have been made. The Presbytery ought not to be judge and prosecutor at the same time.

To obviate this difficulty, the Constitution, Book of Discipline, Section 10, requires the Presbytery to appoint a committee to conduct the prosecution in the name of the Presbyterian Church in the United States of America. This committee, not the Presbytery, represents the whole Church. It is not dependent for its existence on the will of the Presbytery. It does not derive its powers from the will of the Presbytery. It is not limited in its action by the will of the Presbytery. This is evident from the following considerations:

1st. The act of Presbytery in appointing the committee of prosecution is *ministerial* only. The committee of prosecution is in no sense the creature of Presbytery. It owes its existence to the Constitution itself. The Presbytery has no discretion in the matter. Having determined to initiate judicial process, it is under obligation to appoint the committee of prosecution, whose duties are defined by Section 11 of the Book of Discipline.

The President of the United States nominates, and by and with the advice and consent of the Senate, appoints the judges of the Supreme Court. In making such appointments the President and Senate act ministerially, in obedience to a constitutional requirement. The power to appoint and to confirm, in these circumstances, does not give the President or the Senate in any degree, the right of control over the action and tenure of the judges. The judges are appointed according to the provisions of the Constitution; they shape their official life and conduct according to the directions of that instrument, in entire independence of the appointing and confirming power.

This illustrates the position of the committee of prosecution in our judicial system. The mere power of appointment, in a ministerial way, does not give the Presbytery the right to control the action and life of the committee. It is not a presbyterial committee. It is created by the Constitution, which determines its duties and the length of its life.

2d. The language of the Book necessarily implies that the committee of prosecution is to represent the Presbyterian Church in every case where the judicatory initiates the prosecution. Section 11 of the Book makes the tenth Section effective.

Section 10 directs that, when a judicatory initiates prosecution, the Presbyterian Church in the United States of America *shall be* the prosecutor, and an original party; and Section 11 orders that a committee *shall be* appointed by that judicatory " to conduct " the prosecution." The provisions of Section 11 are absolutely necessary to carry those of Section 10 into effect. And the import of these provisions cannot be mistaken. The Presbyterian Church shall be the prosecutor, and the committee shall conduct the prosecution. Since, then, the Presbyterian Church is to conduct its business as prosecutor, through the instrumentality of the committee of prosecution, the relation between the two can be properly expressed in any given case, only, by saying that the committee represents the Church.

3d. It is sufficiently evident that the committee of prosecution, and not the Presbytery, represents the Presbyterian Church, for, according to Section 11, the committee is "to conduct the prosecution, in all its " stages, in whatever judicatory, until the final issue " be reached.'"

This language means that if the case be taken to the higher judicatories, the committee of prosecution must follow it, to conduct the prosecution in all its stages until a final settlement is reached.

But if the committee of prosecution has only a presbyterial relation, and can exist and act only by the will of the Presbytery, then it cannot exercise its functions beyond the bounds of the Presbytery whose creature it is. It would be precluded, by any such relations, from prosecuting in the higher courts. The Presbytery itself has no right to prosecute either at the bar of the Synod or of the Assembly, and cannot, therefore, empower any of its committees to do so, although it may appear through a committee to defend its own action before a superior judicatory.

But the Book's meaning is clear, that the Presbyterian Church shall continue to be the prosecutor at every stage, and shall do its work as prosecutor by means of the Committee of Prosecution. That committee, then, is related constitutionally, not to the Presbytery, but to the Presbyterian Church. For this reason, its duties are defined, and its rights are guaranteed in all the higher judicatories.

The words, "in all its stages, in whatever judi-
" catory," as used in Section 11, involve the right of appeal for both original parties; and since the Presbyterian Church, as an original party, conducts the prosecution by means of the Committee of Prosecution, it is the intent of the Book, that the committee should have the power of appeal, in the name of the Church. The power to appeal is a necessary part of that prosecution, which the committee is directed to conduct in behalf of the Church. It is the only way in which the Presbyterian Church can exercise this right of an original party.

As still further confirmatory of the position that the Committee of Prosecution is not a presbyterial committee, but is constitutionally related to the Presbyterian Church, we have the additional direction of Section 11, "that any appellate judicatory before
" which the case is pending shall, if desired by the
" prosecuting committee, appoint one or more of its
" own members to assist in the prosecution, upon the
" nomination of the prosecuting committee." This provision, alone, suffices to prove the prosecuting committee wholly independent of the initiating judicatory. That committee has the sole right to determine whether or not it will have any addition to its membership,

and then to name those to be added by the superior judicatory. If this were a mere presbyterial committee, having no right to act beyond the will of the Presbytery, then, whenever it might become desirable to have assistance in the prosecution, this committee would have to apply to Presbytery for additional members, since neither Synod nor Assembly has the right to constitute, increase or diminish presbyterial committees.

There can be no doubt, then, that the Committee of Prosecution represents the Presbyterian Church in the United States of America, an original party, so far as the prosecution of any given case is concerned, and that it has the constitutional right to take an appeal in the name of that Church, from the final decision of an inferior judicatory in the case.

Against this conclusion no serious objection is urged except that no precedents, under the new Book, sustain it. The answer to this objection is, that, as this is the first important case of the kind, arising under the present Book of Discipline, there has been no opportunity to establish precedents, *except as was done by the General Assembly of* 1892, *in this case.*

This new procedure was adopted, because the practice according to the former procedure was unsatisfactory.

STEPS LEADING TO THE REVISION OF THE
BOOK OF DISCIPLINE.

The old-school Assembly of 1861, on motion of Drs. Charles K. Imbrie and Jonathan Edwards, sent back to the Synod of New Jersey, the appeal and complaint of the Presbytery of Passaic against the Synod in the case of Mr. Guild, for the reason that the Synod had not heard the *original parties*, the *Committee of Prosecution* being one of them, thus recognizing the right of the committee prosecuting on "common fame" to take an appeal. (Minutes of 1861, pp. 146-177.)

The Assembly of 1877 dismissed the case brought before them on appeal, from the Presbytery of Cincinnati, by the Rev. Dr. Thos. H. Skinner and others, who acted as a committee of prosecution, on the ground that the appellants, not being an original party, were not entitled to appeal. But a strong protest was spread on the Minutes, in which the protestants argue with entire conclusiveness that, according to the old Book, not only personal prosecutors and defendants in a judicial case, but any "aggrieved party," and "all " persons who have submitted to a regular trial in an " inferior, may appeal to a higher judicatory." The protest was not answered, for the simple reason that the positions taken in it were unanswerable. (Minutes 1877, pp. 576 to 580.)

At the very next Assembly after that, the revision of the Book of Discipline was begun ; and the chapter on appeals was reconstructed. Original parties and their rights were more clearly defined, and the right of appeal given to them exclusively. That uncertain quantity, "Common Fame," was banished altogether, and in place of it, the Presbyterian Church in the United States of America, was made the responsible prosecutor, an original party with specific direction to discharge its functions of prosecutor and original party, by means of the committee of prosecution.

In the old Book, "Common Fame" was not declared to be an original party; but in the new Book, the Presbyterian Church is made an original party, and, as such, has the constitutional right to take an appeal by means of the committee through whom it conducts the prosecution.

It is objected that, if the committee of prosecution represents the Presbyterian Church, and is thus virtually independent of the Presbytery, then great evils are sure to overtake us. It is said that the Presbyterian Church as represented in the General Assembly, may itself claim the right of appointing the committee; that the committee, thus entrusted with enormous powers, may use them to the great injury of accused parties; and that we open wide the gates for a perfect deluge of litigation, and so endanger the peace and usefulness of the Church to an alarming extent.

But if all this were true, it would not change the constitutionality of the standing and rights of the committee of prosecution under the Book. It might furnish an argument in favor of changing the Book. But these evils are all purely imaginary. They have never existed, and they are not likely to exist under the present Book of Discipline.

THE PROSECUTING COMMITTEE OF THE BOOK OF DISCIPLINE, A SAFE AND USEFUL AGENCY TO CONDUCT PROSECUTIONS IN BEHALF OF THE PRESBYTERIAN CHURCH.

There are many considerations to warrant the conclusion that a committee of prosecution, with just such relations and powers as are indicated in the Book of Discipline, is not only entirely safe, but also highly desirable as an agency for conducting the prosecution on the part of the Presbyterian Church. For

1. The court which initiates the prosecution, is charged with the duty of appointing the committee. No other body can appoint it, not even the Assembly, since the Constitution does not give it that right. The fact that the committee is charged with grave responsibilities and endowed with a large measure of power, leads to the exercise of caution, first in the initiation of prosecution, and then in the selection of the committee. These are strong safeguards and they are entirely

within the control, in the first instance, of the respective Presbyteries.

The fact that under our Book of Discipline the Prosecuting Committee acting for the Church at large is vested with ample powers to secure prompt decisions, is likely to accomplish very beneficial results.

Presbyteries will be careful not to institute judicial proceedings and appoint such committees, unless, as in this case, strong reasons exist for setting the proceedings in motion.

2. It is not to be presumed that a committee of prosecution, clothed with powers of the kind named, will become an instrument of inflicting wrong upon innocent parties. The presumption is, that a committee of Christian ministers and elders, appointed after prayerful consideration, by a judicatory which is composed of Christian ministers and elders, will be at pains to do only what is just, fair and Christian in the prosecution of any case, and that all the more so, since they are impersonal prosecutors.

The real danger is that, when there may be urgent need for initiating prosecution in a case like this, no body of men will be found willing to serve on the committee of prosecution, as they will thereby make themselves liable to be reviled and traduced, as this Prosecuting Committee has been, for rendering such service to the Church.

3. To illustrate specifically, in a trial for heresy, the Church, through its doctrines, being the party attacked, is in more immediate danger of suffering injury than is the other party. *Her faith, purity and peace, her testimony for the truth, and her ecclesiastical integrity, are all at stake.* The Church ought to have the power to appeal from an adverse decision of an inferior judicatory, whose members may be in sympathy with the

accused or with his erroneous opinions. Such conditions are not impossible.

An accused person, owing to his social or ecclesiastical position, may exert an influence so great in his Presbytery as to render it extremely difficult, if not altogether impossible, to convict him even on the best of evidence. Or a considerable number of the members of that judicatory, through sympathetic or other interests, may so far forget their positions as judges in the case, that they will not only try to retard and hamper the prosecution in every possible way, but actively plan and labor to procure an acquittal, no matter what the evidence may be.

If the Presbyterian Church should have no right of appeal, by its committee of prosecution, from a decision thus reached, by possibly a bare majority vote, then in the language of the Book, "heretical opinions * * * may be allowed to gain ground," with the greatest ease, and to an alarming extent.

This danger is not imaginary in times like our own, when individual liberty of expression is boldly championed at the expense of denominational bonds. The Presbyterian Church must have disciplinary methods such as will enable her to meet threatened dangers of this kind, to defend her faith and to preserve her purity, her integrity and usefulness. To this end the Presbyterian Church was made the prosecutor, and an original party, in certain cases, with the constitutional right of prosecuting by a committee.

APPEAL TO GENERAL ASSEMBLY OF 1892.

The Prosecuting Committee representing the Presbyterian Church as an original party, appealed from the judgment of the Presbytery of New York, dismissing the case, entered on November 4th, 1891, to the General Assembly of 1892.

The Prosecuting Committee based its first appeal from the Presbytery directly to the General Assembly of 1892, upon the special reasons set out therein, which have been substantially repeated in the pending appeal. They also relied upon the provisions of Section 102 of the Book of Discipline, which is as follows: "102. Appeals are, *generally*, to be taken to the judicatory immediately superior to that appealed from." And upon Chapter XII., Sections IV. and V. of the Form of Government, which are as follows:

"IV. The General Assembly *shall receive and issue all Appeals*, complaints and references that affect *the doctrine or constitution* of the Church which may be regularly brought before them from the inferior *judicatories.*"

"V. To the General Assembly also belongs the power of deciding in *all* controversies respecting *doctrine and discipline.*"

This Section IV. of the Form of Government is mandatory and says the General Assembly shall receive and issue all appeals that affect the doctrine or constitution of the Church, which may be regularly brought before them from the inferior judicatories.

This mandatory provision when read in connection with Section 102 of the Book of Discipline leaves but little discretion, when the conditions named by the Book have been complied with. They have been complied with in this case, and it would seem that the Assembly is compelled not only to entertain this Appeal but to issue it as well.

ACTION OF THE GENERAL ASSEMBLY OF 1892 AS TO PROSECUTING COMMITTEE.

The right of the Prosecuting Committee to take an appeal directly to the General Assembly and its status as a Prosecuting Committee, were questioned at Portland and were fully discussed by the Appellant and the Appellee. The record of the proceedings in this branch of the case, will be found at page 90 and following pages in the Minutes of the General Assembly for 1892, as follows:

"The Judicial Committee presented its report in the case of the Presbyterian Church in the United States of America *vs*. Rev. Charles A. Briggs, D. D., which was accepted as follows:

"The Judicial Committee respectfully reports that it has carefully considered the documents submitted to it in this case, and adopted the following resolutions:

"1. That, in the opinion of this Committee, the appeal taken by *the Presbyterian Church in the United States of America, an original party* represented by the '*Committee of Prosecution*,' *appointed under Section* 11 *of the Book of Discipline*, has been taken from the final judgment of the Presbytery in dismissing the case; and *that the said Committee had the right to take this appeal representing the said original party.*

"2. That it finds that the notice of the appeal has been given, and that the appeal, specifications of error, and record have been filed in accordance with Sections 96 and 97 of the Book of Discipline, and the appeal is order.

"3. That, in the judgment of the Committee, the appeal should be entertained, and a time set apart for the hearing of the case.

"In view of these considerations, the Committee reports that the appeal is in order, and that the General Assembly should proceed in accordance with the provisions of Section 99 of the Book of Discipline, by causing the judgment appealed from, the notice of appeal, the appeal and the specifications of the errors alleged, to be read; then to hear the appellant by the Committee of Prosecution; then the defendant in person, or by his counsel; then the appellant by the Committee of Prosecution in reply upon the question 'whether the appeal shall be entertained?'."

In behalf of the Committee,

T. RALSTON SMITH,
Chairman.

That report was brought before the house. A minority of the Judicial Committee presented a report which was also accepted, and, although the Assembly subsequently, after full discussion by the parties, laid the minority report on the table and adopted the report of the majority of the Committee, that minority report and the action of the Assembly thereon, becomes of great interest and importance, in view of what is now proposed. The minority of the Judicial Committee clearly expressed their views in the report, and there is not a word in it suggesting that this Prosecuting Committee was not a duly constituted prosecuting committee. Nor is there any question raised as to the right of the Committee to take the appeal. But what did the minority recommend? They said:

"The undersigned, a minority of the Judicial Committee, would respectfully submit the following report:

'"Whereas, the Book of Discipline requires that appeals are, generally, to be taken to the Judicatory immediately superior to that appealed from" (Sec. 102); and,

Whereas, There are no sufficient reasons for making the appeal against the Presbytery of New York in dismissing the case against Dr. Briggs an exception to this rule;

"Therefore, we recommend to the General Assembly *that the appeal be not entertained;* that the papers in the case be returned to the Appellant, and *that they be advised to bring their appeal or complaint before the Synod of New York.*

Respectfully submitted,

D. R. FRAZER,
THOMAS GORDON,
OSWALD P. BACKUS,
GEORGE W. KETCHAM."

If this Committee was not a Prosecuting Committee and had not the right to appeal to the General Assembly, what right had such a Committee to take an appeal to the Synod of New York? Before passing away from the consideration of this minority report, it may be well to recall the fact, that the Portland Assembly, after hearing the arguments on both sides, and after discussion by members of the Assembly, *did not adopt* the recommendations of the minority report *to refer the case back to Synod*, but laid the minority report upon the table, and adopted the recommendations of the majority of the Committee.

THE ASSEMBLY OF 1892 DECLINED TO RETURN THE CASE TO SYNOD.

The General Assembly of 1892, in declining to send the case down to Synod, acted intelligently and has established a precedent *in this case* which cannot be ignored when that branch of the subject is under discussion.

These questions as to the status of the Prosecuting Committee, its right to represent the Presbyterian Church in the United States as an original party, and its right to take the appeal directly to the General Assembly, were all brought up. After three hours of argument and discussion by the Committee and the Appellee, and by members of the Assembly, action was had as shown by page 118 of the Minutes of the General Assembly of 1892, as follows:

"Resolved, that so much of the report of the Judicial Committee as relates to the appeal being found in order be adopted."

This action adopted all of the committee's report, except the two lines of subdivision 3, which were excluded because their adoption would have carried the adoption of the report, the very thing that was up for discussion, namely, whether the appeal should or should not be entertained. For this reason it was considered that subdivision 3 should be reserved for action, after the arguments had been made and this was done.

THE APPEAL TO THE GENERAL ASSEMBLY OF 1892 WAS ENTERTAINED.

On page 119 of the Minutes of the General Assembly of 1892, you will find the action of the Assembly, on the question of entertaining the appeal, as follows :

"It was resolved that the vote on entertaining the appeal be now taken without debate. *The minority report was read and laid* on the table. The Moderator also announced *that the only remaining part of the majority Report which had not been adopted was*, 'Third, that in the judgment of the committee, the appeal should be entertained, and a time set apart for the hearing of the case.' *This part* of the majority report *was then adopted*, carrying in the affirmative the question of the entertainment of the appeal. It was then resolved, that the Assembly proceed at once with the case in the order prescribed in Section XCIX., Book of Discipline."

THE APPEAL WAS SUSTAINED.

The appeal to the Assembly having been entertained, the question came up as to the action of the Assembly on the merits of the appeal. The merits were then discussed for an hour and a half by each of the parties, and at the end of that discussion a vote was taken and the appeal was sustained by a vote of 431 to 87. (General Assembly Minutes, 1892, pp. 140-150.) "The Moderator announced that the specification of errors in the appeal were all sustained, and the appeal was sustained." A committee was appointed to bring in a minute in the case, the report of which will be found at page 152 of the Minutes of 1892, as follows:

"The Committee appointed to prepare a minute in the judicial case of the Rev. Charles A. Briggs, D. D., presented its report, which was adopted, and is as follows:

"To the General Assembly of the Presbyterian Church in the United States of America:

"Your Committee appointed to draft a form of judgment to be entered in the case of the Presbyterian Church in the United States of America against Rev. Charles A. Briggs, D. D., respectfully report, and recommend for adoption, the accompanying form of decree and order.

Respectfully submitted,
THOMAS EWING,
Chairman."

| "THE PRESBYTERIAN CHURCH in the UNITED STATES OF AMERICA, vs. REV. CHARLES A. BRIGGS, D. D. | *Appeal from the judgment of the Presbytery of New York, dismissing the case.* |

"The General Assembly having, on the 28th day of May, 1892, duly sustained all the specifications of error alleged and set forth in the appeal and specification in this case.

"It is now, May 30, 1892, ordered, that the judgment of the Presbytery of New York, entered November 4, 1891, dismissing the case of the Presbyterian Church in the United States of America against Rev. Charles A. Briggs, D. D., be, and the same is hereby reversed. And the case is remanded to the Presbytery of New York for a new trial, with directions to the said Presbytery to proceed to pass upon and determine the sufficiency of the charges and specifications in form and legal effect, and to permit the *Prosecuting Committee* to amend the specifications or charges, *not changing the general nature of the same*, if, in the furtherance of justice, it be necessary to amend, so that the case may be brought to issue and tried on the merits thereof as speedily as may be practical.

"And it is further ordered, that the stated clerk of the General Assembly return the record, and certify the proceedings had thereon, with the necessary papers relating thereto, to the Presbytery of New York."

The exact status of the Prosecuting Committee was fully recognized and defined in the report of the majority of the Judicial Committee, which was adopted by the Assembly. It was not questioned in the minority report and it was established by the entertainment and sustaining of the Appeal. In the mandate of the Assembly to the Presbytery of New York, the rights of the Committee are recognized in express terms.

No fair-minded man, after reading the record of what was done in this case, by the General Assembly of 1892, can longer question the status of the Prosecuting Committee, but if any further evidence should be required as to what that Assembly did and intended to do, it would be found in a protest presented by the Rev. S. J. McPherson, D. D., and some 53 or 54 others, against the action of the General Assembly, which protest is found at page 205 of the Minutes of 1892. There was no misunderstanding at Portland, on either side, as to what had taken place, as the protest which certain of those who were on the ground and disapproved of the Assembly's action clearly shows, as follows :

"The following protest was presented and ordered to be entered on the 'Minutes' of the Assembly without answer.

"We, the undersigned, ministers and elders, commissioners of the 104th General Assembly, do hereby enter and record our protest against the action of the General Assembly *in entertaining the appeal* in the case of 'The Presbyterian Church in the United States of America against the Rev. Charles A. Briggs, D. D.,' and *so giving to the Committee* which preferred the charges against Dr. Briggs *standing before the Assembly and right of appeal* as an '*original party*,' *beyond the control of the Presbytery and its power to discharge them when dismissing the case.*" * * *

THE GENERAL ASSEMBLY CANNOT REVISE OR REVERSE ACTION TAKEN BY A PREVIOUS ASSEMBLY IN A JUDICIAL CASE.

It must be kept in mind that the action of the General Assembly of 1892, in deciding substantially all of the questions which can be raised in opposition to the entertainment of this appeal, is not to be referred to simply as a precedent, in a case similar to this. It was action taken after full discussion, and in this judicial case. Among the questions thus passed upon and determined by the Assembly of 1892 are the following, which are now *res adjudicata* in this case.

1. That the appeal was taken by the Presbyterian Church in the United States of America, as an Original Party.

2. That the Original Party is represented by the Prosecuting Committee.

3. That such Committee is a Prosecuting Committee appointed under Section 11 of the Book of Discipline.

4. The Original Party, by its Prosecuting Committee, has the right, in this case, to take such an appeal from the Presbytery, directly to the General Assembly.

5. That such an Appeal is regular and in order.

6. The appeal being regular and in order, it must be received and issued by the Assembly and should not be sent down to Synod. (Form of Government, Chap. XII., Sec. IV.)

It is the law of our Church, that it is not competent for one General Assembly to *revise or reverse* the proceedings of a previous Assembly, *taken in a judicial case*. This point, as stated above, has been settled by the General Assembly in the appeal of Samuel Lowry, Minutes, 1824, page 115 ; case of T. F. Worrell, Minutes, 1864, page 398.

The case before us, the Presbyterian Church in the United States of America against the Rev. Charles A. Briggs, D. D., is the same case, the appeal in which was entertained and sustained by the General Assembly of 1892, at Portland, Oregon.

By reference to the printed Record in your hands,

at page 37, you will find the mandate of the General Assembly in that case, reversing the judgment of the Presbytery of New York, entered on the 4th day of November, 1891.

This order of the General Assembly remanded the case to the Presbytery of New York, with directions that the case should be brought to issue and tried on the merits thereof. The mandate also directed that the Presbytery should pass upon and determine the sufficiency of the Charges and Specifications in form and legal effect, and to permit the Prosecuting Committee to amend the Charges and Specifications, not changing the general nature of the same.

The Prosecuting Committee, with the consent of the Presbytery, the Appellee not objecting, filed amended Charges and Specifications, which did not change the general nature of the original charges. The fact that the Presbytery threw out two of the amended charges, Nos. IV. and VII., upon the mistaken ground that they did not conform to the general nature of the original charges, is made the basis of Specifications 1 and 11 under the first ground of the Appeal now pending.

By the mandate of the Assembly of 1892, the Presbytery was restricted in the trial upon the merits to the original charges or to amended charges, which did not change the general nature of the original charges.

The fact that the Presbytery proceeded to trial upon six out of eight of the amended charges, is conclusive evidence, that the judgment now appealed from is in the same judicial case that was entertained and sustained at Portland, remanded to New York, there tried, and from the final judgment in which this appeal was taken.

This appeal is therefore an appeal in the same judicial case as that decided by the General Assembly of 1892, and there is no fact to justify the claim made by the Appellee that this is an appeal in a different case, and that the precedents established in this judicial case, by the Assembly of 1892, are not controlling.

All the points decided by the Portland Assembly of 1892, in the case of the Presbyterian Church in the United States of America against the Rev. Charles A. Briggs, D. D., are decisions in this judicial case, under the same title and with the same parties as the one, the entertainment of which, is now under consideration.

Under these circumstances, the precedents above referred to, established by the Assemblies of 1824 and 1864, which remain unquestioned, absolutely preclude this Assembly from attempting to revise or reverse the action of the Assembly of 1892 upon any point, in this judicial case, passed upon by that Assembly.

ACTION OF SYNOD OF NEW YORK AS TO THE PROSECUTING COMMITTEE.

Subsequent to the proceedings in the Presbytery of New York, on November 4, 1891, which resulted in the judgment dismissing the case, the Rev. Francis Brown, D. D., made complaint to the Synod of New York, against the action of the Presbytery in sustaining the ruling of the Moderator, that the Committee was a Committee of Prosecution under Section 11 of the Book of Discipline.

After the ten days provided for by Section 84 of the Book of Discipline, had expired, and in some cases months after, the names of a number of persons, 113 in all, no one of whom had given notice of complaint, were added to this complaint, and it was claimed for it, that the action of the Presbytery complained of, was had in *a non-judicial case*, and that, therefore, under Section 85 of the Book of Discipline said paper, with the additional signatures, purporting to be a complaint, stayed the *judicial proceedings* until the final issue of the case in the superior judicatory.

This paper, purporting to be a complaint, was presented to the Synod of New York, at its session held at Albany, New York, in October, 1892, and was declared to be in order, but the Synod, after extended discussion, decided not to issue the complaint, and by a vote of 122 to 40 took the following action :

"In the matter of Judicial cases Nos. 3 and 4 (Dr. Brown's complaint) the committee finds the complaints to be in order, *but recommends that it is inexpedient to take action at the present time for the following reasons:*

"1. The case, through the action of the General Assembly and of the Presbytery of New York, is again before the Presbytery, and the complainants will there have their remedy in their own hands.

"2. In case the remedy then be found insufficient, they may afterwards have opportunity by appeal or complaint to bring the case before Synod."

When the matter was again presented to the Presbytery of New York, it was discovered that the complainants did not "have their remedy in their own hands," for the Presbytery, as hereinafter shown, promptly, and for the second time, sustained the ruling of the Moderator, which had been appealed from, as to the status of the Prosecuting Committee.

COMPLAINT AGAINST ACTION OF THE SYNOD OF NEW YORK, NOW PENDING BEFORE THIS ASSEMBLY.

A complaint was made to this Assembly and is now pending before it, against the action of the Synod of New York in declaring the said paper purporting to be a complaint, to be in order, in respect of the 113 so-called complainants, no one of whom had given notice of complaint, as required by Section 84 of the Book of Discipline, and whose signatures were added to the paper purporting to be a complaint, after the expiration of the ten days fixed by the Book of Discipline.

The complaint to the Assembly against the action of the Synod of New York, last above referred to, brings up to this Assembly the only question of the slightest importance, in this case, now before the Synod. When the question raised by that complaint, and the issues in this appeal, have been considered all the questions involved can be at the same time and finally disposed of by the highest Court of our Church.

FINAL ACTION BY NEW YORK PRESBYTERY AS TO THE STATUS OF THE PROSECUTING COMMITTEE.

When in compliance with the mandate of the General Assembly the Presbytery of New York, on the 9th day of November, 1892, proceeded with the trial, the Appellee presented objections to the status, rights and powers of the Prosecuting Committee and asked the Presbytery to apply the remedy which the Synod had said might be in its own hands.

Thereupon the following proceedings were had as recorded at page 262 of Vol. 14 of the Records of the Presbytery of New York :

"A point of order was here raised as to whether any-
"thing is in order except the consideration of the spe-
"cific action of the General Assembly.

"The Moderator decided that the point of order was
"well taken. That the raising of the question of the
"status of the Prosecuting Committee and of its right
"to appear and continue the conduct of this case is not
"now in order for these reasons :

"1st. That this whole question was fully discussed
"and decided by the Judicial Committee of the General
"Assembly.

"2d. That the recognition of the status of the Com-
"mittee and its powers as defined in the appeal were
"embodied in the Judicial Committee's report, recom-
"mending the entertainment of the appeal.

"3d. That in the minutes of the General Assembly "giving its findings in the case, the Committee's status "is clearly recognized.

"4th. That the protest recorded in the minutes of "the General Assembly by those objecting to its action, "was based on the fact, that its action in entertaining "the appeal gave the committee the standing and "powers claimed for it; and

"Lastly. That the order sending the case again to "this Presbytery, requiring us to proceed to pass upon "and determine the sufficiency of the charges and "specifications, as to form and legal effect, and to "proceed with the trial, this being the single point "before us to be acted upon, therefore the Moderator's "decision is, that this question is out of order.

"An appeal to the house against the Moderator's "decision was then taken. On a vote being taken, a "division was called for, which resulted in 73 to 58 in "favor of the Moderator's decision."

By thus, a second time, sustaining the Moderator's ruling the Presbytery of New York gave a very decided answer to the Appellee's request. It confirmed its previous action, and based the same upon the action of the General Assembly of 1892, which fully sustained the status, rights and powers of the Prosecuting Committee at every point.

In view of the above, it is not creditable to our intelligence, nor loyal to the decisions of our highest Court, that we should give this matter further consideration.

An Alleged Constitutional Limitation.

Great weight has been given to a technical question raised in the interest of the Appellee and of delay, based upon a clause contained in the Fifth Amendment to the Constitution of the United States, which is as follows: * * * "Nor shall any person be subject for the same offense to be twice put in jeopardy of life or limb." It has been claimed that this constitutional provision prevents an appeal from the final judgment of the Presbytery of New York in this case, and that such an appeal would place the Appellee's "ecclesiastical life" in jeopardy a second time. This somewhat ingenious but inappropriate use of the term "ecclesiastical life" seems to have confused the minds of some, as to the character of proceedings under the Book of Discipline.

THE ORDINATION VOW A COVENANT AND AGREEMENT.

When the Appellee was ordained as a minister, and as a condition precedent to such ordination, certain questions were addressed to him, among others the following (Form of Government, Chapter XV., Section XII.):

"1. Do you believe the Scriptures of the Old and New Testaments to be the Word of God, the only infallible rule of faith and practice?

"2. Do you sincerely receive and adopt the Confession of Faith of this Church, as containing the system of doctrine taught in the Holy Scriptures?

"3. Do you approve of the government and discipline of the Presbyterian Church in these United States?

"4. Do you promise subjection to your brethren in the Lord?

* * * * * * * * *

"6. Do you promise to be zealous and faithful in maintaining the truths of the Gospel, and the purity and peace of the Church; whatever persecution or opposition may arise unto you on that account?"

To each of these questions the Appellee gave an affirmative answer and these questions and answers thenceforth were part of a sacred covenant, contract or agreement between the Appellee and the Presbyterian Church and all the parties in interest.

The relation then established was a purely voluntary one of contract or agreement. Good considerations moved each of the parties and the questions and answers established the agreement or meeting of the minds of the parties.

THIS NOT A CRIMINAL CASE, BUT A PROCEEDING TO DETERMINE WHETHER THE APPELLEE'S AGREEMENT HAS BEEN CARRIED OUT.

This judicial proceeding is to determine whether that covenant, contract or agreement of the Appellee has been complied with or not. The inaccurate use of the term "ecclesiastical life" cannot change the nature of this proceeding under the Book of Discipline.

These are not criminal proceedings involving peril to the life or limb of the Appellee. They are proceedings to enforce a contract, or rather to determine whether the contract has been maintained in all its integrity. Preservation of "ecclesiastical life" in this case means simply the privilege to enjoy the benefits of a certain contract. If it should be shown that the Appellee has not maintained the contract in all its integrity, the loss of his "ecclesiastical life" would mean simply the loss of the benefits which he at one time enjoyed under the contract which he had broken.

As a matter of law, the distinction upon which I am insisting is so simple as to require only very brief illustration. A citizen of the United States is engaged by contract to perform certain services, for which he receives an official position and adequate compensation. It is at length alleged, by the other party to the contract, that such services have not been properly performed, and the matter is brought into the Courts, the bill praying that the contract, because of its nonperformance by the other party, should be cancelled or terminated. A decision is reached in the Court of first resort, in favor of the citizen first alluded to, and the other contracting party appeals.

Would the appellee, in such a case, be justified, or could he successfully plead that the Constitution of the United States protected him, and that he need give no attention to the appeal? Might he claim that the Constitution of the United States precluded the appellate Courts from considering a second time, on appeal, the points involved in the alleged breach of contract? There is probably no lawyer in this country, there is certainly no lawyer in this assembly, who would answer these questions in the affirmative.

The failure of the appellee in such a case, to comply with the terms of his contract, injures the other contracting party. He may not wish or pray for damages; he simply asks for relief from a contract that has not been fulfilled by the other party and from a relation which has therefore become intolerable. But the question whether the contract has been broken, is a proper one for the appellate Court to consider in determining whether the appellant is entitled to the relief asked for.

The appellee, in such a case, might say that as he was dependent upon the business position and income secured through the contract, that his "business life" and his "financial life" would be placed in jeopardy a second time by the appeal. But the twice-endangered business life or financial life could not be made a ground of objection to the appeal as such.

Not only every lawyer, but every man of affairs will assent to that. What has been called a man's "ecclesiastical life" is a matter of great importance, but it should not be urged as a ground against an appeal in a case where an ecclesiastical covenant is involved. It would, indeed, be unfortunate if a higher code of ethics prevailed in the civil Courts of this country than the code which is recognized in the courts of this Church.

THE CONSTITUTIONAL LIMITATION, ABOVE REFERRED TO, DOES NOT APPLY IN THIS CASE.

The provision of the amendment to the Constitution referred to, is the outgrowth or remnant of the struggle for security and safety on the part of the subject against the despotic and arbitrary power so often exercised by kings and rulers in the past, over their subjects. It originated as a constitutional and very proper safeguard to protect the subject against the power of a sovereign. This provision was introduced as an amendment to the Constitution of the United States, simply to guard against the power of the Federal Government and the Federal Courts, at a time when alarm was felt about the tendency towards Federal centralization of power. It is still an eminently wise constitutional provision, and properly controls in the administration of justice in all criminal cases where the death penalty or other serious legal penalty is enforced, but it has no place or influence in the orderly enforcement of discipline under the Constitution of a voluntary association like the Presbyterian Church.

No one is forced to accept the doctrines of the Presbyterian Church. No one is forced to remain in a position where one is subject to its discipline. But when any one has voluntarily entered into covenant or agreement with that Church, he is honorably and morally bound to submit to the orderly enforcement of its law. So long as he remains in this ecclesiastical fellowship and communion, it is not lawful or right to invoke the provisions of any civil law or constitution to delay the orderly enforcement of the discipline of the Church, or to prevent it.

THE CONFESSIONAL POSITION AS TO CIVIL LAWS AND CONSTITUTIONS.

The Confession of Faith enforces this distinction with the utmost clearness. Chapter XXIII., Subsection III., is as follows: "Civil magistrates may not * * * * * * in the least, interfere in matters of faith. * * * * * * And, as Jesus Christ hath appointed a regular government and discipline in his Church, no law of any commonwealth should interfere with, let, or hinder, the due exercise thereof, among the voluntary members of any denomination of Christians, according to their own profession and belief." * * * *

DECISION THEREON OF THE SUPREME COURT OF THE UNITED STATES.

This position so fully and clearly stated in the Confession of Faith, has in effect, been adopted by the Supreme Court of the United States in the leading case of Watson against Jones, reported in 13 Wallace, pages 679-738. This case is commonly known as the Walnut Street Church case and the opinion is given in full in Moore's Digest, 1886, pages 251-262.

In this decision the Supreme Court of the United States holds, that when the General Assembly as the Supreme Court of the Presbyterian Church has decided *any question of doctrine or discipline* according to the Standards and Book of Discipline, *the legal tribunals must accept such decision as final as against the decision of any Civil Court or Constitution*, and that the Civil Courts will not even look into or question such decisions. This opinion of the Supreme Court of the United States says:

"There are in the Presbyterian system of ecclesiastical government, in regular succession, the Presbytery over the session or local church, the Synod over the

Presbytery and the General Assembly over all. These are called in the language of the Church organs, judicatories, and they entertain appeals from the decisions of those below, and prescribe corrective measures in other cases."

"In this class of cases we think the rule of action which should govern the civil courts, founded in a broad and sound view of the relations of Church and State under our system of laws, and supported by a preponderating weight of judicial authority, is that, whenever the questions of discipline or of faith or ecclesiastical rule, custom or law, have been decided by the highest of these church judicatories to which the matter has been carried, the legal tribunals must accept such decisions as final and as binding on them in their application to the case before them."

"The right to organize voluntary religious associations, to assist in the expression and dissemination of any religious doctrine, and to create tribunals for the decision of controverted questions of faith within the association, and for the ecclesiastical government of all the individual members, congregations and officers within the general association, is unquestioned. All who unite themselves to such a body, do so with an implied consent to this government, and are bound to submit to it. But it would be vain consent and would lead to the total subversion of such religious bodies, if any one aggrieved by one of their decisions could appeal to the secular Courts and have them reversed. It is of the essence of these religious unions, and of their right to establish tribunals for the decision of questions arising among themselves, that those decisions should be binding in all cases of ecclesiastical cognizance, *subject only to such appeals* as the organism itself provides for."

The opinion of the Supreme Court continues as follows:

"In the case of Watson *vs.* Farris, 45 Missouri, 183, that Court held *that whether a case was regularly or irregularly before the Assembly, was a question which the Assembly had the right to determine for itself,* and no civil court could reverse, modify or impair its action in a matter of merely ecclesiastical concern."

"We cannot better close this review of the authorities than in the language of the Supreme Court of Pennsylvania in the case of the German Reformed Church *vs.* Siebert, 5 Barr, 291; 'The decisions of ecclesiastical courts, like every other judicial tribunal are final, as they are the best judges of what constitutes an offence against the word of God and the discipline of the Church. Any other than those Courts must be incompetent judges of matters of faith, discipline and doctrine; and civil courts if they should be so unwise as to attempt to supervise their judgments on matters which come within their jurisdiction, would only involve themselves in a sea of uncertainty and doubt which would do anything but improve either religion or good morals'."

THIS DECISION THE LAW OF THE LAND.

This decision of the Supreme Court of the United States still stands. It has been frequently cited with approval by the same Court and is the law of the land upon the questions decided therein. *This decision of the Supreme Court of the United States makes final and conclusive any decision reached by the General Assembly of the Presbyterian Church as to matters that concern theological controversy, Church discipline, ecclesiastical government or the conformity of the members of the Church to its Standards.*

Even if the provision of the Constitution of the United States referred to, did apply to proceedings under a

Book of Discipline like that of the Presbyterian Church, such a provision would not be in point. The Constitution of the United States declares, indeed, that no person shall be subject to be put in jeopardy of life or limb, twice for the same offence. But the Supreme Court of the United States has held in ex-parte Lange, 18 Wallace, 163, that this constitutional provision was mainly designed *to prevent a second punishment* for the same crime or misdemeanor and not a second trial. Where, as in this case, *no punishment has been inflicted upon the Appellee*, the Constitutional provision is not to be invoked. It is not to interfere. It has reference only to restraints upon the general government, and its courts. (Baker on the Constitution, page 182.)

[Here the argument was interrupted by adjournment.]

Before resuming my argument at the point of interruption at the adjournment of this afternoon, I should say something as to the concluding part of Dr. Briggs' argument.

The declaration of his faith made by the Appellee at the close of his plea, may or may not be fully in accord with the accepted forms of belief in the Presbyterian Church. One point should be noted in it, however. He has modified his answer to the questions of Union Seminary, for he now declares that he accepts the Scriptures as true, as to historical facts, a modification sufficiently broad to allow of acceptance even by one who believes that Jonah, or Ruth, or Esther, or Job, or all of them, are unhistorical characters.

In any event, the Appellee's confession here made, is no stronger than that which he made just before delivering the Inaugural Address, so that the question remains as it did, before this new statement was altered as it has been to-day. In the Appellee's judgment his inaugural is fully in accord with the confession. The question for you to decide, is whether or not the two can be in full accord.

The Appellee referred sharply to the fact that on page 6 of the Record the Appellants had omitted the series of questions and answers included in the preamble to the resolution. Stars were placed in the record to indicate an omission, as should always be done when an extract is not full and complete.

An examination of the page will show to any candid man that everything covering the matter at issue is given there, and given in fullness. That matter was introduced, not to tell anything respecting Dr. Briggs' soundness or unsoundness, nor even to tell anything that Dr. Briggs had said, but solely and only to prove that an attempt was made to dismiss the case because of statements made by Dr. Briggs, not on the floor of the Presbytery, not in response to queries offered by the Presbytery, but made to a body of gentlemen who in their corporate capacity bore no direct relations to the Presbytery.

With reference to the confession or declaration as made by the Appellee to-day, I was very glad to hear it. I have heard it in somewhat similar forms on other occasions. But those categorical answers were given and were replied to, after the Inaugural Address had been delivered, but before the proceedings in the New York Presbytery were begun.

During the first trial declarations of principles were made by the Appellee and the case was dismissed. Keep in mind the only thing that these proceedings are based upon is the Inaugural Address.

If any one has the volume in his possession, and will look at the preface of the third edition of Dr. Briggs' Inaugural Address, which bears imprint or date of November 5th, 1891, the day immediately following the first trial in Presbytery—the day after the case had been dismissed—he will find these words:

"I have seen nothing in the hostile criticism to lead me to make any change whatever, either in the matter or the form of the address. But it seems to me wise to republish the address in a second edition under my own responsibility, with some additional notes and explanations. This third edition contains the charges made against me before the Presbytery of New York, Oct. 5th, and my answer thereto of Nov. 4th."

The fourth edition of the Inaugural, which is dated in the following year, June 24th, 1892, contains the above words, reaffirming at that date the declarations of the Inaugural Address.

The charges are based upon the Inaugural Address only; and the Inaugural Address, as you see by the preface of the succeeding editions, stands not retracted, not withdrawn—stands just as delivered.

I will now resume, Fathers and Brethren, at the point at which the argument was interrupted.

The Alleged Plea that an Acquittal by a Lower Court Bars the Right of Appeal.

It has been frequently claimed of late, that "by the law of the Presbyterian Church the acquittal of an accused person by a lower court, bars the right of appeal to a higher court."

Such a claim is not true in fact nor sound in law. Some have been led into mistake in this matter from not distinguishing the very marked difference between some of the provisions of law and the procedure followed in civil and ecclesiastical trials.

By the Amended Charges and Specifications in this case, the accused was charged with delivering an Inaugural Address, in which it was claimed, that he taught doctrines which are contrary to the Holy Scriptures and the Standards of the Presbyterian Church. Upon the trial the accused admitted the fact that he had delivered the Address containing the words set out in the Specifications to the Charges. But at the same time he made a denial, which, in the Civil Courts, would be called a demurrer, as to the legal effect of the teaching with which he was charged.

In a trial in a civil court, the facts as to what he had taught, which were admitted, would have been passed upon by the jury; the legal effect of the teaching which he denied, would have been passed upon by the Court. It is at this point that confusion comes to some minds. I ask you to carefully distinguish the difference between the organization and practice of the civil and ecclesiastical courts.

Under our Presbyterian polity, the members of a Judicatory are both jurymen and judges. By the admissions of the accused, that he did deliver the address and did use the words charged, the case passed at once out of the hands of the members of the Judicatory in their capacity of jurymen, for the facts were all settled by the admissions of the accused. The questions of law had been already determined when the Presbytery accepted the charges and specifications, as sufficient in form and legal effect, if proved, to be an offence and sufficient to put the accused on his defence. (Records Presbytery of N. Y., Vol. 14, page 369.)

After hearing the arguments on both sides the Judicatory went into private session and determined that the accused should be "fully acquitted." Thereupon the case was taken on appeal to the Supreme Court of the Church on the legal questions involved.

It would not be proper for me, at this time, to discuss the further steps in the appeal, but it is sufficient to say that while such proceedings are seldom taken in our ecclesiastical Courts, corresponding proceedings are taken every day in our Federal and State Courts.

As the Form of Government and the Book of Discipline of the Presbyterian Church make full and exact provision for appeals to the General Assembly on doctrinal and constitutional questions, making no distinction as to whether the decision appealed from was for or against the accused, no good, sound or legal reason exists why such an appeal having been taken should not be entertained by this Assembly.

It is affirmed that, if this right of appeal, especially appeal from a verdict of acquittal, in the name of the Church, be granted to the Committee of Prosecution, it will be in gross violation of the Constitution, and result in the rankest kind of injustice. Surely this objection is not intended seriously. How can that be a violation of the constitution for which the constitution makes express provision ? The absence of precedent for the exercise of this right by the Committee of Prosecution, does not make its exercise unconstitutional, for, as has been stated already, there may have been neither time nor occasion for making precedents on this point. To affirm that everything for which there cannot be found a precedent is unconstitutional, is to elevate precedent above the Constitution, and to deny the possibility of constitutional reforms or changes.

The Constitution of the Presbyterian Church does not regard the verdict of acquittal in the lower Judicatory as a completion of the case, in the sense that the jeopardy ceases with such acquittal. An accused person has never been in jeopardy, technically, until the case reaches Synod, in matters of ordinary discipline, or reaches the Assembly in cases of doctrine and Constitution.

This right of appeal from any decision of an inferior judicatory by any of the parties has never been seriously questioned. It has been uniformly exercised. Under the Old Book, "a party aggrieved," and all persons who have submitted to a regular trial in an inferior, may appeal to a higher judicatory. Any one or more of a minority |had the right to appeal from any final judgment of a lower to a higher judicatory. Moore's Digest, 1873, p. 548, says: "Before the " adoption of the Constitution in its present form, " in 1821, no distinction was made between an appeal " and complaint. The Common form was, 'we appeal " and complain.' Under this broad title *any decision* " *whatever* was carried by *any parties* from the lower " courts to the higher. *Appeals* are limited by the " present Constitution to the original parties to a case " who may deem themselves aggrieved, and to cases " which have been judicially decided by a lower judi- " catory. Under this head, however, are included all " cases of whatever character which have been the " subject of a decision by an inferior judicatory."

The assembly of 1833 endorsed the principle of appeal from a sentence of acquittal, in the case of Mr. Griffith. (See Moore's Digest, 1873, p. 548.)

"The Synod of New York decided that the death of " Rev. Mr. Griffith should be no bar in the way of the " prosecution of an appeal by his prosecutor from the " decision of the Presbytery of Bedford, acquitting " Mr. Griffith. With these (this) exceptions (excep- " tion) the Committee recommended that the Records " be approved. Their report was adopted. Minutes " 1833, p. 400." (Moore's Digest, 1873, p. 548.)

In the case last referred to the Synod of New York decided that a prosecutor had the right to appeal from the decision of the Presbytery acquitting the accused, and that part of the Synod's proceedings the Assembly of 1833 approved.

A well-known Elder of our Church, when recently discussing this question, aptly says: "It has always

"been the law of the Church that the prosecutor, at
"least in judicial cases involving doctrine and consti-
"tutional law, may take an appeal from the decision of
"the Court in which the case originated, to the Supe-
"rior Courts, although the decision in the lower Court
"may have acquitted the accused of the charge pre-
"ferred against him; and that up to 1821 any one or
"more of a minority had the right to appeal from any
"decision whatever of a lower Court to a higher. Yet
"no one ever claimed or imagined until now, that
"there was the slightest injustice in this. On the con-
"trary, it was recognized as the only way in which
"doctrinal and constitutional questions could be
"authoritatively determined.

"In view of these facts I think that it will be ad-
"mitted that the right of a prosecutor to appeal to a
"superior Court from a judgment of acquittal in an
"inferior Court, is not a novelty, an innovation, sought
"for the first time to be made a feature of our Church
"discipline." (Open letter of William Ernst, Esq., to
Prof. Willis J. Beecher, D. D., in the "Presbyterian,"
April, 1893.)

AN APPEAL DIRECT FROM THE PRESBYTERY TO THE ASSEMBLY, BEING ALLOWED BY THE BOOK OF DISCIPLINE, IS REGULAR.

This is not the ordinary, but the extraordinary, mode of procedure, and is to be taken only for special reasons. But it should be distinctly noticed that the extraordinary feature does not render it irregular, since the Constitution provides for it.

Section 102 of the Book of Discipline reads: "Appeals "are, generally, to be taken to the judicatory imme- "diately superior to that appealed from." The use of the word "generally" leaves room for exceptional cases, in which "the judicatory immediately superior" may be passed by; and this is no novelty; it was not introduced by those who remodelled the Book; it was in the old Book; it is part of the time-honored practice of our church.

According to Section 70 of the Book of Discipline, there are four ways in which a cause may be carried from a lower to a higher judicatory, viz.: General Review and Control, Reference, Complaint and Appeal. Sections 71 and 83 make it plain that Review and Control and Complaints must invariably be by or to the next superior judicatory.

But it is different with References and Appeals. Section 77 states that a Reference is "made by an "inferior to a superior judicatory," and Section 94 that an appeal is "from an inferior to a superior judicatory." In both cases the language of the Book carefully refrains from naming the judicatory next superior, as in the case of Review and Control, and of Complaints. The *next* superior judicatory may or may not be resorted to in case of a reference or an appeal.

These provisions of the Book of Discipline conform with the directions of the Form of Government. By Chapter XI., Section IV., of the Form of Government, the Synod is debarred from giving a final decision on matters which affect the doctrine and constitution of the Church. I refer to this here particularly for the reason that an overture has come to this Assembly, from some of the Presbyteries, in which the Assembly is urged not to entertain this appeal, as that would be " an ignoring of that important body, the Synod, and " a virtual slight upon synodical privileges and " dignity." But how can Synod be ignored, or its privileges and dignity be slighted by withholding from it a matter respecting which it cannot make a final decision? The appellants have disclaimed any intention to ignore the Synod, or to cast a slight upon its privileges and dignity.

The rights, privileges and dignity of the Synod of New York are not touched in any way by direct appeal to the Assembly, since neither that nor any other Synod has the constitutional power to settle doctrinal or constitutional questions for the whole Church. Besides, the fact, pointed out in the appeal, that all but one of the thirty-one Presbyteries of the Synod of New York will now, in the Assembly, have a voice in the final settlement of these questions, should have due consideration. In no other way can the Synod of New York exert so large an influence in the final determination of this matter.

The Constitution (Form of Government, Chapter XI., Section IV.), in express terms limits the powers of the Synod by providing that its decision shall be final, only, in cases which "do not affect the doctrine or constitution of the church." Such a constitutional limitation does not ignore or reflect upon the dignity of the Synod.

No intelligent man would claim that the provisions of the Constitution of the United States (Article VII., Section I.), that "All bills for raising revenue shall originate in the House of Representatives," is a reflection upon the character or dignity of the Senate of the United States. This provision was made so as to carry out consistently, the theory upon which a Constitution providing for a complete system of political government was based.

So this constitutional limitation upon the power of the Synod, not to make final decisions upon doctrinal and constitutional questions, was most properly made to secure a consistent, fair, well-rounded system of ecclesiastical government.

If time permitted, this might be illustrated in many ways, but one example will be sufficient. When an effort was made to revise the Confession of Faith, in compliance with the mandatory provisions of the Form of Government the overtures in relation to the proposed doctrinal changes, were sent down, not to the Synods, but to the Presbyteries, and the answers of the Presbyteries were transmitted, not through or by way of the Synods, but directly to the General Assembly.

No one pretends to claim that such a constitutional proceeding is a slight upon the character or dignity of the Synods. It is the constitutional method of dealing with overtures relating to doctrinal changes.

In exactly the same way the constitution provides that appeals in judicial cases, relating to doctrine, need not go to the Synod, but may go directly to the General Assembly.

There is no justification in fact or law, for the statements which have been made, *first*, that this appeal should not, as a matter of right, be brought directly to the General Assembly, or, *second*, that in acting within the limits of constitutional authority, the Prosecuting Committee, representing the entire Church, have intentionally ignored the powers or prerogatives, or reflected upon the character and dignity of the Synod of New York.

This case, as such, has never been before the Synod of New York. That Synod has not assumed jurisdiction of this case. All that it has ever done is to declare in order, two certain complaints which relate to collateral questions, to give to these complaints the legal effect claimed for them by the Complainants they had under Section 85 of the Book of Discipline to allege, that they were not taken in the *judicial case*, although they claimed, as soon as the complaints were made, that the judicial case was thereby stayed.

The Synod of New York has never received or entertained, or heard in its official capacity, of the case of The Presbyterian Church in the United States of

America against the Rev. Charles A. Briggs, D. D. Consequently, in taking this Appeal to the General Assembly, there is no intended slight to the Synod of New York; there is nothing that could be reasonably construed into such a slight. In coming to the General Assembly, the Appellant is doing simply what the Constitution says it may do, and what, as representing the Presbyterian Church in the United States, it was the duty of the Prosecuting Committee to do. The Committee would have subjected themselves, very properly, to censure from this body, if they had taken any other course. If this Court should, in its wise discretion, think that this matter should go to the Synod, the first steps toward that result must be to entertain this appeal. You cannot act or take any act in disposing of this matter until you have first voted to entertain the appeal. Until all preliminary and jurisdictional questions have been settled and jurisdiction has been assumed, this Court cannot make any order as to the disposition of the case. When you have taken the vote to entertain the appeal, then the members of the Court should consider the obligation placed upon them by the Constitution of this Church, to dispose of this case in such manner as will conserve the truth and best protect the interest of the whole Church.

As Commissioners to this General Assembly you are under very solemn obligations and responsibilities. You have not come here to act in obedience to special resolutions of your respective presbyteries, if any such may have been passed, upon questions which may come before this General Assembly.

You have been called to this high court by the mandate of the Constitution of our Church. You are members of a supreme Court of Commissioners, each member bearing, not a resolution of instructions as to how he shall vote upon questions arising here, but which have not come judicially before your respective Presbyteries.

You bear a solemn commission to this Assembly, which by its express terms authorizes and directs you "to consult, vote, and determine on all things that may "come before that body, according to the principles and "constitution of this Church, and the word of God," and not according to anything else. (Form of Government, Chapter XXII., Section II. Minutes 1877, page 577).

Section XII. of the Form of Government directs that "the General Assembly shall receive and issue all " appeals, complaints, and references that affect the " doctrine or constitution of the Church, which may " be regularly brought before them from the inferior " judicatories, * * * and they shall constitute " the bond of union, peace, correspondence and mu- " tual confidence among all our churches." According to Section V. of the same Chapter, "To the " General Assembly also belongs the power of deciding " in all controversies respecting doctrine and disci- " pline ; of reproving, warning, or bearing testimony "against error in doctrine ; * * * of suppressing " schismatical contentions and disputations ; * * and " the promotion of charity, truth and holiness, through " all the churches under their care." The constitution puts especial responsibility on the General Assembly, respecting all matters which affect the doctrine, discipline, the purity and peace of the Church.

It is very evident then, that the framers of our Book of Discipline and of the Form of Government, intentionally left the way open for passing the intermediate judicatories, so that cases affecting the doctrine and constitution of the Church, might be taken directly to the Assembly, if such a course seemed necessary. When, therefore, we come to the Assembly with our appeal we are following the constitutional method of procedure, for which precedents are not wanting.

The General Assembly of 1824, in answer to a petition of certain members of the Tammany Street Church of Baltimore, stated: "It is unquestionably the priv-
" ilege of individuals and members of the Presbyterian
" Church, when they think they see the peace, purity,
" or prosperity of the Church in danger, either from an
" individual, or from an inferior court, to apply to the
" General Assembly, in an orderly manner, for redress
" and direction." (Minutes 1824, p. 113.)

The Assembly of 1833 (Minutes 1833, p. 396), responding to an overture from the Presbytery of Baltimore in reference to the practice of inferior judicatories in carrying appeals and complaints directly to the Assembly, adopted the following resolution: "That the constitution of our Church is so explicit that
" it requires no order of the Assembly in relation to
" the case brought to view in this overture." Dr. Moore, in the Presbyterian Digest, 1886, p. 740, states in reference to this deliverance, that "the principle
"guiding the Assembly seems to be that where there
" is no sufficient reason for passing the next superior
"court, the case should go there. But where good
" reasons for carrying it directly to the Assembly are
"assigned, it will be entertained."

The uniform practice of the General Assembly, in judicial cases, has been to receive appeal coming to it without first going to Synod, if good reasons were adduced.

1. The Assembly of 1816 (Minutes 1816, p. 626) thought it reasonable to receive the appeal of the Rev. George Bourne from the Presbytery of Lexington, on the ground that he *preferred* to be tried by the Assembly rather than by the Synod (Baird, p. 166). And the Assembly of 1818 refused to approve the minutes of the

Synod of Virginia expressing censure on the Presbytery of Lexington for allowing the appeal of Mr. Bourne to pass the Synod. (See Baird, p. 152.)

2. In the Assembly of 1883 (Minutes 1883, p. 617) the Judicial Committee reported that since the Rev. W. W. McLane had not given sufficient reasons for coming direct to the Assembly with his appeal from the decision of the Presbytery of Steubenville, the case and the papers pertaining to it be referred to the Synod of Ohio ; but the Assembly declined to adopt the report, and returned it to the Judicial Committee with instruction "to prepare and issue the case before the Assembly." (Moore's Presbyterian Digest, 1886, p. 741.)

3. The Assembly of 1884 stated, in reference to the appeal of the Rev. Jared M. Chavis, from the Presbytery of Atlantic, "that the appellant has shown a sufficient reason for bringing his appeal to the General Assembly, without first going to the Synod of Atlantic." They reversed the decision of the Presbytery, and then, since no testimony had been taken by the Presbytery, referred the case to the Synod, with instructions to take the proper action in the premises. (Minutes 1884, p. 108.)

I call attention to this citation, as it is, I believe, the only *judicial case*, since the revision of our Book of Discipline, which has been sent down by the Assembly to Synod. This exceptional action strongly confirms, if it does not completely establish, our position, that a *judicial case involving doctrine* cannot be sent down by the Assembly to Synod.

The charges in the Chavis case were for alleged immorality—a case in which the decision of Synod is final. In that case the Presbytery had failed in its duty as a trial court. The appeal disclosed such irregularities in the matter of discipline that the General Assembly sent a special committee to visit the Presbytery of Atlantic, to investigate and do anything in its power to correct the same. The Minutes of the Assembly (1884, p. 108) declare "that the appellant had shown a sufficient reason for bringing his appeal to the General Assembly without first going to the Synod of Atlantic." But as the Form of Government makes the decision of the Synod final in all such cases, the Chavis case was returned to the Synod for action, as should have been done in a case involving *moral* and not *doctrinal* questions.

If this case should be referred by this Assembly, to the Synod of New York, and the majority of that Synod should be unwilling to take up and give full consideration to it, they might be ready to listen to the technical objection that the Synod would have no authority to hear the case, upon the ground that the right of appeal to Synod had been lost, because notice of appeal had not been given within the ten days fixed by Section 96 of the Book of Discipline.

Under these circumstances, the final adjudication of the case would be deferred for two years, because a complaint against the actions of Synod on this purely technical ground would have to be settled by the next Assembly, the case again returned to Synod, and the appeal from Synod's decision would come before the Assembly two years hence.

I only make this as a suggestion as to what is likely to happen in case this Venerable Body should, for any reason, take a course which I hope I have convinced the Commissioners is not warranted by the facts or by the Constitution of the Church.

4. In the New School Assembly of 1839 a motion to send the appeal of Mr. Lewis Tappan from the Third Presbytery of New York to the Synod, was lost, and the appeal was then entertained and issued. (Moore's Digest, 1st Ed., p. 225.)

These examples sufficiently indicate what the practice of the Assembly has been with regard to entertaining appeals which have come to them without having first been before the Synod. Whenever appellants have given good reasons, the Assembly has received the appeal.

The contention that, while an appeal of the defendant may thus be received for special reasons, no such privilege can be accorded to that of a prosecutor, introduces a distinction which is not recognized by the constitution of the Church. The right of appeal is secured to both of the original parties without distinction. We have already shown that in a trial for heresy the Church has far greater interests at stake than any defendant can possibly have, and is liable to suffer vastly more from delay than he. The Presbyterian Church has an equal right, with the humblest as well as with the most distinguished of its members, to make use of all constitutional provisions for the preservation of its interests.

THERE ARE SPECIAL REASONS WHY THIS APPEAL SHOULD BE RECEIVED BY THE ASSEMBLY WITHOUT HAVING FIRST BEEN TAKEN TO THE SYNOD OF NEW YORK.

In addition to the reasons set out in the appeal, the following may be stated:

1. The appeal relates to doctrines which are absolutely fundamental to our system.

The attempt to convince the Church that the doctrines at stake are non-essential or unimportant, and that the contention about them is but a "strife of "tongues," has not been successful. The Christian world, and especially the people of our own communion, very largely consider them vital. From the time when Dr. Briggs delivered his Inaugural Address until now, a strong conviction in all parts of our Church has been growing stronger that his blow struck at fundamental doctrines.

The sole supremacy of the Holy Scriptures in matters of faith, the veracity, genuineness and trustworthiness of that Scripture, and the question whether the process of redemption is limited to this life, or is to be extended to the world beyond the grave, are involved in this discussion. These are considered vitally important by evangelical Protestants, and particularly by Presbyterians, since they concern not only our creed, but also our entire method of presenting the Gospel. The publication of Dr. Briggs' views has given rise to widespread alarm and contention. It is the duty of the Assembly to receive and issue this appeal for the sake of the purity and peace of the Church.

No Presbytery or Synod can settle these doctrines for the Presbyterian Church; the Assembly alone represents that Church; it is the only court to which this appeal should come. Since the Assembly is not a court of original jurisdiction, it was necessary that the matter should first be passed on by such a court; but now, since it has been tried by a court of original jurisdiction, there is no reason why it should be sent to another inferior judicatory which, under the Constitution, cannot render a final decision.

2. The case is fully ripe for final judgment by this Assembly. If the Commissioners were not acquainted with the merits of the case, there might be reason for delay. But, aside from the fact that the questions involved have been before the Church for more than two years, and have been discussed both by the secular and the religious press, the Defence of Dr. Briggs and the Arguments of the Committee of Prosecution have been put into the hands of all of our ministers, and of many of our elders; there is good reason for concluding that the brethren are well informed on the subjects

involved in the case. Like the children of Issachar, the members of this Assembly have "understanding " of the times, to know what Israel ought to do."

3. It is imperatively necessary that a final decision in this case be reached at the earliest possible date. This is requisite alike for the purity and peace, and the prosperity and usefulness of the Church. Debate, contention, and uncertainty should not be protracted any longer than is absolutely necessary. Only a little while ago, all seemed to be agreed, respecting this matter.

Not a few of those urging the now famous "peace and work" plea were so deeply impressed with the fact that this conflict interferes seriously with the peace and work of our churches, that they desired the matter to be dropped immediately after the Presbytery of New York had rendered its decision in this case.

We did not agree with them in detail, believing that it would be better to wait four months longer, bring the case to this Assembly, and obtain a decision which would be more potential in allaying the unrest and disquiet of our people than that of the Presbytery of New York could possibly be.

But we agree with them as to the necessity of disposing of this matter finally and authoritatively as soon as possible ; and since the Assembly alone can render a final and authoritative decision on questions of this kind, we ask it to render that decision here, and at this time.

Consistency is not the distinctive quality of those brethren, who less than four months ago insisted with intense earnestness that, for the sake of peace, work and liberty, the discussion should cease at once. They now insist with a zeal no less earnest, that, to guard the interests of our beloved Church, the case should be delayed another year, and first be sent to the Synod of New York. If their judgment of four months ago was correct, then their present judgment cannot be, for no evident change of sentiment in either Church or defendant has taken place since that time.

But why this determined purpose to keep this case from coming before the General Assembly, and to send it to the Synod? There would be reason in this were it a case respecting morality, for then the Synod would have the constitutional right to make a final decision. It cannot do so in this case, since it involves the doctrines of the Church, which the Assembly only can finally decide. This shows that there is no desire, on the part of those just referred to, to secure a settlement of the matter at issue by the only body which constitutionally can settle it for the Church. The prerogatives and privileges of our judicatories have been mentioned; but the court, whose prerogatives, privileges and dignity have been attacked in connection with this case, is not the Synod of New York, but the General Assembly itself.

So earnest is the attempt to keep this case from coming before the Assembly for decision, that the disruption of the Church is threatened if the Assembly should entertain and issue it. But this threat argues on the one hand, conscious weakness on the part of those who make it, and on the other, a deliberate intention to unduly influence the Assembly so as to prevent it from giving an honest expression of opinion.

A wise and manly settlement of this case by the Assembly will purify and strengthen our Church and be the beginning of a long period of peace and prosperity.

4. This case involves the legal construction of the ordination vow of every minister, elder and deacon in our Church; it involves what they may believe and teach as the faith of the Church, under the terms of that vow. The Presbytery of New York has decided

in the case of Dr. Briggs that a Presbyterian minister, elder or deacon may believe and teach, in harmony with that vow, certain doctrines. The Presbytery of Cincinnati has held in the case of Dr. H. S. Smith that certain of these views cannot be taught without a violation of the ordination vow. What the faith of the Church, as to the fundamental doctrines involved in this case, is, and what is embraced within the terms of the ordination vow, and the liberty in teaching allowed by the Church, can only be determined by the General Assembly.

The importance of an immediate decision of these matters will be recognized at once, when we consider that during the coming year at least two hundred and fifty ministers will be received into our Church and from three to five thousand elders and deacons elected and ordained. Those ministers, elders and deacons who take the ordination vow, according to the decision of the New York Presbytery in this case, have a right to believe, until that decision is reversed, that they can hold the views of Dr. Briggs and teach them without transgressing the limits of liberty allowed under our Constitution to scholarship and opinion.

Is it fair or just to leave the terms of the ordination vow and the doctrines involved in this case, unsettled for another year, for this would be the result of not entertaining the appeal or, after it has been entertained, sending it to the Synod? Would it be right or honest to permit ministers, elders and deacons to enter the Church during the next year, believing, as they would have a right to believe, with the judgment of the New York Presbytery unreversed, that, under the terms of their ordination vow, they can believe and teach the views held by Dr. Briggs? Then, in case the Assembly of 1894 should reverse the judgment of New York Presbytery, it would place those who have become ministers, elders and deacons in the position of being compelled either to renounce their views, or to retire from the Church, or subject themselves to discipline to expel them from the Church.

The Church, in all its agencies, must go on, it must license more ministers, elect and ordain more elders and deacons. If no other consideration existed than this, it would be of paramount importance. Fairness and justice to those whom the Church invites into official station would seem to require this Judicatory to entertain this appeal and determine what the Church holds upon the fundamental questions at issue.

5. As a final reason why the Assembly should entertain this appeal now, we urge that great and widespread injury is certain to come from protracted delay. It will tend to unsettle faith, especially among our young people; it will injuriously affect the training of our young men for the ministry, and will result in the spread of false doctrines.

The Presbytery of New York, in the final judgment, says: "There are truths and forms with regard to "which men of good character may differ." No one disputes that. But the statement necessarily implies that there are also truths and forms in regard to which good men, especially ministers of the Presbyterian Church, should not differ; and the question is whether or not the truths and forms contained in this case are of that kind. The great majority of Presbyterians believe that they are. The verdict of the Presbytery of New York confirms that belief rather than otherwise; for, while they acquit him, they distinctly disapprove the critical and theological views of Dr. Briggs, for which he has been put on the defence. Why disapprove these truths and forms if Presbyterian Ministers and elders may differ in regard to them?

If the doctrines presented by Prof. Briggs be erroneous, as we verily believe, then, through delay, "heretical opinions" are sure to "gain ground," and our Church will be affected injuriously through the continuance of uncertainty and doubt, and of suspicion and strife.

In closing, Moderator, let me thank you and the General Assembly for your indulgent attention to this long and sometimes technical argument. The laws of our Book may be imperfect, for they are human laws; our interpretation of the law may be defective, because it is a human interpretation; but these laws and their interpreters may be the means of advancing the Kingdom of God. And, having been faithful to the rights and laws of His Church on earth, you shall doubtless see the effects of this fidelity in that heavenly empire, the realm of glory, to which He will one day summon His elect.

VII.

Preliminary Statement of Mr. McCook, of the Prosecuting Committee, as to Procedure and Designating the Portions of the Record to be used by the Appellant during the Argument of the Appeal.

Moderator, Fathers and Brethren:

Upon the suggestion of the Judicial Committee, and with the assent of the parties, it has been arranged that the Appellant shall present, in the opening argument, its entire case, with citation of authorities, and reference to so much of the record as it relies upon to sustain the same.

The Appellant gladly acts upon this suggestion of the Judicial Committee, as it is likely, in this case, to save the time of the Assembly. This procedure is, however, contrary to that which has, so far as I can learn, always been followed in ecclesiastical courts, where the Appellant has been permitted to dispose of his time and present his case, opening and closing his argument, in the manner which commends itself to his best judgment, being restricted only by the limit of time fixed by the Court.

This practice has always been followed, so far as I can learn, under our Book of Discipline, wherein Sec. 99 provides in Subsection 2 that "The parties shall be heard, the Appellant opening and closing."

In assenting to this suggestion of the Judicial Committee, the Appellant, to prevent the establishment of a precedent which might work to the disadvantage of parties in other cases of appeal, and especially where the Church at large, as in this case, is the Appellant, calls attention to the matter, now and in this public manner, so that the facts may appear upon the Stenographic Record of the judicial proceedings, showing its exceptional character, and so that a stipulation or consent of parties as to the order of procedure, in a single case, should not be quoted as authority or as establishing a precedent, contrary to the direct, affirmative, constitutional right of Appellants under Section 99 of the Book of Discipline, to open and close the argument on appeal, and to present the same as they may think best.

So as not to break in upon or interfere with Dr. Lampe's opening argument, I will now cite, as briefly as possible, the authorities and so much of the record as will be used by the Appellant in its arguments to support the Appeal and the specifications of error alleged.

To give full information to the Appellee as to the portion of the evidence and of the record in the case, to be used by the Appellant, and to save the time of the Court, as far as possible, reference will be made to the books submitted in evidence, by title and also to the volumes and pages used, but the extracts therefrom will not be read to the Court, unless it appears necessary or advisable to the Appellant to do so.

The Prosecuting Committee has prepared and placed in the hands of the Commissioners, for their information, a printed document containing a copy, certified by the Stated Clerk of the Presbytery of New York, of the final judgment, notice of Appeal and of the Appeal to the General Assembly, with the specifications of error alleged, together with a record of all proceedings had in the Presbytery of New York as shown by the minutes of that judicatory during the trial of the case.

Upon pages 86, 88 and 89 of the printed document (pages 92, 94 and 95 of this volume) will be found reference to the evidence introduced, at the trial, by the Appellant. On pages 89, 90, 91, 92 and 93 (pages 95 to

99 of this volume) will be found reference to the evidence introduced by the Appellee, all of which having been received as competent evidence by the lower Court may be referred to and used by the parties in the argument of this Appeal.

When sitting as a judicatory in a judicial case, the members of the Court are charged with judicial knowledge of the contents of the Constitution of the Presbyterian Church in the United States of America, consisting of the Confession of Faith, the Larger and Shorter Catechisms, the Form of Government, the Book of Discipline and Directory for Worship, a copy of which was introduced in evidence, in the Court below, by the Appellant, marked F.

The members of the Court are also charged with judicial knowledge of the contents of the Holy Bible, a copy of which was introduced in evidence, in the Court below, by the Appellant, marked G, and any portions of the Bible and the Constitution of the Presbyterian Church may be quoted, referred to and used by the Appellant, without any previous designation of the part or parts thereof to be so used.

The Minutes of the General Assembly, being a public document and an official record of the Church, the Court must also take judicial knowledge of the contents thereof, and the Appellant proposes to use portions of pages 57 and 235 of the Minutes of the General Assembly of 1892.

Use will also be made, as a part of the record in this case, of portions of the original Charges and Specifications in this case, presented to the Presbytery of New York on the 5th day of October, 1891, and of all or any part of the Amended Charges and Specifications (pages 44 to 73 of the printed document, pages 50 to 79 of this volume) presented to the Presbytery of New York on the 9th day of November, 1892, including the quotations from the Inaugural Address and the citations of proofs from Scripture, the Confession of Faith and the Larger and Shorter Catechisms.

The Appellant will also refer to or use the final judgment of the Presbytery of New York, entered on the 9th day of January, 1893, the Notice of Appeal, the Appeal and the Specifications of Error alleged, all of which have already been read to the Court and will be found in the printed document at pages 3 to 34 inclusive. (Pages 11 to 42 of this volume.)

The Appellant will also refer to or use the following pages, or parts thereof, of the Minutes of the Presbytery of New York: Vol. 14, pages 227, 228, 265, 276, 285, 286, 291, 292, 294, 303-305, 310, 313, 319, 355, 356, 361, 378, 384, 385, 395, 396, 397 and 500 *et sequitur*.

The Appellant will also refer to or use the following pages, or parts thereof, of the Stenographic Report of the trial in the Presbytery of New York from November 9th, 1892, to January 9th, 1893, as follows: Pages 121, 122, 123, 148, 187, 188, 405, 411, 451 *et sequitur*, 470-472, 475, 476, 477, 478, 784, 900, 993, 1009, 1010, 1028-9, 1035, 1036-1038, 1153, 1174, 1210, 1212, 1214, 1225, 1228, 1341, 1343-1351.

The Apellant will also refer to or use the preface to Dr. Briggs' Inaugural Address, Third Edition, with the Appendix thereto, and the whole or parts of the following pages thereof: 25, 26, 27, 31, 32, 33, 34, 35, 41, 53, 55, 88, 89, 103, 104, 105, 106, 107, 147.

The Appellant will also refer to or use the following works of Dr. Briggs:

Whither, pages xi., 211, 221.

Biblical Study, pages 161, 243.

Who Wrote the Pentateuch? pages 23, 25, 28, 29, 75, 79, 101, 106, 124, 157, 158, 159, 162.

Who Wrote Isaiah? pages 135, 137, 138.

Dr. Briggs' article in the Presbyterian Review for April, 1884, page 384.

Dr. Briggs' article in the Andover Review, volume 13, page 59.

The Appellant will also refer to or use in their arguments portions of pages 1 and 4 of Newman's Apologia Pro Vita Sua, in the volume submitted in evidence, in the Court below, by the Appellant, marked D.

The Appellant will also refer to or use portions of Book I., Chapters 1 and 2; Book II., Chapter 2, and Book IV., Chapter 2, of Martineau's Seat of Authority in Religion, in the volume introduced in evidence, in the Court below, by the Appellant, marked E.

The Appellant will also refer to or use Kuenen's Prophets and Prophecies in Israel, 1877, pages 448, 449.

I shall not take the time of the Court to read any of the citations at this time, but they may be read and will be referred to by the Prosecuting Committee, representing the Appellant, from time to time during the arguments.

Dr. Lampe will now present the Appellant's opening argument.

VIII.

ARGUMENT OF THE REV. JOSEPH J. LAMPE, D. D., A MEMBER OF THE PROSECUTING COMMITTEE, ON THE MERITS AND IN FAVOR OF SUSTAINING THE APPEAL.

MR. MODERATOR, FATHERS AND BRETHREN :
In accordance with Section 95 of the Book of Discipline, the Appellants assign five grounds of appeal, viz. : Irregularity in the proceedings of the Presbytery of New York ; receiving improper, and declining to receive important testimony; manifestation of prejudice in the conduct of the case ; and mistake or injustice in the decision.

Some of the specifications under these grounds have reference only to the order of procedure. Your attention is called to them for the reason that errors of procedure should not be allowed to become precedents for future cases.

1st. The first ground is that of irregularity in the proceedings of the lower judicatory.

1. The first important error was the rejection of Charges 4 and 7 of the amended form ; for if these charges were essential parts of the original charges, sent down

by the General Assembly of 1892 to the Presbytery of New York, to be tried on the merits thereof, and, if Dr. Briggs has really not disavowed the serious errors charged against him in them, then it was irregular for the Presbytery to order the Committee of Prosecution to strike them out, and the Appellants were in duty bound to bring them here, as has been done in the first and second specifications under the first ground of appeal.

Two principal objections were made to these charges : 1. That they were new charges. 2. That the defendant had disclaimed the teaching with which these charges were concerned.

The substance of Charge 4 was originally a specification under the first of the original charges (Spec. 7). It was objected to as being vague and indefinite, and, in accordance with Dr. Briggs' own criticisms, it was made definite. It was objected that it did not charge the contravening of any essential doctrine, and so an explanatory clause was added to show the essential character of the doctrine which had been contravened.

The 7th specification of the original first charge accused Dr. Briggs of teaching that much of predictive prophecy had been reversed by history, and that many predictions had not been and could not be fulfilled. Charge 4 is more specific. It relates principally to Messianic prophecy. It refers to the exact words of Dr. Briggs. The general nature so far is not changed ; the general nature of Specification 7 was predictive prophecy, and, as Messianic prophecy is a species of predictive prophecy, it is not changing the general nature to raise the question of the species instead of the question of predictive prophecy generally.

But objection was made to the explanatory clause in the 4th amended charge. Does this make the charge new? If so, then one must ask this question:

Why is it an offence to deny the fulfillment of the great body of Messianic prediction? Well, your answer may be either (a) Because the word of God is infallible, in which case you assume the infallibility of the Bible as the ground for belief in the Messianic prophecy, or (b) Because of the attributes of God. Dr. Briggs affirms that the great body of Messianic prediction not only has not been fulfilled but cannot be fulfilled. If that be the correct view, it must be asked, What is to be thought of Him who inspires a false prophecy, and of the words of Jesus Himself that all things must be fulfilled? Inasmuch as Dr. Briggs had denied the truthfulness of Scripture, and yet had admitted its Inspiration, the only possible essential reason which could be adduced for the doctrine of the fulfillment of all Messianic prediction was that it came with the authority of God. That God being true could not lie; that God being omniscient could not be ignorant; that God being immutable could not change. Undoubtedly the charge was serious; possibly the defendant was not aware of what he had been denying. But, if innocent of the charge, it was for him to retract the assertion, or to meet the evidence of the Committee with proper evidence of his own. On the contrary, he asserts before the testimony is taken, that he does not hold any such doctrine, and yet reaffirms the doctrine by declining to retract the original statement. Can any one say that such a manner of dealing with the subject did not demand the judicial decision of the Presbytery?

This brings us to the other ground upon which Charge 4 was struck out. It was because of the alleged disclaimers and disavowals of the defendant.

All the eight amended charges alleged certain offences. The evidence for these allegations was contained in verbatim citations from the writings of Dr. Briggs, which he himself put in evidence, and which he declined to withdraw or retract. Prior to being called upon to plead "guilty" or "not guilty" to the charges, and while the sufficiency of the charges was under discussion, his alleged disclaimers and disavowals, which were not at that time in evidence, were brought forward as a ground upon which Charge 4 and also Charge 7 should be struck out. He objected, and Dr. George Alexander objected on his behalf, to going to trial on Charges 4 and 7, because he had never taught the doctrines with teaching which he is therein charged. Why, then, did he consent to go to trial on the remaining charges? Was it because he has taught the doctrines therein alleged? If that is the reason, then why did he plead not guilty to these remaining charges? Why did he not disclaim these as he disclaimed Charges 4 and 7? But, if he has not taught any of the doctrines alleged in the amended eight charges, why not go to trial on all eight of them, or else disclaim having committed the offences contained in all eight of them? The Committee had no wish to find more errors in the Inaugural than were really there; but the duty of the Committee was to the church, to come to a decision as to these doctrines taught explicitly in the Inaugural Address, which had never been withdrawn or retracted by the defendant. A plea of not guilty is not sufficient evidence in a man's defence. Still less is a plea of not guilty sufficient evidence when it is not introduced as evidence, but is brought forward irregularly as a preliminary objection to the indictment.

Much fault was found with the committee for noticing this doctrine of predictive prophecy in connection with Dr. Briggs' doctrine of Scripture, but the mandate of the Assembly was that the case should be tried on its merits, and this was a part of the original case. The Inaugural Address had been put in evidence by the defendant himself; it was no injustice to discuss that evidence.

Having discussed so especially Charge 4, but little remains to be said with respect to the amended Charge 7. It will be sufficient to inquire whether it was a new charge. Charge 7 of the amended charges is a subdivision of Charge 2 of the original charges.

The latter charged the defendant with teaching a doctrine of " the character, state and sanctification of believers " after death." Notice the exact words. It is not a doctrine of the *sanctification* of believers after death alone, but is a doctrine with respect to the state and character after death. What is the state and character of the believer after death? Is he one who has already believed in this life, or has he come to faith and penitence beyond the grave? On this subject the teaching of the Inaugural Address is definite, although it might be said that the second original charge was indefinite. To make the accusation definite, so that the defendant might have knowledge of the specific offence with which he was charged, the original Charge 2 was divided into amended Charges 7 and 8. The general nature of original Charge 2 was eschatological. It was also so closely related to Dr. Briggs' doctrine of Redemption, that one of these doctrines could not be understood to the exclusion of the other. The Committee was prepared to show that the defendant had taught that other processes than sanctification were continued in the life to come, and they summed these up in the words, state and character, as distinguished from sanctification. Dr. Briggs has expressly taught that more than one of the processes of redemption may go on in the future state. The Committee were prepared to prove this at the time when the original charges were presented, and they are prepared to prove the amended Charge 7, to which Dr. Briggs, in advance of being called to plead, made the alleged disclaimer. Judicial process was necessary to determine whether his written words upon which the charges are based or his verbal disclaimer were to be taken as the truth. The language of the

Inaugural is on this point unambiguous, and has never been retracted.

The original Charge 2 deals with the subject-matter of both amended Charges 7 and 8.

Under the specification to the original charge is cited that passage of the Inaugural Address where it is said: "Another fault of Protestant theology is in its limitation " of the process of redemption to this world." The process of redemption is a process which corresponds to the "character and state" referred to under original Charge 2. The process of redemption, according to the defendant, is a manifold process. It includes regeneration, faith, as well as sanctification. The denial of Dr. Briggs, as it is called, in answer to the question on this subject as propounded by the Directors of Union Seminary, took place before the General Assembly of 1892 sent the case for full trial to the lower judicatory. The Prosecuting Committee reappears here with the same complaint, that being ready to prove the charge with respect to the defendant's views of the future life, in spite of the opinions of judges who were his advocates on the floor of the Presbytery, the general nature of original Charge 2 was so changed by the order of the court that the mandate of the General Assembly has been disobeyed in one of the most important particulars.

The changes made in extracts from the Confession cannot change the general nature of the charge. The references to the Confession in both series of charges and specifications are practically the same, the changes being comparatively few. But it matters not whether they are few or many, for references to the Standards are proofs to the charges, not part of the charges themselves. In any event, it must be remembered that the Standards are always in the Court, both as law and evidence, and that any part of them can be cited at any time in support of a charge.

2. The second error was in compelling transfer of the proofs from their proper place after the specifications to a place immediately following the charges. Since the Presbytery was to vote on the matter contained in the specifications, either to sustain or not to sustain the charges, it was the Committee's duty to show that the statements contained in the specifications are in conflict with Scripture and the Standards. The order to transfer the references to Scripture and the Standards from the specifications to the charges was made with the evident purpose to place them where they could not be used effectively as proofs. This order therefore was a gross error in procedure on the part of the Presbytery as pointed out in the third specification.

3. The insertion of a large amount of matter into the official stenographic report, at the request of the defendant and with the approval of the Moderator, after the adjournment of the Court and after both parties had given notice that they had presented all the evidence which they intended to offer, was grossly irregular and therefore

more than a mistake, as indicated in Specifications 7 and 8. It needs no discussion to convince the Assembly that evidence can be introduced regularly only in open Court and at the proper time.

4. The vote to strike from the record the request of the Committee of Prosecution, as stated in Specifications 9 and 10; the refusal to permit the members of the judicatory to vote to sustain in part, as indicated in the eleventh specification; and the decision to give to the unsworn statements, explanations and disclaimers of the defendant the force of sworn, approbated and subscribed testimony as noticed in the sixth specification, were all flagrant errors of procedure. The bare mentioning of them makes plain their irregularity.

5. The sixth specification refers to the new matter alleged to have been introduced in the argument replying to that of Dr. Briggs. If that contention had any force, it obliges us to make the terms " new matter " equivalent to new evidence. A reference to the argument will show any thoughtful man that no new evidence was introduced. That new matter, in the way of varied presentation of the case, in the way of illustration and argument was brought in, there can be no doubt, otherwise the closing argument would have been but a repetition of the opening. The argument was confined strictly within the limits of the evidence submitted, and in every case was directed against the pivotal positions of the Appellee. It was unnecessary to follow the defence step by step. It was no

less the Committee's duty than its privilege to show in any legitimate way which seemed most effective that he had evaded the main issue and had not harmonized his views with the Holy Scripture and the Standards.

The defendant errs in maintaining that we had only the right of rebuttal. The Committee's argument was not in rebuttal, but was the closing argument of the prosecution, in which all the evidence submitted by both was at our disposal for use in answer to that of the defence.

The Appellee also errs in speaking of illustration in argument as the introduction of new evidence. It is a well-settled principle of ecclesiastical procedure that authorities quoted in illustration have the force, not of evidence, but of argument.

It was therefore irregular to allow the defendant to reply to the closing argument of the prosecution.

6. The twelfth specification calls your attention to the order of the inferior judicatory, directing that each item of the several charges should be voted on separately, for the alleged reason that each charge contained as many offences as it contains direct references to doctrines of the Standards. But this is clearly a mistake. Each one of the five charges contains but a single offence as any one will see from a single glance at them.

The double or triple reference to doctrines of the Confession does not multiply the offence to that extent, but furnishes so many proofs to establish the one offence.

Had we cited a dozen doctrines of the Confession in support of a charge and in addition a hundred texts from the Bible, they would not have made so many different offences in the charge, but would have been merely so many added proofs to establish the one offence of the charge. If the position taken by the Presbytery be correct, then it will be impossible ever to cite more than one proof in support of an offence.

2d. The second and third grounds of appeal refer to the question of testimony, and they may be considered together.

1. That large amount of matter which, by the request of the defendant and with the approval of the Moderator, was inserted into the official stenographic report, after the adjournment of the Presbytery, cannot, in any proper sense, be called testimony at all. And yet it was allowed by the Presbytery to remain on the record as competent evidence.

In regard to the other evidence offered by Dr. Briggs, it should be said that he declined to verify it under oath. He denounced the request that he be required to do so as an outrage. He was both counsel and client, and, as counsel, he made statements, explanations and disclaimers in regard to the language which his client had used, to which the inferior judicatory, contrary to the directions of Sections 61 and 62 of the Book of Discipline, gave the full value of competent evidence for making up their final verdict.

This was especially unfortunate, as it has been all along evident, we are not so much concerned with the form of the defendant's statements as with the meaning which he puts into the form. Had the Presbytery ordered Dr. Briggs to put his client on the witness-stand to make affirmations under oath, as the Book directs, it might have been possible to determine more exactly the value and meaning which are to be attached to his statements.

2. Furthermore, the Presbytery erred in declining to receive important testimony. We have shown that the fourth and seventh charges properly belong to the amended series, since the matter contained in them was essentially in the original charges.

In these charges Dr. Briggs is accused of teaching grave errors. The Committee of Prosecution offered to produce testimony to prove those charges; and whether competent to prove them or not, it was certainly important testimony, and for that reason should have been received and examined by the Presbytery. But instead of that the Presbytery ordered the charges to be stricken out on the ground principally of some general disclaimers which Dr. Briggs was alleged to have made, but which were not specified and were not presented to the Court as testimony.

3rd. The state of things to which your attention is called in the specifications given under the fourth ground of appeal, shows conclusively that prejudice was manifested in the conduct of the case. I need not speak of them at length. Similar conduct by members of the Presbytery of New York was declared by the Assembly of 1892 to be a manifestation of prejudice.

A number of the members of the lower Court showed a deep personal interest in the case of the defendant. Some manifested all the zeal of advocates instead of maintaining the calmness and equipoise of judges.

One of the judges allowed his zeal to carry him so far that he affirmed and re-affirmed that some of the charges gave Dr. Briggs the lie direct.

The names of some of the judges are introduced because of a principle which is here involved. It is not simply that in assuming the rôle of advocates they exhibited prejudice. It is especially on account of the grounds upon which they made prejudiced appeals to the Court. Their remarks also have especial interest from the time at which they were made.

In the closing argument for the prosecution citations by way of argument and illustrations were made from many eminent writers as expressive of the views which the speaker was maintaining. It was not new evidence, for the time of taking evidence was past. This kind of argument was characterized by Dr. George Alexander as a "fresh assault" upon Dr. Briggs, and another judge insisted that new matter had been introduced. They were called upon to specify the "new matter." They did not and could not do so.

Their objection was to the quotations which illustrated

the speaker's denial of the claim of Dr. Briggs that his views represented the belief of historic Presbyterianism. These extracts made every drop of Anglo-Saxon blood in the brethren named " to protest and boil." The quotations were from men like Augustine, Luther, Calvin, Baxter, the Westminster divines, and especially from the writings of American Presbyterians like Jonathan Dickinson, Samuel Davies, Jonathan Edwards, John Witherspoon, Ashbel Green, Archibald Alexander, Thomas H. Skinner, Albert Barnes and Henry B. Smith. If the time has come when Presbyterian blood boils at the words of such men as these, I insist that the attention of the General Assembly should be called to the fact; especially since the blood of the same judges did not "protest and boil" when the defendant introduced a large number of names as authorities in support of his doctrine of an errant Bible, many of whom advance rationalistic, if not infidel, views, and none of them, in my opinion, hold the true Presbyterian doctrine respecting the Holy Scripture.

This claim on the part of the Committee, that there was prepossession of opinion and prejudiced judgment on the part of certain officials of Union Seminary, is not essentially different from the declaration of the Directors themselves. This declaration was made through Mr. Kingsley, their representative in the General Assembly in 1892. According to him, previous to the regular trial in the Presbytery of New York there had been an investigation of the charges brought against Dr. Briggs. This investigation was made by the officers of Union Seminary. The result was the questions put by the Directors of Union Seminary and answered by Dr. Briggs, to which allusion has so often been made. I quote from the report of the Directors read by Mr. Kingsley before the Portland Assembly:

"This board had carefully investigated the charges " which the Presbyteries were bringing against Dr. " Briggs and had received from him a clear and positive " denial of each charge, on the ground of which denials " the board resolved to sustain him, saying that 'we will " stand by him heartily on the ground of this report' (i. e., " the report of his denials received from the committee of " investigation)."

And again in his remarks on the report Mr. Kingsley said: "It was due to ourselves and to Dr. Briggs that " we should be true to the promise we had made 'to " stand by him.'"

Prejudice was also manifested by the Presbytery in allowing the defendant the largest liberty for introducing improper testimony; in declining to receive important testimony offered by the Committee of Prosecution; in throwing out Charges 4 and 7; in expressing a desire to relieve the Committee of Prosecution from any further responsibility in connection with the case; and in stating it to be their "earnest conviction that the grave " issues involved in this case will be more wisely and " justly determined by calm investigation and fraternal " discussion than by judicial arraignment and process."

As the issues involved are acknowledged to be "grave,"

it would be reasonable for unbiased judges to conclude that those issues would be more wisely and justly determined by judicial process rather than by the calm investigation and fraternal discussion, by which nothing can be determined authoritatively.

4th. The facts presented in the specifications under the fifth ground of appeal show that mistakes and injustice have entered into the final judgment of the inferior judicatory.

A brief consideration of a few of these facts cannot fail to convince you.

1. According to Section 58 of the Book of Discipline, if the specifications of fact on which a charge is based have been shown to be true, then the charge is to be considered as sustained. Dr. Briggs offered no proof to show that he had not made the statements which are cited in the specifications. On the contrary, he admitted and authenticated them all. The charges were based on these statements and sustained by them. Under such circumstances, a verdict of acquittal could be justified only on the ground that the charges themselves were not relevant or that they contained no valid offences. But when the Presbytery declared the charges and specifications to be sufficient in form and legal effect, it thereby decided that the charges severally alleged an offence. Otherwise, the charges and specifications would not have been sufficient in form and legal effect. And therefore, since the charges were sustained by the facts stated in the specifications,

it must be that the verdict of acquittal was not reached in accordance with the law and evidence in the case.

2. That the charges were proved becomes still more evident from the statement made in the verdict rendered by the inferior judicatory to the effect that in acquitting Dr. Briggs, the Presbytery is not to be understood as "expressing approval of the critical and theological views "embodied in his Inaugural Address." A resolution to that effect was introduced on the floor of Presbytery when the voting was about to commence, possibly with the intention of securing votes for acquittal which otherwise might be conscientiously withheld.

But why this caveat if the views of Dr. Briggs are in harmony with received truth? Manifestly, the majority of Presbytery do not desire to burden themselves or cloud their reputation by an espousal of those views. They must consider the influence of such doctrines baneful to no slight extent.

For those critical and theological views, Dr. Briggs was put on trial. He not only approves them, but diligently propagates them. And it was the duty of the lower Court, by a calm and impartial investigation, to ascertain whether or not, those critical and theological views are in harmony with the Holy Scripture and the Standards; and to condemn them if they did not find them in harmony with those authorities, and thus to check their spread and influence in the most effective way.

The fact that they felt disinclined to acquit the defendant, without expressing a distinct disavowal of his critical and theological views, for which he is on trial, leads to a very strong presumption that the decision is contrary to the evidence not only, but that those rendering the decision recognize the views of the defendant as conflicting with the Scripture and the Standards; for, certainly, no body of Presbyterian ministers and elders need be at pains to disavow views which are in accord with the Bible and our Creed. The inferior judicatory, in this final judgment, has not given us either good Presbyterian law or doctrine.

3. The presumption that the charges were proved is strengthened by reference to the method by which the verdict was reached. This was by "giving due consid-
" eration to the defendant's explanation of the language
" used in his Inaugural Address, accepting his frank and
" full disclaimer of the interpretation which has been put
" upon some of its phrases and illustrations," and "cred-
" iting his affirmations of loyalty to the Standards of the
" Church and to the Holy Scriptures as the only infallible
" rule of faith and practice."

This can only mean that they have taken Dr. Briggs at his own word. By their own confession, therefore, they have not decided the case on the law and the evidence.

It is well known that Dr. Briggs entered a plea of " not guilty"; that he claims to be orthodox and that he subscribes to an orthodox creed. But, in spite of all that, he has made and persists in making the statements for which he has been called in question, and which have alarmed the whole Church.

The question to be determined is, whether or not the views of Dr. Briggs can be tolerated under the orthodox creed to which he subscribes ; and to take his word for it is to evade the whole issue. The explanations and disclaimers referred to have not been indicated in the verdict. One wonders where and what they are. They are certainly not competent evidence. Dr. Briggs has, in fact, disclaimed nothing, but has distinctly reaffirmed all the views of his Inaugural Address of every kind.

Is it to be expected that, if the statements of Dr. Briggs did not relieve the minds of his devoted personal friends in the New York Presbytery, they can bring assurance and peace to the Church ?

4. The lower judicatory, in its final judgment, makes also a number of vague, misleading and contradictory statements which give further evidence of mistake and injustice in that judgment.

It is intimated in the verdict that the present controversy is unjustifiable ; that the principles at stake are non-essential, belonging with " truths and forms with regard " to which men of good character may differ," and are within the limits allowed under the constitution to " scholarship and opinion "; and that there has been an effort made to convict the defendant by " inference and

" implication," and by the unfavorable interpretation of
" ambiguous expressions."

Is it true then that doctrines such as the sole supremacy of the Holy Scriptures as an authority in matters of religion, their entire veracity and absolute trustworthiness, and the question whether the process of redemption is confined to this life, or is to be extended to the life beyond the grave, are matters about which Presbyterian ministers and elders may differ, or mere matters of opinion which the scholars of our Church may adopt or reject? May one who has assumed the ordination vow of a Presbyterian minister teach that the Church, as a great Fountain of divine authority, can savingly enlighten men and give them religious certainty apart from the Holy Scripture ; that the Reason as a great fountain of divine authority can savingly enlighten and give religious certainty to those who not only reject the Scripture, but the entire body of distinctively evangelical truth? May he teach that the process of redemption extends into the next world? It is neither candid nor honest to evade these questions.

The majority of Presbytery hesitate indeed, and, while they acquit, enter a caveat. They say that "grave issues" are involved in the case. But if the issues are grave, then there must be something more than mere "inference," "implication," and non-essential principles, as to which Presbyterian ministers may differ.

5. It is further evident from the language used in the final judgment, that the inferior judicatory did not make a decision on the merits of the case. They declare it to be their " earnest conviction that the grave issues involved " in this case will be more wisely and justly determined " by calm investigation and fraternal discussion than by " judicial arraignment and process." What is this but to say that they threw the case out of Court for the reason that they have an " earnest conviction against settling the " grave issues involved in it by judicial arraignment and " process?"

The Presbytery was constituted a Court to try the case by judicial process, and the acknowledgment that the members had an " earnest conviction" against determining the issues involved in that way amounts to a confession on their part that they were disqualified to sit as judges. The Presbytery of New York, in the first instance, decided that the case was a proper one for judicial investigation; the General Assembly sent it back to Presbytery with direction to try the case on its merits, and the members of the Court were solemnly charged to determine the issues of the case by judicial process; if the majority of the lower Court were prepossessed against determining such issues in that way, they should have withdrawn from the Court and thus have permitted the case to be tried by those who believe in determining important questions of doctrine by means of judicial arraignment and process, as the constitution directs.

But it is certain that a body having this earnest conviction against settling the questions in dispute by judicial process, could not give a righteous or even intelligent judgment on the merits of the case. The verdict is self-contradictory. In effect, the opinions of Dr. Briggs are declared to be in harmony with the Scripture and the Standards, but discredit is thrown on the judgment by the refusal to approve the very views which form the basis of the trial. Such a verdict is unjust to all and can do nothing to allay the disquietude which pervades the Presbyterian Church.

We are now to show by an examination of the merits of the case, that the final judgment rendered in it by the Presbytery of New York, is not in harmony with the Holy Scripture, the Standards, and with the evidence submitted.

Dr. Briggs has disavowed nothing. He expressly declares that he holds firmly to all the views contained in the Inaugural Address. He says: " The Inaugural Ad-
" dress was simply a concentration of opinions expressed
" more at length in other places and under other circum-
" stances. The defendant is altogether unconscious of
" any substantial change of opinion on the subject-matters
" of the charges for many years. * * * The defendant
" has not asked for toleration. He claims his rights un-
" der the constitution of his Church to teach anything
" and everything that he has ever taught." (Defence, Preface, p. 18.)

Nor has he made any statements or explanations which show the views, which are the subject of these charges, to be in harmony with the Bible and our Standards.

The bare categorical replies by Dr. Briggs to a series of questions put to him by sympathetic professors and directors of the Union Seminary, neither explain or disavow anything; for all but one of the questions are susceptible of more than one meaning, and the answers can be made by one holding the doctrines of Dr. Briggs. They give us no more light than does his orthodox subscription.

It is conceded freely and cheerfully that Dr. Briggs has made many orthodox statements and that he has supported them efficiently. No accusation is made against him for these. But he has been charged with the propagation of views which are believed to be heretical. For these he has been put on trial.

In his Defence, Dr. Briggs made a number of statements in reference to the law by which he is to be judged, which, if accepted, reduce that law as nearly as possible to a nonentity.

He contends that the Court must determine whether or not the doctrines are essential to our system; but he contends also that the decision must depend upon the extent of the system as understood by the Westminster divines, so that in so far as the doctrines of that system are differently understood now than they were by those divines, he is not to be tried by them. He forgets that we have nothing to do with the opinions of the Westminster divines. If we have to do with any, we should follow those of the American divines, who adopted the Presbyterian Standards of 1788 as representative of their own views.

He maintains also that he is not to be tried by the Bible except so far as it has been embodied and defined in our Standards. But he does not wish to be tried by the Standards except in so far as they can be proven to be true by express statements of the Scripture; nor would he be tried by all that part of the Standards which is supported by express statements of Scripture. The measuring-rod, according to Dr. Briggs, must consist only of those doctrines which are stated in the Confession and in both of the Catechisms. If a doctrine of the Confession be not restated in both Catechisms, then it is not to enter into consideration even though it be shown to be true from the Holy Scripture. This fencing about the law gives the impression that the defendant is conscious of inherent weakness.

There is no need of hedging and fencing. The Book of Discipline gives the law by which a person is to be tried in our judicatories. Sections 3 and 4 tell us, " An " offence is anything in the doctrine, principles or practice " of a Church member, officer or judicatory, which is con- " trary to the Word of God ; or which, if it be not in its " own nature sinful, may tempt others to sin, or mar their " spiritual edification. Nothing shall, therefore, be the

" object of judicial process, which cannot be proved to be " contrary to the Holy Scriptures, or to the regulations " and practice of the Church founded thereon." It is clear that anything which can be shown to be contrary to the *Holy Scriptures*, is an offence and may be made the object of judicial process, even though it be not embodied or defined in the Standards ; and in like manner that *anything* which can be shown to be contrary to the *Standards* is an offence which may be made the object of judicial process, even though it be not supported by express statements of Scripture, for the Standards accept doctrines derived from Scripture by necessary inference.

The prosecution therefore have to prove the offence either against the Scripture or the Standards or against both ; but let it be distinctly observed that proof from either Scripture or Standards alone is sufficient to establish the offence.

The degree of the offence and the measure or kind of discipline to be inflicted for it, are not for us, but for the Court to determine. We have never said, and do not now, say a word about the kind of discipline which should be exercised if the offence were established ; but we contend that the offence is one which merits discipline.

The Craighead case, to which Dr. Briggs has referred, was essentially different from the one in hand and does not apply to it ; but it is maintained by all alike that if the statements of Dr. Briggs are capable of two constructions, he must have the benefit of the more favorable construction, should he claim that as his, even if the more evident construction, is plainly heretical; and also that he is not to be charged with an opinion which he disavows.

FOUNTAINS OF DIVINE AUTHORITY.

The first and second charges refer to the subject of divine authority and may be considered together. In them he is charged with teaching: "*First*, that the Rea-
"son is a fountain of divine authority which may and
"does savingly enlighten men, even such men as reject
"the Scriptures as the authoritative proclamation of the
"will of God and reject also the way of salvation through
"the mediation and sacrifice of the Son of God as re-
"vealed therein." "*Second*, that the Church is a fountain
"of divine authority which, apart from the Holy Scrip-
"ture, may and does savingly enlighten men." We ask you to notice the statements contained in the citations made from the Inaugural Address in the specifications under these charges, as amply justifying these charges.

On page 24 of the Inaugural, after having referred to the imperfection and errancy of all the forms of human authority, he states in definition of divine authority, "The
"earnest spirit presses back of all these human authorities in
"quest of an infallible guide and of an eternal and immutable
"certainty. Probability might be the guide of life in the
"superficial 18th century, and for those who have inher-
"ited its traditions, but the men of the present times are
"in quest of certainty. Divine authority is the only

"authority to which man can yield implicit obedience, "on which he can rest in loving certainty and build "with joyous confidence." * * * There are historically three great fountains of divine authority—the Bible, the Church and the Reason."

The Bible, the Church and the Reason, then, are equal in being great fountains of divine authority. The quality of divinity, and the right of divine authority belong alike to all three ; and, as such, each can be to man an infallible guide of life, and speak to him with eternal and immutable certainty, for he can yield to each implicit obedience, rest on each with loving certainty and build with joyous confidence.

It does not in the least relieve the matter to say that the Bible differs from the other two fountains of divine authority in being in addition also an infallible rule of faith and practice, for according to Dr. Briggs' own definition, the Church and the Reason, as infallible guides, can do for men precisely the same things which the Bible does for them as an infallible rule.

We have to do with the Church and the Reason. In respect to them Dr. Briggs affirms : *first*, that they can conduct men to a saving acquaintance with God ; and *second*, that they can give to men immutable certainty or assurance in matter of religion. Martineau and the rationalists are examples for the Reason. Newman and the Churchman for the Church.

"Newman could not reach certainty through the Bible, "striving never so hard." He and the majority of Christians from the apostolic age have found God through the Church. "Martyrs and saints, fathers and schoolmen, "the profoundest intellects, the saintliest lives, have "had this experience. Institutional Christianity has "been to them the presence-chamber of God." Dr. Briggs affirms this to be true categorically, although, he remarks : "It is difficult for many Protestants to regard "this experience as any other than pious illusion and de-"lusion." (Inaugural, p. 25.)

"Martineau could not find divine authority in the "Church or the Bible, but he did find God enthroned in "his own soul." (Inaugural, p. 27.) To him and the rationalists, the Reason is the Holy of Holies of human nature, in which God presents Himself to those who seek Him. (Inaugural, p. 26.) And therefore, although it is well known that they reject the Scriptures as the authoritative proclamation of the will of God and the way of salvation through the mediation and sacrifice of the Son of God as revealed therein, Dr. Briggs nevertheless would not "refuse these Rationalists a place in the "company of the faithful." (Inaugural, p. 27).

That Dr. Briggs conceives of each one of the three fountains of divine authority as capable of imparting a saving knowledge of God is evident from his own statements on the subject. He says : " Unless God's authority "is discerned in the forms of the Reason, there is no ground "upon which any of the heathen could ever have been

" saved, for they know nothing of Bible or Church. If " they are not savingly enlightened by the light of the " World in the forms of the Reason the whole heathen " world is lost forever." (Inaug., 2d ed., pp. 88, 89.) The divine authority in the Reason therefore does savingly enlighten men in the view of Dr. Briggs.

Again he says: "Spurgeon is an example of the "average modern Evangelical, who holds the Protestant "position and assails the Church and Reason in the in-"terest of the authority of Scripture. But the average "opinion of the Christian world would not assign him a "higher place in the Kingdom of God than Martineau or "Newman. May we not conclude on the whole, that "these three representative Christians of our time, living "in or near the world's metropolis, have, each in his way, "found God and rested on Divine authority? * * * "Men are influenced by their temperaments and environ-"ments which of the three ways of access to God they "may pursue." (Inaugural, p. 28.) Here Dr. Briggs not only teaches that men may and do find God savingly through any one of the three fountains of divine authority, but admits that the Bible, as the *only* way for obtaining salvation and certainty, as held by Spurgeon, is the Protestant doctrine. And therefore, since the Presbyterian Church is a Protestant Church, he convicts himself of teaching doctrines which are not Presbyterian.

The labored argument made by Dr. Briggs in his Defence to show that according to the teaching of both the Bible and the Standards, the Church and the Reason are great fountains of divine authority, is wide of the mark and wholly unsuccessful.

The facts that God can give evidence of himself to man's soul and that man has the power of verifying truth, that he can receive communications from God, and be the subject of gracious influences, show that as created in the image of God, man is endowed with a moral and rational nature, but does not at all prove that his reason is a great fountain of divine authority.

The Church, as shown by the citations which Dr. Briggs made from the Standards, has no authority except such as Christ has delegated to it, and prescribed for it in his word. The Church is guilty of usurpation whenever it attempts to exercise authority not so delegated or prescribed, so that it may become a curse instead of a blessing, as abundantly shown in the history of the Church.

Christ is supreme in the Church and in all matters of faith and life. But we know nothing about Him, except through the Bible story. The truth by means of which He saves and assures His people is treasured up in the Scriptures, so that we are shut up to them, both for a saving knowledge of God and for assurance. The Bible alone tells us what we need to know about God, ourselves, the plan of salvation, our duty and the conditions of eternal life and destiny. For this reason, the Bible alone, as against the Church and Reason, gives light in the moral and spiritual realm. It is a light to man's pathway and a lamp to his feet, by which he discovers his way through the darkness of this world to the world of eternal light. The Bible is as the bread of God to give life to men's souls, for man shall live by every word that proceedeth out of the mouth of God. The Church is constituted of errant men and women only partially sanctified, and the Reason, unless enlightened by the word of God, gropes in the darkness of sin. Neither has power to enlighten, assure and quicken a human soul, but light and life come from the Holy Scriptures to believing hearts, for in them the Holy Spirit speaks with divine love and power.

In harmony with all evangelical Protestants, Presbyterians believe that salvation and assurance are obtained through belief of truth revealed in the Holy Scripture; they do not hesitate to say that, since the Holy Spirit bears witness by and with the word of this blessed book which has expressly set down in it the whole counsel of God concerning all things necessary for His own glory, man's salvation, faith and life, men who tell us they cannot find God and certainty in these Holy Scriptures are, as those Scriptures declare, dead in trespasses and sins.

The Scripture expressly declares that men by wisdom, that is through the forms of the Reason, have not known God. History shows that to be absolutely true. Reason, unaided by revealed truth, has never been able to bring man out of the bondage of sin to God. And, therefore, "it pleased God by the foolishness of preaching to save " them that believe." God begets men to a new life by the word of truth and saves them by the belief of that truth, "for how shall they believe on Him of whom they have "not heard and how shall they hear without a preacher?" (Rom. 10; 14.)

Any discussion in respect to the salvation of infants, incapables and exceptional cases of heathen, through the working of the Spirit, is immaterial here—no question is raised in the charges in reference to them. The matter in hand is wholly different. Can one having the Bible and rejecting it find the way to God through either Church or Reason? The Bible teaches that those possessing the revealed truth which it contains are saved through belief in that truth, and not otherwise. The Holy Spirit has given the Bible to enlighten men savingly, and it is hardly to be supposed that He will enlighten in other ways those who reject the Holy Scripture, or find it an unsatisfactory source of comfort. There is nothing in the Church and Reason, apart from the Bible, by which the Spirit can savingly enlighten men. He bears witness *by and with the Word* in the hearts of those who believe unto salvation. Albert Barnes states very truly on 1 Peter, 1:23: "It is " the uniform doctrine of the Scriptures that divine truth " is made the instrument of quickening the soul unto " spiritual life."

The same is true in reference to the question of certainty. Assurance stands solely on the truth of Scripture, on God's promises. Christian assurance, resting on a firm belief in doctrines respecting Christ and salvation, must stand or fall with faith in Scripture's truth. It is absurd to suppose, and dangerous to teach, that the Holy Spirit would give this assurance through Church or Reason to those who either reject or turn away from the Holy Scripture. As Albert Barnes states in 2 Thess., 2 : 13 : " No one who is not a believer in the truth can have " evidence that God has chosen him."

That the Holy Scriptures claim for themselves supreme authority in matters of faith and life is indicated by texts which we have cited in connection with these two charges and their specifications. These texts are to be taken in their obvious meaning, and not in the strained interpretation which Dr. Briggs puts upon them.

Christ and the New Testament writers invariably appeal to the Holy Scripture as the ultimate authority for the settlement of all religious and moral questions. "*It is "written"* was with them a final settlement, since for them God speaks in what is written. Christ convicted the rationalistic Sadducees of error respecting the resurrection, and the churchly Pharisees of error respecting divorce, due in each case to ignorance of the Scriptures. (Mt. 22 : 29 ; 19 : 3–6.)

With Christ and the Apostles the Bible alone held the place of absolute and final authority. They never appealed to either Church or Reason, but brought both Church and Reason to the bar of Scripture for judgment and light.

In harmony with this truth of Scripture, our Standards as cited by us affirm that "the whole counsel of God "concerning all things necessary for His own glory and "man's salvation, faith and life, is either expressly set "down in Scripture, or by good and necessary con- "sequence may be deduced from Scripture," so that all who will may become savingly acquainted with God and gain assurance of his love; that the Holy Scripture is "*most necessary*," as it makes the full discovery of the "*only way*" of man's salvation, the Holy Spirit bearing witness "*by and with the word*" in the heart for the conversion and comfort of the soul; and that all matters of religion are to be authoritatively settled by an appeal to the Holy Scriptures, since the Holy Spirit speaks in them as the " Supreme Judge."

Dr. Briggs' teachings conflict with both Scripture and the Standards. They touch matters which are vitally essential to Presbyterians, whose faith and practice are based solely on the authority of Holy Scripture.

According to these views we must recognize the Church of Rome as a great fountain of divine authority, able to give men, without or above the Bible, a saving knowledge of God and divine assurance. This would be a complete abandonment of the Reformation position; and for the Presbyterian Church it would mean denominational suicide. Whether or not Dr. Briggs would regard this as in any sense a calamity, cannot be determined with certainty, for he regards it to be the duty of the hour, in the interest of the broadest comprehension, to destroy all denominational barriers which separate Protestants, and to form an "alliance between Protest-"antism and Romanism and all other branches of Chris-"tendom." (Whither, p. XI.)

The positions taken in his Inaugural certainly entitle him to the dignity of chief Apostle in such a movement.

Dr. Briggs' teachings respecting the Reason are even worse than those respecting the Church. In referring to Martineau as an illustration, he has made his meaning unmistakable. Martineau's late work shows that he rejects the entire Bible as a revelation from God, and all the distinctive doctrines of grace, rejects Christ Himself as Lord and Saviour, and consigns the account of His Incarnation, Resurrection and other miraculous events to the wonders of an invented Messianic Mythology or popular apotheosis. The Bible states: "That if thou shalt " confess with thy mouth the Lord Jesus, and shalt be-" lieve in thy heart that God hath raised Him from the " dead, thou shalt be saved." (Rom. 10: 9.) Christ declared: "If ye believe not that I am He, ye shall die in " your sins." (Jno. 8: 24.) "Whosoever shall deny " Me before men, him will I also deny before my Father " which is in Heaven." (Mt. 10: 33.) "No man cometh " to the Father but by Me." (Jno. 14: 61.) Martineau, therefore, in refusing to believe in the resurrection of Christ, and in rejecting the Saviour, puts himself among those to whom Christ and the Scripture deny salvation. Yet Dr. Briggs, with a full knowledge of these facts, states, in his Defence : " It is plain to me that Martineau " has gained a higher stage of Christian freedom and " direct communion with God, and it is immaterial how " he gained it." (Defence p. 67.)

If men of that type are to be heralded as representative Christian men, if after rejecting Christ and the Scripture, they have entered into friendly communion with God and obtained divine assurance through the forms of the Reason, then our entire Church life and activity is a mistake and of all men we are most miserable. It would be wise to close our Churches and Theological Seminaries and to devote our money to causes better adapted to human advancement than Home and Foreign Missions can be.

Surely it is clear that the final judgment of the New York Presbytery on the first and second charges, is not in accordance with the law and evidence in the case, and that it should be reversed.

THE TRUTHFULNESS OF THE BIBLE.

The third charge has reference to the subject of inspiration. In it Dr. Briggs is charged with teaching that errors may have existed in the original text of Scripture, as it came from its authors. Dr. Briggs admits the correctness of the facts cited in the specifications, and that the charge correctly states his teaching on this point, but denies that it is an offence.

Our Standards assert that the Holy Scriptures are the Word of God ; therefore to say that there may have been errors in the original text, is to assert that God may have put into that text that which is not true.

Dr. Briggs' view of inspiration does not give assurance of entire truthfulness in the genuine text of the Holy Scripture. On the contrary, it enables him to teach, as we shall show from the evidence submitted, that the genuine text of the Bible contains errors.

It is in evidence that Dr. Briggs maintains three propositions in regard to the Holy Scripture which, if true, render not merely possible, but even quite certain, that errors pervade its contents. They are vitally connected with his view on this question.

1. He contends that instead of saying the Scriptures *are* the Word of God, the true statement is, that they "*contain*" the Word of God, using that expression not in the Shorter Catechism sense which is equivalent to the statement that the Scriptures are the Word of God, but in the sense, that some parts of their contents are not the Word of God. (The Bible, the Church and the Reason, p. 99).

2. He makes the anti-confessional statement that there are in the Holy Scripture certain circumstantial and non-essential elements which, whether inspired or not, are pervaded by errors. (Inaugural, pp. 35, 36.) In our Standards some portions of the Bible are

regarded as more important than others; but all alike are regarded as truly inspired and entirely truthful.

3. He affirms that not the language of the Bible but the concept or thought conveyed by the language is inspired. (Inaugural, pp. 31, 32.)

In his view "we cannot term the providential care of "God over the *external production* of His Word" inspiration. (Inaugural, pp. 31, 32. Biblical Study, p. 161.)

Thus the entire text of the Bible from beginning to end is exclusively of human and not of divine origin. It is the human setting in which the "divine jewel" of the substance of the thought or the concept is held. The writers of the Bible received concepts of divine truth which they were left to dress up in human language. The Bible is therefore only the fallible expression of divine truth of which the concepts were imparted to the writers by God. As no one has ever seen or known those concepts in their naked reality, we can never be entirely certain, according to Dr. Briggs, that the human authors of the Bible received anything more than a fallible impression of the truth. At all events, if the divine inspiration did not extend to the language of the Bible then the revelation which God made to the writers perished with them. The record of that revelation at least is only human and fallible and the Scriptures are but the human account of the Word of God—not that Word itself. If so the Bible is only one of the many good books which contain divine truth, and is not the Book of books, which Christians have always considered it to be.

Holding such views, Dr. Briggs naturally enough teaches that the genuine text of Scripture may contain errors and he need find no difficulty in holding that it must contain errors since nothing human is free from error.

So after having pointed out a number of cases of what he regards as biblical errors, Dr. Briggs states (Defence, p. 114), "The number of such instances as I "have given above might be increased to an indefinite "extent, extending over a large part of the Old Testa- "ment and the New Testament."

Dr. Briggs teaches then that the number of errors in the Bible extending over large parts of both Testaments, is very great, and the connection clearly shows that he holds those errors to be in the genuine text of Scripture. This conclusion is supported by the evidence in the case, for he states, in The Bible, the Church and the Reason : "These human features render it improbable that the " Bible should be free from errors in its human setting. * * " How could it be otherwise if the divine revelation was "to come through such men as the ancient times were " capable of producing ? Holy Scripture does not claim "inerrancy in its human setting, and it does not in fact "possess it." (p. 108.) Further on he states : "The " Evangelist seems to have overlooked the fact that one " of these passages is from Malachi 3 : 1. Here are two "slips of memory on the part of the Evangelists, such "as any writer is liable to make." (The Bible, the Church and the Reason, p. 109.)

It will be conceded that what the Evangelists wrote belonged to the genuine text of Scripture, yet, according to Dr. Briggs, such a text is marred by errors of memory. It is clear that inspiration, as understood by Dr. Briggs, did not keep the writers of the Bible from making such errors "as other men are liable to make."

This doctrine of Dr. Briggs conflicts irreconcilably with the doctrine respecting the Holy Scripture as formulated in the Standards of our Church. There it is affirmed that the writings, not the concept merely, were inspired throughout, and that they are entirely truthful for the reason that they are inspired.

In regard to the text of the Bible, as we have it, the Confession makes mention of the marvelous fact that by God's "singular care and providence" it has been "kept "pure in all ages"; but of the genuine text it affirms that "the Old Testament in Hebrew, and the New Testament "in Greek were *immediately inspired by God.*" Of the one, as cared for by the singular providence of God it affirms relative accuracy, for the general providential care of God does keep men from all error; but of the other, as coming immediately from God, it asserts absolute accuracy, as we shall see.

The Confession states that the Scripture, in its genuine text, was committed "wholly unto writing" by the Lord

Himself, so that the entire series of canonical books constitute the one "Holy Scripture," or "the Word of God "written," having all of them been "given by inspiration "of God to be the rule of faith and life." And it further declares that "the authority of the Holy Scripture, for "which it ought to be believed and obeyed, dependeth "wholly upon God (who is truth itself) the author thereof; "and therefore it is to be received, because it is the word "of God." And this declaration is made in reference to the entire written contents of all the canonical books. The books were written by men, yet the God of truth is in such a deep sense their author, that everything written therein is to be received, believed and obeyed because it is His word. A statement so sweeping and solemn could not be made if the Scriptures were only partially inspired and were mixed with error. But that the Confession does not tolerate the idea of the presence of errors in the Holy Scripture is still further evident from the fact that the "entire perfection" of the Scripture is given as proof that it is the word of God, while the assertion is made that the Holy Spirit assures the believer of the "infallible truth and divine authority thereof." A book which contains errors cannot have the quality of "entire perfection" and the Holy Spirit could not assure us of its "infallible truth." Our Standards teach the truthfulness of the entire written Bible because it is the "very word" of the God of truth.

This is the doctrine of the Holy Scripture itself. That Scripture claims full inspiration throughout for both matter and form. If the inspiration stopped in the writer and did not extend through him to the language, then are the writings themselves not inspired and we have no Holy Scripture.

But the Bible affirms inspiration of the language as well as of the thought. "All Scripture is given by inspiration "of God," not merely the substance of truth, but the Scripture or writing itself. And it matters not whether we take the rendering of the Revised Version, "*every* "*Scripture*," or the "*all Scripture*" of the Authorized Version, for the word Scripture was used only of inspired writings, and we must take it in the obvious sense in which Paul employed it. There can be no question that he meant the entire Old Testament, all of which Timothy had known from his childhood, and recognized as entirely God-inspired.

Again the Scripture states that "God, who at sundry "times and in divers manners spake in time past unto "the fathers by the prophets, hath in these last days "spoken to us by His Son." (Heb. 1 : 1, 2.) God, then, did not speak merely to the prophets and His Son, but by them, through them, to men. He not only revealed truth to them, but controlled their language in conveying the truth. It is also evident that what God delivered by the prophets is put on an equality with what He spake "to us by His "Son." It is all His Word commended to our faith by the same divine authority. The entire Epistle to the Hebrews carries out this idea that the statements of Scripture are the sayings of God.

Peter and Paul unite in affirming that both the thought and language of the Scripture are inspired: " The prophecy " came not in the old time by the will of man; but holy " men of God spake as they were moved by the Holy " Ghost." (2 Pet. 1 : 21.)

Paul declares : " Now we have received, not the spirit " of the world, but the Spirit which is of God ; that we " might know the things which are freely given to us of " God. Which things also we speak, *not in words which* " *man's wisdom teacheth, but which the Holy Ghost* " *teacheth.*" It is then the positive teaching of the Scriptures themselves that their entire contents are inspired, both in respect to matter and form.

In the New Testament, a large number of quotations from the Old Testament are attributed to God or the Holy Spirit, even when the Old Testament text does not represent them as the speakers. Even narrative parts are in this way attributed directly to God. Mt. 1 : 22 ; 2 : 15 ; Acts 4 : 25 ; 13 : 34 ; Rom. 1 : 2 ; Acts 1 : 16 ; 28 : 25 ; Heb. 3 : 7 ; 4 : 7 ; 9 : 8 ; 10 : 15, etc.

In many places the phrases, "*it is written*" and "*the Scripture saith,*" are used as equivalent to what God says. The human authorship is not excluded. The Scripture is the joint product of a human and divine authorship ; but infinite knowledge pervades the whole Scripture, and the human authorship was so under the control of the divine that the entire Scripture bears the stamp of divine authority and is absolutely reliable.

Writers of the most advanced school of Theology admit that the authors of Scripture claim inspiration for the Holy Writings as such and not merely for the substance of truth contained in them. Richard Rothe, quoted in my argument before the Presbytery, is an example. He says of the New Testament writers : "They see nothing in the "sacred volume which is simply the word of its human "author, and not at the same time the very word of God "Himself. * * * They refer the prophetic inspiration "to the *actus scribendi* of the biblical authors."

The biblical writers also teach the entire truthfulness of the Holy Scripture for the reason that it is fully inspired. It is impossible for God to lie. Everywhere this is assumed and arguments are enforced on it as the basis. Paul supports an important Christological argument in Gal. 3 : 16, on the fact that the singular instead of the plural number of a word is used in the Old Testament. The Word of God "is true from the beginning." Christ declared to God in prayer, "Thy word is truth," and affirmed, "Till heaven and earth pass, one jot or one "tittle shall in no wise pass from the law, till all be ful- "filled." (Mt. 5 : 18). He based the fact that a certain statement had been made in the olden time on the absolute infallibility of the record of the Scripture, in which it is reported, when He said : "Is it not written in your "law, I said, Ye are gods? If he called them gods, unto "whom the word of God came, *and the Scripture cannot* "*be broken.*" According, then, to the infallible opinion of

Jesus Christ, absolute truthfulness of any sentence or statement is proved if it be a constituent part of the Scripture. Christ and the Apostles teach therefore the inerrancy of the entire written Word of God. Not an utterance did they make which can warrant the belief on our part that they thought the Holy Scriptures tainted with errors. They referred to them always as absolutely true, and taught that disbelief in them is sin.

The full inspiration and the entire truthfulness of the written Scripture is therefore a doctrine which is clearly taught in the Bible itself, and is to be received, like all other biblical doctrines, for the reason that the Holy Scripture teaches it. The doctrine is obtained from Scripture by application of the strictest principles of exegesis and by the broadest induction from all the relevant facts, statements, claims and allusions of the Scripture in reference to the subject; it is supported by the entire evidence showing the New Testament writers to be trustworthy teachers of Christian doctrine. Ultimately this evidence rests on the authority and trustworthiness of Christ Himself, for He refers us to them for His statement of doctrine, assuring us that He fitted the writers by giving them the Spirit of truth, to guide them into all truth and to teach them whatsoever He desired them to communicate.

This doctrine of the truthfulness of the Scriptures due to their full inspiration, as taught in the Bible, has been held by the Church of Jesus Christ from New Testament times until now. Dr. Briggs has misunderstood the faith of the Church on this point. All the great historic names which he has cited in favor of an errant Bible are on record in defence of the opposite doctrine. Origen, Jerome, Augustine, Calvin, Luther, Baxter and the Westminster divines have left their testimony that the whole Bible is the inerrant word of God.

It is preposterous at this late day to advance the claim that insisting on the truthfulness of the Bible is tantamount to setting up a new test of orthodoxy. The Church has never believed anything else. Especially is this true of the Presbyterian Church. It will not be possible to point to a single representative Presbyterian divine, from the Westminster period down, and especially among American Presbyterians, who has taught the doctrine of the errancy of the Holy Scriptures. All sides, parties and schools in our Church have been agreed in affirming the inerrancy of the Word of God. Green, Alexander and Hodge cordially unite with Richards and Barnes in subscribing to the statement of Dr. Henry B. Smith that inspiration extends to both thoughts and words and gives us "truth without error" in the Bible. Our Church has always held that, when we have determined the exact historic-grammatical meaning of a statement in the Bible, we have then the absolute truthfulness of that statement certified to us by the Spirit of God.

The issue before this Assembly is whether or not the Presbyterian Church will abandon the historic faith of the

Church of Jesus Christ and affix its imprimatur to the doctrine that the Bible is permeated with errors to "an "indefinite extent."

To sum up, the teaching of Dr. Briggs in this matter constitutes an offence as defined in the Book of Discipline, for several reasons :

1. It conflicts with the teaching of both Scripture and Confession.

2. If this teaching be true, the Holy Scripture cannot be an infallible rule of faith and practice, since, according to it, we cannot say the Bible is the Word of God, but only that it *contains* the Word of God. Webster defines the word infallible as " not fallible ; not capable of " erring ; entirely exempt from liability to mistake ; un- " erring ; inerrable." In plain English, therefore, a book which is pervaded by errors "to an indefinite extent," cannot be an infallible rule. It lacks the one essential of infallibility, viz., absolute truthfulness for all its contents.

3. This teaching subjects the Bible to the reason. For if the Scripture has any erroneous circumstantials, and if the entire visible text is simply human, each man must determine for himself by his own reason or conscience how much may be accepted as the Word of God. Thus the Bible can have practically no objective authority, for it will have to each man only such authority as he may be pleased to accord it.

4. It undermines the trustworthiness of the whole Bible. For if the writers of the Holy Scripture were not

enabled to make correct statements on matters of history and every-day occurrence, in which it is comparatively easy to avoid errors, most men must feel that the statements of such writers respecting the more difficult questions of faith and morals are unworthy of acceptance.

Furthermore, the doctrine of the truthfulness of the Holy Scripture is supported by the entire evidence, which commends all its other doctrines to our faith. If this evidence is not trustworthy in the case of one, it is not trustworthy in respect of any doctrine.

The final judgment of the Presbytery, therefore, on this charge, is not in accord with the law and testimony in the case, and it should be reversed.

GENUINENESS AND AUTHENTICITY.

I. In the fourth charge, the fifth of the amended series, relating to the genuineness and authenticity of the Pentateuch, Dr. Briggs is charged with denying the Mosaic authorship of the Pentateuch. He admits that both specification and charge are accurate, but denies that his teaching on this point constitutes an offence.

In his Response to the original charges and specifications, Dr. Briggs affirmed that Mosaic history, Mosaic institutions and Mosaic legislation lie at the base of all the original documents. In his Defence he asserts that a Mosaic code exists in Chapters 12 to 26 of Deuteronomy; that some Mosaic laws are contained in Chapters 20 to 23 of Exodus, and that some general principles for direction to the priesthood were given by Moses, the place of which he does not indicate. (Who Wrote the Pentateuch? pp. 23, 158, 159.)

This legislation, however, was merely rudimentary. The Pentateuch, as we have it, was a development. Deuteronomy did not attain its present form until in the times of King Josiah ; the Priest code not until the times of Ezra, and the code of holiness came " into the historic " field first in connection with Ezekiel." (Who Wrote the Pentateuch? pp. 124, 157.) Yet, because a few rudimentary laws given by Moses were the basis of the small original documents, we are told that " the " name of Moses pervades the Pentateuch as a sweet " fragrance."

Dr. Briggs maintains that such elaborate codes as those of the Pentateuch could not have originated in the early national existence of Israel. " Several generations are " necessary," he says, "to account for such a series of " modifications of the same law." (Who Wrote the Pentateuch? p. 106.) Again he states : " There " seems to be no room for them (the laws), in " the times of Moses or Joshua or Samuel or David. " The providential historical circumstances did not admit " of obedience to such elaborate codes before we find " them in the history of the times of Josiah and Ezra. " A priestly code seems to require its historical origin in " a dominant priesthood. A prophetic code seems best

" to originate in a period when prophets were in the pre-
" eminence. A theocratic code suits best a prosperous
" Kingdom and a period when elders and judges were in
" authority." (Who Wrote the Pentateuch? p. 124.)

Thus Dr. Briggs declares the great body of laws and regulations which are contained in the Pentateuch to be not merely post-Mosaic in origin, but to be post-Mosaic by several centuries, so that, naturally enough, he can call the Pentateuch an "anonymous" book, and Deuteronomy a "pseudonym." He reaches this result by using processes based on naturalism and evolution, which enable him to determine at what period in the history of Israel the literature and laws of the Pentateuch could have arisen and come to their present form. By the same processes, he is enabled to declare the laws of the Pentateuchal Codes mutually inconsistent (Who Wrote the Pentateuch? pp. 101, etc.) ; and to speak of the histories of the patriarchs, as well as some later Mosaic history, as stories derived from an unreliable tradition. (Who Wrote the Pentateuch? pp. 75, 79.)

Dr. Briggs informs us that these results are endorsed by a virtual consensus of biblical scholarship. This we deny. A large number of biblical scholars does not consent. All the leading names in the list, given by Dr. Briggs, are, in my opinion, not biblical, but anti-biblical scholars, since they deny the presence of the Supernatural in the Bible ; and the rest do not hold to a true doctrine of inspiration.

But there is in fact no consensus among the higher critics in regard to the source of the Pentateuchal documents, their number, the times of their composition, and the results reached from an investigation of them. And when further, we remember that the higher critics conduct their inquiry by principles which are purely subjective to themselves, and that the results which they have reached are not only contrary to all known historical facts, but also to the obvious teaching of the Word of God, it is preposterous to ask Christian people to put confidence in their conclusions.

Criticism of this type ignores the one great fact in the life and history of Israel, which harmonizes and verifies everything in the Pentateuch as the work of Moses; it fails to recognize the visible presence of Jehovah with the Israelites to control their entire national life, whether civil or religious.

The Holy Scripture, as shown by the texts appended to the specification of this charge, gives an account of the origin of the Pentateuch, altogether different from that given by Dr. Briggs.

The Pentateuch itself points to Moses as its author. It speaks of him as a maker of books, in which he wrote history and laws by the command of Jehovah.

A great part of the document is ascribed to the pen of Moses. Exodus, Leviticus, Numbers and Deuteronomy are credited to him, as the medium through whom God communicated them to his people, when Israel was in the Wilderness, and when Aaron and Eliezer were high-priests. The laws of all the codes appear in the Pentateuch as a unit on the background of Israel's wilderness life, not mutually conflicting, but mutually supplementary to each other.

It is conceded that Genesis has a common authorship with the other four books. So that we must accept the conclusion that the Pentateuch claims Moses as its author. Scholars like Kuenen freely admit this.

If this claim be not true, then the Pentateuch is neither genuine nor authentic, and it must be untrustworthy. If the Pentateuch's claim of Mosaic authorship be false, and the work originated piece by piece during centuries after the death of Moses, the document as it has come to us is a fraud, and no dependence can be placed upon it.

Dr. Briggs would have us believe that a book thus constructed may still be spoken of as inspired. Thus he says, on page 121 of the Defence: "If Ezra can be "shown to be responsible for our present Pentateuch, is " he not as truly a well-known biblical and inspired " man and as capable of producing a rule of faith and " practice as Moses?" Well, we should say not. For we would have to change our ideas completely, not only of Ezra, but of inspiration, to suppose that he, as an inspired man, could palm off on a credulous people, a piece of deceit and fraud as the truth of God. If Ezra could do that, then we say without hesitation that he was not as capable of producing a rule of faith and practice as Moses.

Inspiration, as understood by Dr. Briggs, is clearly not that kind of inspiration which will keep the inspired writer from making mistakes or telling lies.

But the Pentateuch is not alone in asserting that Moses is its author. The other books of the Old Testament concur in that claim. The entire body of the Mosaic legislation seems to have been in existence immediately after the death of Moses in the times of Joshua, for the people are commanded by the Lord to guide their life and conduct by it. The Book of Joshua gives evidence of the existence at that time of Mosaic regulations, which Dr. Briggs assigns to succeeding centuries; as, for instance, the command to the 3½ tribes to help their brethren in conquering the land (1:13), the rule that the Levites should have no inheritance (13:14); that Hebron should be given to Caleb (14:6); that the land should be divided by lot (14:2); that cities of refuge should be set apart; and many other regulations. The same can be said of the other preexilic books, especially of Hosea and Amos, and of some of the Davidic Psalms. They testify to the existence of the Mosaic laws as a whole by direct statements, and by revelations of the life and customs of the people in their respective periods. Indeed, all the books of the Old Testament testify in favor of the Mosaic authorship of the Pentateuch.

Wellhausen says that in the time of Chronicles, Moses

was already taken to be the author of the Pentateuch. (Encyclopedia Britannica. Pentateuch.)

It must then either have existed and been believed in as Mosaic in the time of the Kings before the Exile as the book states ; or the account must have been worked into Chronicles fictitiously by Ezra after the Exile. If the latter supposition be true, as the critics assert, then Ezra perpetrated a fraud; and he did it so well that not only did none of his learned contemporaries detect it, but neither Jews nor Christians for many centuries since then had the slightest suspicion of its being a fraud.

The Jewish people for 3,000 years have given their united testimony in behalf of the Mosaic authorship of the Pentateuch. The Christian Church has always united in that testimony. This singular unanimity of God's people on this question for so many centuries is of such great value that it cannot be sneered out of Court as mere traditionalism.

Such a consensus is not to be cast aside for the trivial reason that it does not accord with the subjective impressions of the higher critics, which impressions are those of men as fallible as the rest of us.

Prof. Thayer, of Harvard, himself a progressive critic, says that the recent discovery of the Gospel according to Peter "affords conjectural criticism some edifying lessons." He states, it "consigns the staple of books like ' Super- " natural Religion,' with their conjectural criticism on the " Gospels, 'to the Museum of biblical antiquities.'"

Conjectural criticism on the Pentateuch is likely to be consigned some day to the same museum of biblical antiquities. It has not established its claim to our confidence. For not all of those who use it attain to good results when working in fields where the rest of us can follow.

Thus Dr. Briggs has misapprehended completely the teaching of the Fathers, Reformers, and Westminster divines respecting the truthfulness of the Bible. If he has not been unable to understand them on a point which they make so clear, how can we trust ourselves to him in the more difficult task of ascertaining what kind of Hebrew history and doctrine, holy inspired men ought to have written in the Bible?

But Christ and the writers of the New Testament give unqualified testimony to the Mosaic authorship of the Pentateuch. When speaking of "*the law,*" "*the law of Moses,*" "*the book of Moses,*" and "*Moses' writings,*" they used those terms, in the accepted meanings of that time, as referring to the entire Pentateuch. They charged the Jews with sin in not believing and obeying what Moses had written. They accepted and endorsed the belief of the Jews that Moses was responsible for the whole Pentateuch.

Christ refers to Moses by name eighteen times, not as referring to a book of that name, but to him personally, as a great national leader, his own forerunner, who gave laws and commandants, and also wrote of Him.

In assigning to Moses the patriarchal institution of circumcision (John 7: 22); laws like those concerning divorce (Mark 10: 5); and the account concerning the burning bush (Mark 12: 26); he credits Moses with being the author of the Pre-Mosaic, the legislative and the historical parts of the Pentateuch. That includes the entire document. He certainly assigns the whole body of Pentateuchal laws to Moses (Luke 16: 29; Jno. 7: 19; Mt. 8: 14; 19: 8; 23: 2; John 7: 23); and never spoke of any part of the Pentateuch in a disparaging way; but by what he said and did not say, made it clear that He regarded the whole of it to be the Word of God, reliable and true in all its parts.

The higher critics feel the force of this testimony of Christ, and feel called upon to explain how it is that their statements about the Pentateuch are in conflict with the teaching of Christ. Dr. Briggs maintains that when Christ assigns a particular law or statement to Moses, it and no more belongs to the great law-giver. He minimizes the testimony of Christ on this point, thus: " When Jesus uses Moses as another name for the law or " Pentateuch, it is by no means certain that Jesus meant to " say that Moses wrote the Pentateuch." (Who Wrote the Pentateuch? p. 25.) But why should it not be certain? That is what He was understood to say, and it certainly did not behoove Him, as the great Teacher of truth, consciously to leave a false impression on the minds of His hearers.

The critics have two ways of explaining this discrepancy between their teaching and that of Jesus Christ :

1. One is, that He knew Moses not to be the author of the Pentateuch, but, since all His contemporaries believed Moses to be its author, He accommodated Himself to their belief and way of speaking.

Dr. Briggs says : "Jesus was not obliged to correct all "the errors of His contemporaries." (Who Wrote the Pentateuch? p. 29.) Well, if that is true, then it is a great pity that Dr. Briggs did not follow so good an example so as not to disturb the peace of a great Church.

But this explanation cannot be accepted. It would not be creditable to Christ, especially from Dr. Briggs' point of view. For Dr. Briggs holds the Mosaic authorship of the Pentateuch to be one of the barriers set up by theologians to deprive men of the Bible, and states that we shall not be able to see "the magnificent unity of the whole " Bible, to capture all its sacred treasures and to enjoy all " its heavenly glories," until this mischievous error is removed from the face of the earth by the destructive process of the higher critics. If Christ knew that the belief in the Mosaic authorship of the Pentateuch would prevent the Bible from being understood and would rob people of its treasures and heavenly glories, then should He not have exploded that error at once? We can believe nothing less of Him.

2. The other and more commonly adopted view, is

that Christ did not know the real author of the Pentateuch, and so fell into the common error, with His contemporaries, of believing and teaching that Moses was its author. He never enjoyed the advantage of going to Oxford or to Germany to acquire a scientific and conjectural theory for searching out the truth of the Bible. He did not know the Scriptures, and the higher critics do. Dr. Briggs speaks approvingly of this theory, as follows: "If we "should say Jesus did not know whether Moses wrote "the Pentateuch or not, we would not go beyond His own "saying that He knew not the time of His own advent. "Those who understand the doctrine of the humiliation "of Christ and the incarnation of Christ, find no more "difficulty in supposing that Jesus did not know the "author of the Pentateuch than that He did not know "the day of His own advent." (Who Wrote the Pentateuch? pp. 28, 29.) Conscious ignorance of that distant future day is one thing; but the unconscious teaching of error is quite another. The one would not detract from the truthful testimony of Christ, the other would. He made no disclaimer of knowledge on this point, but claimed and made the impression that He did know all about the Pentateuch and its author. He is the truth. He came into the world to bear witness to the truth, and positively asserted that He always spoke the truth. He declared to the Jews: " He that sent me is true; and I speak to the " world those things which I have heard of Him." Could He affirm in a more solemn way the entire truthfulness of all that He said?

The New Testament gives a large amount of evidence that, as sinlessly perfect and as filled with the Holy Spirit, the knowledge of Christ was universal. And to affirm that when He declared Moses to be the author of the Pentateuch, He erred through ignorance, is a reflection upon His mental as well as upon His moral character, which discredits the New Testament representation of Him as in all respects perfect.

This teaching of Dr. Briggs in regard to the non-Mosaic authorship of the Pentateuch is in vital conflict with the teaching of the whole Bible. It necessarily involves the positions that the Pentateuch, as we have it, is not only erroneous, but also fraudulent; that the writers of the other Old Testament books either knowingly connived at the fraud, or unintentionally perpetuated it; and that the testimony of Christ and the writers of the New Testament must be discredited.

This teaching is far more dangerous than affirming the Scripture to be in error in matter of minor importance; it tends to a total destruction of faith in the Bible. It has done that already for many. It is entirely at variance with the confessional doctrine of the Holy Scripture.

II. The question concerning the book of Isaiah involves the same principles as does that concerning the authorship of the Pentateuch.

The matter is formulated in the fifth charge, or the sixth of the amended form, in which Dr. Briggs is charged " with teaching that Isaiah is not the author of half the "book that bears his name." He admits this to be his teaching but denies that it is an offence.

In his Defence, he points out the 26 Chapters which he allots to Isaiah, and the 39 which he takes from him, although bearing his name.

He is led to this result, not by historic facts, but, as shown in his Defence (pp. 132–146), by subjective impressions whereby he finds himself able to determine the style in which a man like Isaiah ought to have written, what theological ideas it was possible for him to express, and from what historical situation it was possible for him to utter predictive prophecies. The last, however, is the decisive test. It is with the critics a canon of infallible authority that a prophet of God can predict future events only from his own historical point of view, and to the needs of the people of his age. Chapter 13 to 14 : 23 is taken from Isaiah for the reason that that section cannot stand this test of their canon of criticism. The style and theological ideas are correct enough, but it contains a predictive prophecy which Isaiah could not have given from his own historical situation, and the passage can therefore not be assigned to him. But the Scripture credits Isaiah with it. It begins with the statement : " The burden of Babylon, which Isaiah the son of Amos " did see." (Isa. 13 : 1.) The explanation by which Dr. Briggs seeks to nullify this distinct affirmation of the Bible is weak, far-fetched and entirely unsatisfactory. In the same way the entire book could be taken from Isaiah.

But it shows that any statement of the Bible, which comes in conflict with the theory of higher criticism, must be discredited; and thus we see here again, as in the case of the Pentateuch, that this criticism undermines the trustworthiness of a biblical writing by denying its claim about itself. If Isaiah did not write Chapter 13 to 14 : 23, then that section is neither genuine nor authentic. It makes a false claim. It pretends to be what it is not, and so is wholly unworthy of confidence.

The assumption of the critics by which this result is reached also destroys the evidential value of prophecy. For, if a prophet can only speak from his own historical point of view and to the needs of his own times, then predictive prophecy requires no more divine help than that long foresight by the help of which wise statesmen have often been able to point out needed lessons for the future from the drift of present events. Here again we see the damaging nature of the theory of higher criticism. It aims to explain supernatural phenomena in biblical history and prophecy on merely naturalistic principles.

But this division of Isaiah is in direct conflict with the statements of Christ and the writers of the New Testament. They assign quotations from all parts of the book to him, as a person. With reference to the disputed parts it is said : " For Esaias saith, Lord, who hath believed our " report?" But Esaias is very bold, "I was found of " them that sought me not; I was made manifest unto " them that asked not after me. These things said " Esaias, when he saw His glory and spake of Him."

It is clear that, with all his contemporaries, Christ believes Isaiah to be the author of the entire book which bears his name, as He held Moses to be the author of the Pentateuch; and it must destroy confidence in Him as the great Teacher of the New Testament dispensation, if He was so ignorant respecting the character and origin of the Old Testament, which He pretended to know thoroughly, which He came to fulfill, and on which He claimed to found the doctrines of the Gospel. This teaching must bring discredit on Christ as the Teacher.

These declarations of Dr. Briggs in reference to the authorship of the Pentateuch and of Isaiah, but especially of the former, create distrust of the entire Bible. His teaching necessarily involves that. He says: "Higher " criticism comes into conflict with the authority of " Scripture when it finds that its statements are not au- " thoritative and its revelations are not credible." (Biblical Study, p. 243.)

Dr. Briggs here admits that higher criticism does come into conflict with the authority of Scripture to the extent of finding some of its statements not authoritative and some of its revelations not credible. And how is it possible to keep the whole Bible from being involved in distrust if higher criticism finds its statements not authoritative and its revelations not credible?

This teaching of Dr. Briggs is contrary also to our Confessional statements. " The consent of all the parts," can bear no testimony to the entire perfection of such a Bible as the higher criticism gives us. In fact, all the parts dissent as we have seen, and Dr. Briggs' position comes to this, that the Bible is so full of conflicting and mutually inconsistent elements, that it requires to be cut to pieces by the higher criticism and reconstructed on a different basis before the different parts will consent harmoniously.

This criticism also contravenes that statement of our Confession which says : " The infallible rule of interpreta-" tion of Scriptures is Scripture itself," for it does not interpret Scripture by "other places of Scripture which " speak more plainly," but by the evolutionary principles of the conjectural theory. If we allow Scripture to interpret itself we find confirmed the authorship of the Pentateuch and Isaiah by Moses and Isaiah respectively.

But our Standards assert that the entire written Bible is to be believed, received and obeyed, for the reason that it is the word of God, the God of truth being the author thereof, and that the Christian shows his faith by believing " to be true, whatsoever is revealed in the word, for the " authority of God Himself speaking therein."

It is impossible to require such faith in a Scripture which is not only erroneous but also tainted with fraud.

The verdict of acquittal by the inferior judicatory on these two charges is therefore contrary to the law and evidence in this case and should not be allowed to stand as the judgment of our Church.

The rejected charges may be considered at this point. We claim that the inferior judicatory erred in ordering these two charges to be stricken out. It was an error for the reason that they allege valid offences, as we will now show.

1. PREDICTIVE PROPHECY.

In the fourth of the amended charges, Dr. Briggs is charged "with teaching that many of the Old Testament " predictions have been reversed by history, and that the " great body of Messianic prediction cannot be fulfilled."

He complains that he is misquoted, and that invalid inferences are drawn from his statement, but the complaint is not well founded. The entire statement is given in the specification, and it sustains the charge. The qualifying clause concerning "the details of predictive prophecy of " the Old Testament" in no wise modifies the statement that "many of these predictions have been reversed by " history."

The statement was originally made by Kuenen, and when Dr. Briggs adopted it as his own, he failed to state that he did not use it with Kuenen's meaning. Kuenen sustained his position by denial of the reality of predictive prophecy, the inspiration of the prophet and the presence of the supernatural in the Bible. He says: " It is the " common conviction of all the writers of the New Testa- " ment that the Old Testament is inspired of God, and is " thus invested with divine authority. The remark, made

" as it were in passing, in a passage from the fourth Gos-
" pel, that the Scripture cannot be broken, is assented
" to by all the writers, without distinction. In accordance
" with this they ascribe divine fore-knowledge to the
" Israelitish prophets. And far indeed from limiting this
" fore-knowledge to generalities, and thus depriving it of
" all its importance, they refer us repeatedly to the
" agreement between specific prophetical utterances and
" single historical facts, and have no hesitation in declar-
" ing their conviction, both that the prophet spoke of
" these specific facts, and that they, under God's direction,
" occurred in order that the word of the prophet might be
" fulfilled. * * * The New Testament judgment
" concerning the origin and nature of the prophetical ex-
" pectations, and concerning their relation to historical
" reality, may be regarded as *diametrically opposed to
" ours.*" (Kuenen, Prophets and Prophecy in Israel,
pp. 448, 449.)

Kuenen here acknowledges that all the New Testament writers without distinction believed in the fulfillment of the details of predictive prophecy and that he aimed to disprove the details, the *specific prophetical utterances and single historical facts*, for the purpose of destroying the value of the prophecy itself.

It must be conceded that whenever predictive prophecy may become an actual occurrence, there must be a sufficient number of details to make that event possible; and hence, to deny details is to deny the actual occurrence of the event predicted.

But even if admitting that the qualifying clause covers the last sentence, the case is not changed. Dr. Briggs categorically asserts all that is charged against him, for he says, that "the great body of the Messianic prediction "has not only never been fulfilled, but cannot now be "fulfilled"; and also that "the prediction of Jonah is not "the only unfulfilled prediction in the Old Testament." These utterances of Dr. Briggs have caused alarm and justly. The leaders of the higher criticism school are, for the most part, avowedly hostile to that supernatural element in Scripture which predictive prophecy calls for; consistently, therefore, they deny the existence of such prophecy, and hold that the prophets of Scripture were nothing more than men of extraordinary genius and illumination, whose utterances concerning the future were based on a far-seeing foresight of the providential drift of things in their historical situation.

The Scripture contains a large number of predictions. Some of them have been fulfilled, while others remain thus far unfulfilled. It is possible that both the matter and form of some predictive prophecies have been misunderstood, and thus misinterpreted, but it is impossible to misunderstand the Scripture position, that all which the Lord has spoken by the mouth of His holy prophets is to be fulfilled. Joshua states the biblical point of view in these words : "Ye know in your hearts and in all " your souls, that not one thing hath failed of all the good " things which the Lord your God spake concerning "you; all are come to pass unto you, and not one thing "hath failed thereof." How different this from Dr. Briggs' position.

The New Testament writers repeatedly assert that the Scriptures contain predictive prophecy, take for granted that every part of it will be fulfilled, and give detailed instances where either it has come to pass or will yet surely take place. They thus refer to the ministry of John; the fact that Christ was born of a virgin, and at Bethlehem, and resided at Nazareth; that He rode on an ass into Jerusalem; was forsaken by His disciples; was sold for thirty pieces of silver, and that lots were cast for His vesture. (Isa. 40:3, and Mt. 3:3; Isa. 7:14, and Mt. 1:23, 24; Micah 5:2, and Mt. 2:5, 6; Mt. 2:23; Zech. 9:9, and Mt. 21:4, 5; Zech. 11:12, 13, and Mt. 27:9; Zech. 13:7, and Mt. 26:31; Ps. 22:18, and Mt. 27:33.) Similarly, allusion is made to the abomination of desolation spoken by Daniel the prophet as certain to be fulfilled. (Dan. 9:27, and Mt. 24:15.) Here the fulfillment of Old Testament predictions are cited to the minutest detail.

The language of Christ is still more emphatic. He came not to destroy, but to fulfill the law and the prophets, and most solemnly affirmed that rather would heaven and earth pass away than that one jot or one tittle of them should remain unfulfilled. (Matt. 5:17, 18.) He claimed the fulfillment in Himself of what the Spirit foretold by the mouth of David in Psalm cx., and told His disciples, after the resurrection : "That all things must "be fulfilled, which were written in the law of Moses, "and in the prophets, and in the Psalms, concerning me." (Luke 24 : 44.) Our Lord here affirms that there is a *divine necessity* that, not merely prophecy in general, but *all things* concerning Him must be fulfilled ; "All things" must surely include Messianic predictions. Much more might be cited to the same effect, but this is sufficient.

If, in view of all this, the statements of Dr. Briggs are to be considered as correct, that "many predictions of "the Old Testament have been reversed by history"; and that "the great body of the Messianic prediction has "not only never been fulfilled, but cannot now be ful-"filled," then the plain utterances of Scripture coming ostensibly from the Lord by the mouth of His servants the prophets, together with the declarations of Christ concerning prophecy in general, and Messianic prophecy in particular, are contradicted. It is the Bible and Christ against Dr. Briggs. The attributes of God, pointed out in the charge, are here involved.

These statements of Dr. Briggs being in conflict with the declarations of Scripture and the citations from the Standards should be condemned by this Court and be disavowed by him.

2. REDEMPTION AFTER DEATH.

The other rejected charge is the 7th of the amended form, in which Dr. Briggs is charged "with teaching that

" the processes of redemption extend to the world to
" come in the case of many who die in sin."

It is claimed that he disavowed this doctrine by categorically answering a question propounded to him in private by directors of Union Seminary. But such a categorical answer under such circumstances proves nothing and disavows nothing ; the more so, because since that time Dr. Briggs has affirmed his adherence to everything which he has stated in the Inaugural both as to "matter " and form."

We therefore ask this Venerable Body to consider whether the facts pointed out in the specification do not, in the light of the evidence submitted, prove the charge.

He accuses Protestants of the fault of not extending the process of redemption to the vast periods of time in the middle state between death and the resurrection. (Inaugural, p. 53.)

" The processes of redemption," he states, "ever keep " the race in mind. The Bible tells us of a race origin, a " race ideal, a race Redeemer and a race redemption." (Inaugural, p. 5o.)

According to Dr. Briggs, redemption is not limited by election. He says, "The Bible does not teach universal " salvation, but it does teach the salvation of the world, of " the race of man, and that cannot be accomplished by " the selection of a limited number of individuals from the

" mass. * * * The salvation of the world can only mean the world as a whole, compared with which the unredeemed will be so few and insignificant and evidently beyond the reach of redemption by their own act of rejecting it and hardening themselves against it, and by descending into such depths of demoniacal depravity in the middle state, that they will vanish from the sight of the redeemed as altogether and irredeemably evil and never more disturb the harmonies of the saints." (Inaugural, pp. 55, 56.)

If Dr. Briggs does not teach in this passage that some men who die impenitent might have been redeemed in the middle state but for their " descending into such depths of " demoniacal depravity in the middle state," then certainly when he tried to clothe his concept with language, he puts its clothes on upside down. The unmistakable drift of the entire passage is that the redemption of the world, of the race of man, is largely to be accomplished by means of the opportunities which will be given them in the middle state.

And this agrees with what Dr. Briggs has stated concerning "a judgment immediately after death." (Inaugural, p. 54.) He calls it a " hurtful unchristian error," a " bugbear," which " makes death a terror to the best of men." This points unmistakably to another chance after death, since the issues of life are not to be regarded as final at death. It is a hurtful error which he renounces.

In line with this, Dr. Briggs terms the statements of

Dr. Dorner concerning the possibility of repentance in the next world, "excellent thoughts." (Whither, p. 211.) His remarks about the unpardonable sin cited in the specification, point in the same direction. He says of some classes of people that not until they reach the middle state "are they justified, for there can be no justifi-
" cation without faith for them any more than for others.
" The intermediate state is for them a *state* of *blessed pos-*
" *sibilities* of redemption." (Magazine of Christian Literature, Dec., 1889, p. 110.) "We are opening our
" minds," he says, " to see that the Redeemer's work upon
" the cross was the beginning of a larger work in the
" realm of the dead, and from His heavenly throne
" whence the exalted Saviour is drawing all men to
" Himself." (Andover Review, vol. 13, p. 59.) And again, "If life in this world is brief, and life in the middle
" state is long, we must rise to the conception of the love
" of God as accomplishing even greater works of redemp-
" tion in the middle state than in this world." (Magazine of Christian Literature, Dec., 1889, p. 106.)

These are dangerous utterances, all the more so because they come from a professor of a prominent Theological Seminary. They are calculated to make men careless about their eternal welfare and lead them to presume on the mercy of God. The Scriptures and the Standards of our Church, as shown by the citations annexed to this charge, confine the work of redemption to this life under the dispensation of the Gospel. Both

Scripture and Standards agree in declaring that "*now* is " the accepted time, behold *now* is the day of salvation "; that "it is appointed unto men once to die, but *after this* "*judgment*," and that there is an impassable "gulf fixed " immediately after death between the righteous and the wicked. (2 Cor. 6 : 2 ; Heb. 9 : 27 ; Luke 16 : 26.)

This teaching of Dr. Briggs should be condemned by this Court, and be retracted by him.

PROGRESSIVE SANCTIFICATION AFTER DEATH.

The last or 8th charge of the amended form refers to the subject of Progressive Sanctification after death, in which Dr. Briggs is charged "with teaching that Sancti- " fication is not complete at death."

He admits the charge, but denies that it constitutes an offence, alleging not only that the doctrine is not contrary to the Scripture and Standards, but also that it is the very doctrine taught in them.

Sanctification has for its aim, the removal of sin from the nature of believers with all its effects. "Sanctifica- " tion is a work of God's free grace, whereby we are " renewed in the whole man after the image of God, and " are enabled more and more to die unto sin and live " unto righteousness." And when we are completely dead to sin, when it has been entirely exterminated from the soul, then sanctification has completed its work, and the believer, having been renewed in the whole man after the image of God, will live unto righteousness, and be perfectly holy. He will be no longer in need of either sanctification or redemption.

Adam, before he sinned, as created in the image of God, was perfectly holy, and did not need to have any part of the process of redemption applied to him. It was possible for him to advance in the breadth and intensity of holy life to all eternity, but such an onward growth in holy life cannot be called a process of sanctification.

Christ was perfectly holy when He was born. After that He grew, as the God-man, into a larger and fuller life, but He was at no time more holy or morally perfect than on the day of His birth. In the same way the believer will, when at death he has been made perfect in holiness, advance along all the lines of holy life forever. That is not the question at issue.

That Dr. Briggs uses the term sanctification in the sense of eliminating sin from the soul of believers is plain from the language of the Inaugural. In order to maintain his doctrine of progressive sanctification after death, he finds it necessary to attack the Protestant doctrine, which limits the process of redemption to this world, and refuses to extend it to the vast periods of the world beyond the grave. (Inaugural, pp. 53, 54.) The Protestant doctrine, according to which the believer is made perfectly holy at death, stands in the way of Dr. Briggs' doctrine.

He affirms that progressive sanctification after death is necessary, "in order that the work of redemption may be "complete." (Inaugural, p. 54.)

He terms the transformation of the saint, in the dying hour, a magical illusion, which should be banished from the world and renounced as a hurtful unchristian error. (Inaugural, p. 54.) He maintains that believers, after death, " are still the same persons, with all the gifts and graces, " and also the same habits of mind, disposition and temper, " which they had when they left the world. Death de-" stroys the body. It does not change the moral and " religious nature of man." ("Evil Habits," in Magazine of Christian Literature.) Sin, therefore, remains still in the higher nature of man, and it is the office of progressive sanctification after death to overcome sin in that nature. (Inaugural, 2d ed., p. 108.)

"The intermediate state," he says, "is for all believers, " without exception, a state for their sanctification. They " are there trained in the School of Christ, and are pre-" pared for the Christian perfection which they must " attain ere the judgment day." (Magazine of Christian Literature, Dec., 1889, p. 112.) He assures us that believers are, in the middle state, "delivered from all " temptations such as spring from without, from the world " and the devil. They are encircled with influences for " good such as they never enjoyed before." (Inaugural, p. 107.) Therefore, "we may justly hold," he states, "that " the evil which still lingers in the higher moral nature of

" believers will be suppressed and modified with an energy
" of repentance, humiliation, confession and determination
" that will be more powerful than ever before, because it
" will be stimulated by the presence of Christ and His
" saints." (Magazine of Christian Lit., Dec., 1889, p. 114.)

These statements show that, in the view of Dr. Briggs, believers do not enter the next world free from sin. If they were without sin, then certainly there could be no place for confession, repentance and humiliation for sin, and endeavors to suppress it.

His reference to Abraham, in illustration of the doctrine, confirms this view. In his earthly life, Dr. Briggs tells us, the old patriarch lived on a plane of moral advancement so low, that, were he living now, we could not receive him into our families; nay, we might be obliged even to imprison him lest he should defile the community by his example. But when he "went into
" the abode of the dead, he held his pre-eminence among
" the departed. He made up for his defects in this life by
" advancing in the school of sanctification there open to
" him." (Inaugural, pp. 56, 57.) Abraham was freed from sin and moral imperfection in the intermediate state.

This is still further confirmed by the naturalistic principle of evolution which, in the opinion of Dr. Briggs, necessitates the extension of the process of sanctification into the next world. He states : " It is unpsychological
" and unethical to suppose that the character of a disem-
" bodied spirit will all be changed in the moment of
" death." (Inaugural, pp. 107, 108.)

In his Defence, he maintains the same position. He states that the best of Christians leave this world weak and imperfect (Defence, p. 177); that they are still impure, in need of Christ as their Priest, and of cleansing by His blood (Defence, pp. 166-8); and that they are morally imperfect in nature and conduct. (Defence, pp. 166, 169, 170, 172, 173, 175.) Those who are impure and morally defective in character and life are sinful; for sin does not consist merely of positive transgressions, but any want of conformity to the law of God is sin. He does in fact affirm that not until the judgment day shall believers be fully and forever freed from all sin (Defence, p. 156); and therefore when he says, "I see believers enter "the middle state still imperfect, but they are cleansed "by the blood of Christ from all sin, and are therefore "sinless" (Defence, p. 177), he must in consistency be understood to mean that sin is not imputed to them, as it is not to believers in this world. This accords perfectly with his statement on pp. 158, 159 of Defence, where he says: "I do not doubt that the fountain which flows "from the Redeemer's side cleanseth from all sin in the "hour of death *as in any hour of life*, when the sinner "opens his heart in faith and repentance to the saving "love of Jesus." All believers are thus imputatively sinless.

The whole contention of Dr. Briggs, in his Defence, is that the Bible and the Standards favor the view that the work of making believers pure, morally perfect and holy, is accomplished by means of progressive sanctification after death. In discussing one of the rejected charges, it was shown that, according to his teaching, the exercise of faith and the act of justification may possibly take place after death ; so that, as sin cannot be removed before justification nor before the exercise of faith and repentance, it is clear that believers can enter the next world sinful and morally imperfect.

This doctrine is contrary to the teaching of the Holy Scriptures. The two passages of Scripture appended to this charge, show in the one case that the spirits of just men in the state between death and the resurrection are perfect; and in the other, that the transformation of the saints, who shall be on the earth when Christ shall come again, from their imperfect and sinful condition in this life to perfect holiness shall take place instantly, "in the " twinkling of an eye." It is easily possible for the Spirit of God to work the same change in the souls of all believers instantly at their death, in spite of any natural principle of psychology or ethics.

But the Bible teaches in many other places that believers enter immediately after death into a state of perfect holiness. It represents them there as the "in-" heritors of the promises," as arrayed in white robes with palms in their hands, as having entered into the perfect rest of God and exchanged the mortal for the immortal. It speaks of them as housed in heaven, where only the undefiled can go, and as having gone to be forever with Christ, whom only the holy shall see. The

Bible gives no intimation of any process of redemption or sanctification in the next world.

The Standards of our Church, too, are as silent as the Bible respecting any Gospel work, processes of redemption or ministrations of the Spirit in the life after death. They confine redemption in all its processes to this life.

The Confession states that "the souls of the righteous" immediately after death, "being then made perfect in "holiness, are received into the highest heaven"; the Larger Catechism tells us, "The Communion in glory "with Christ which the members of the invisible church "enjoy immediately after death, is in that their souls are "then made perfect in holiness, and received into the "highest heavens, where they behold the face of God in "light and glory," and the Shorter Catechism asserts, "The souls of believers are at their death made perfect "in holiness and do immediately pass into glory"; by no violence can such language be made consistent with the doctrine of progressive sanctification after death; it is impossible to conceive that the authors of our Standards could have intended to teach any such doctrine, for they held the opposing doctrine, which they have expressed so well in the statements quoted. They say in L. C., 85, that the righteous "even in death are delivered from the "sting and curse of it; so that although they die, yet it "is out of God's love, to *free them perfectly from sin and* "*misery*."

This doctrine of Dr. Briggs then is an offence according to the Book of Discipline for the following three reasons :

1. The doctrine is contrary to the Bible and the Standards. It is injected into them at the behest of a naturalistic principle of psychology and ethics according to which the instant change of a saint of God at death to perfect holiness by the divine Spirit is declared to be a magical illusion.

2. It is separated from the Roman Catholic doctrine of purgatory by so frail a barrier that it will easily pass into it.

3. It will lead to graver departures from the faith. The doctrine of redemption after death is advocated at present principally in the interest of the doctrine of Second Probation, Dr. Briggs entertains the largest hopes in respect to the possibilities of redemption in the middle state.

He says, in Whither, p. 221 : "The question which " we have to determine as Calvinists is—whether the " divine act of regeneration may take place in the middle " state or not."

Certainly, if we once admit that one of the processes of redemption takes place in the middle state, we will be compelled, ere long, in logical consistency, to affirm that all the processes of redemption may be carried on there.

The verdict of acquittal, therefore, on this charge, is

contrary to the evidence and to Presbyterian doctrine, and should be reversed.

We have shown that the Presbytery of New York has rendered a decision contrary to the law and evidence in giving its verdict of acquittal in this case. As not in accord with true Presbyterian doctrine, the verdict should be reversed and another should be formulated in harmony with our doctrines and the evidence in this case.

The Presbytery, while not approving the erroneous views of Dr. Briggs, suggests that they should be tolerated in the interest of scholarship and liberty.

The Presbyterian Church favors the best scholarship and insists that its ministers shall be thoroughly educated. It welcomes the deepest research, but it requires also a reverent handling of the Word of God. The type of higher criticism which is before us has no monopoly of scholarship. Scholars who in knowledge and skill are at least easily the peers of those who claim to be the higher critics dispute their claims. Since the methods of higher criticism are uncertain and its results so far not large, it becomes its apostles to be modest. They have, however, laid themselves open to suspicion by inordinate conceit and utter recklessness.

The Presbyterian Church is the friend of liberty. It has always been foremost in efforts to promote religious, civil, social and individual freedom. It demands the freest and fullest honest investigation of all the facts and phenomena of the Bible.

But as in all other relations and institutions, divine and human, liberty in our Church or in any other Church must be regulated liberty. It has its limitations. The freedom of one's house does not mean the right to pull out its foundation. And liberty in a denomination cannot mean the right to destroy its denominational life and doctrines.

No one restrains the liberty of Dr. Briggs. He is as free to go as he was to come. On his own responsibility he can proclaim his theological and critical views from the house-tops. The whole world will give him a hearing. But he may not exercise this liberty in the denomination, at the expense of that of his brethren. They have an equal right with him to the enjoyment of liberty.

The Presbyterian Church is also entitled to her share of the blessings of liberty. If she feels in conscience bound to maintain her unbroken testimony for doctrines which were taught by Christ and the Apostles, and which have been held by the Church of Christ from New Testament times to the present, then in God's name, the liberty to do this should be freely accorded to her. No man may wrench from her hand her imprimatur and affix it to doctrines which are abhorrent to her membership and destructive of her denominational tenets, genius and life.

At three different times the General Assembly has warned the churches against the baneful influence of that kind of biblical criticism, which Dr. Briggs champions, as tending to undermine faith in the Holy Scripture; and enjoined the Presbyteries to see to it that our students for the ministry were not subjected to this criticism during their theological training. The Church has been very patient in this matter, and Dr. Briggs, not having heeded the warning of the Assembly, has now no right to complain that his liberty is unduly interfered with, if they refuse longer to be responsible for the destructive opinions which he propagates.

Greater things than mere liberty and scholarship are involved in this issue. Truth, honor and fidelity to great trusts committed claim our attention. We are in a crisis. Not only are great doctrines of our faith emasculated; the Bible itself is in peril. It is assailed from unusual quarters. It is wounded in the house of its friends. Our people are profoundly stirred. They are greatly troubled, and look to this Assembly for relief.

A great responsibility rests on you to-day, Mr. Moderator and Brethren. It is for you to decide whether our great Church shall continue her faith in the sole supremacy of the Holy Scriptures as the source of authority in religion for salvation and certainty; or admit the Church and the Reason to an equality with the Scriptures in this matter; whether we will continue our testimony for the absolute truthfulness and trustworthiness of the Word of God, or tolerate the propagation of the doctrine of an errant Scripture; whether we will still affirm the plenary inspiration of the Holy Scripture to the extent of entire truthfulness, or so lower the doctrine of inspiration as will permit us to say that an inspired writer in penning the Bible not only committed errors but stated what he knew to be false, and whether we shall still teach that the work of redemption is confined to this life, or that it is to be extended to the vast periods of time which intervene between death and the resurrection.

These questions have hitherto not been relegated in the Presbyterian Church to the domain of liberty of opinion. They have been regarded as of such vital importance that those who have assumed the vow to which Presbyterian Ministers subscribe might not differ in respect to them.

The Presbytery of New York concedes that "grave " issues" are involved. Truly, truly. Tolerate the errors, say the Presbytery, but be careful not to approve them. Strange delusion. Now, our people not only, but Christian people generally, are anxiously waiting to hear what answer this great Assembly will give to these questions. And the opportunity is offered to this Venerable Body to allay anxiety, to restore confidence and to re-establish peace, by wise counsels, by bearing clear testimony for the truth of God, by speaking with no uncertain sound, by contending "earnestly for the faith " which was once for all delivered unto the saints," and by firmly holding " fast the form of sound words."

IX.

MR. MCCOOK'S CLOSING ARGUMENT IN REPLY TO DR. BRIGGS, ON THE MERITS OF THE APPEAL.

MODERATOR, FATHERS AND BRETHREN:
In the printed document before you, prepared by the Prosecuting Committee, for the information of the Court, at page 44 (page 50 of this volume), you will find the Amended Charges and Specifications upon which the Appellee was tried in the lower Judicatory.

THE AMENDED CHARGES AND SPECIFICATIONS.

Section 15 of the Book of Discipline provides: "The charge shall set forth the alleged offence; and "the specifications shall set forth the facts relied upon "to sustain the charge." You will notice that in drafting each charge, the Committee has carefully followed the provisions of the book.

Section 15, further provides that "Each specification "shall declare, as far as possible, the time, place, and "circumstances." Each one of the specifications begins with a recital of the time, place and circumstances under which the Inaugural Address was delivered. Following, and as a part of each of the specifications, you will find extracts from the Inaugural Address delivered by the Appellee, at the time and place charged. Following these extracts are the quotations from the Scriptures, the Confession of Faith and Catechisms, to which the words of the Inaugural Address set out in the Specifications are directly opposed.

Under the provisions of the Book of Discipline, a charge can be sustained, only, by first sustaining the specifications presented to support the charge. Section 23 of the Book of Discipline, provides that "the judi-"catory shall proceed to vote on each specification and "on each charge separately."

The Prosecuting Committee, in preparing the amended Charges and Specifications, endeavored to follow, in so far as they properly might, every suggestion made by Dr. Briggs in his Response to the original Charges and Specifications. And yet the Committee has been accused by the Appellee of inconsistency, because they complied with some of the Appellee's suggestions in this behalf. For the sake of clearness and to define the issue to the narrowest limit, we tried to make the amended Charges and Specifications so plain, that there could be no question as to what was charged and what the Prosecuting Committee intended to prove.

To avoid issues of fact, the substance of each Specification was expressed in the words of the Appellee. Dr. Briggs was compelled to admit before the lower Court, as he has admitted before this Assembly, that the Specifications set forth by the Committee were expressed in the very language of the Inaugural Address.

In this way, questions of fact were for the most part eliminated from the case. I regret, however, that at a later stage of the proceedings, in his argument before this Court, when referring to the Specifications, the Appellee asserts: "Yes, these are my words. I admit "that, but I do not admit the facts stated therein."

In the ordinary affairs of life, such a statement would be looked upon as a quibble, I will not use a stronger word, but I do most earnestly object to a Presbyterian Minister and Professor of Theology delivering an elaborate Inaugural Address, and then, when challenged before the Courts of the Church, answering: "Yes, these are my words. I admit that, but I do not "admit the facts stated therein."

I shall give you but one other illustration of the style of defence resorted to in his argument, by the Appellee. It is in connection with Charge VIII., which you will find on page 69 of the printed document (page 75 of this volume). There Dr. Briggs is charged with teaching "that Sanctification is not complete at death." The Charge alleges that this is contrary to the doctrine of Holy Scripture and the Standards of the Church, "that the souls of believers are at their death *at* "*once* made perfect in holiness." Notice that the Charge says "at once."

On page 72 of the printed document (page 78 of this volume) will be found the citations from the Standards upon which the Prosecuting Committee relied to sustain its position.

The Appellee holds that there is nothing in the Standards to justify such a claim. You have heard his argument. In addition to the strong and explicit statement of Section I., Chapter XXXII. of the Confession of Faith, there quoted, where the word *immediately* is used, the answer to Question 86 of the Larger Catechism, as cited, contains these words: "The Com-" munion in glory with Christ, which the members of " the invisible Church enjoy *immediately* after death." "Immediately," according to Dr. Briggs, does not mean "at once." In addition to the quotations from the Confession of Faith and the Larger Catechism, the Prosecuting Committee also cited the answer to Question 37 in the Shorter Catechism: "The souls of " believers are at their death made perfect in holiness, " and do *immediately* pass into glory."

It is difficult for men who are familiar with, and accept in sincerity the Confession of Faith and Catechisms of the Westminster Standards, to discover any basis for such a claim as that made by Dr. Briggs in this matter. If the Standards of the Presbyterian Church are ambiguous at this important point, they undoubtedly need revision.

I will pass from the question of the regularity and sufficiency, both as to form and legal effect, of the amended Charges and Specifications upon which the Appellee was arraigned in the Court below, and to which he has made such extended reference in his argument before this Court, by simply assuring you that these Charges and Specifications, every one of them, were drawn in the strictest compliance with the provisions of the Constitution of the Presbyterian Church, which you have all vowed to sustain. The Charges are clear; the words of the Specifications, as alleged, are admitted by the Appellee to be true; the proofs cited from the Scriptures and the Standards, placed beside the specifications, show that the Appellee's words in the Inaugural Address are contrary to the Scriptures and the Standards of the Presbyterian Church, and therefore each of the amended Charges and Specifications should have been sustained by the Presbytery.

THE DOCTRINES OF THE CHARGES ARE ESSENTIAL.

A great deal has been said by the Appellee about the doctrines, with which the Charges are concerned, not being essential. The fact that any doctrine is formulated and set forth in the Standards of the Presbyterian Church, is presumptive evidence that such doctrine is essential, when taken in connection with judicial proceedings conducted under our Book of Discipline. When a prosecution like this has been begun, in compliance with its Constitution, the Presbyterian Church is not required to prove that its Standards are right. The burden of proof is upon the accused, and he must show that his teaching is within the Standards. The fact that the doctrine is in the Standards, makes it incumbent upon one who has taken the ordination vow, to show that his views, when thus challenged, are in harmony with or not contrary to the doctrines of the Standards.

THIS IS NOT A CRIMINAL PROCEEDING.

I will pause to illustrate this for a moment. It has been claimed by the Appellee and his supporters, that this is in the nature of a criminal proceeding. I do not like, and have always resisted that suggestion. It is, I insist, rather a question of contract, of whether the Appellee's ordination vow has been complied with. I have never used this illustration before, and would not do so now, if it had not been so frequently urged by the other side in this case.

Suppose, when a prisoner is brought into a criminal court, the judge being on the bench, the prosecuting officer presents the proof to sustain the charge, and the prisoner says, "I admit the facts as charged." What is the result? The judge says the statute is clear. The facts are admitted. Judgment will pass.

But what if the prisoner should say, "Oh, Judge, don't give that judgment. I am not at all convinced that the law under which your Court is sitting, or the section of the statutes that you are construing, is a beneficent or good law, or that you have construed the law aright. I must be convinced upon all these points before you can pass sentence upon me"? The judge would probably say: "Prisoner, your duty is to conform to the law. My duty is to determine, upon the evidence before me, whether you are guilty or not." What court would listen to such a plea from a prisoner? "You cannot convict me, you cannot sentence me, until you have satisfied me of the soundness of the law, or that the statute you propose to enforce is the law, or that it is essential, or that in the interest of justice it ought to be enforced." No intelligent judge would listen to such words for a minute. The prisoner would pass forth and the Court would proceed to its other and usual duties.

The Grounds of Appeal and Specifications of Error.

I now wish to direct your attention to the grounds of appeal and the specifications of error alleged, which have already been passed upon, found in order and entertained by this General Assembly.

There are several grounds of appeal; there are many specifications of error. This is no fault of the Prosecuting Committee. It is simply because so many errors were committed by the Court below. In the performance of its duty to the whole Church, the Prosecuting Committee did not feel at liberty to exercise its judgment and eliminate or not notice any of the errors committed at the trial by the Presbytery. Those errors have been specified and brought here on appeal, in strict compliance with the provisions of the Book of Discipline, not because the Committee wished to do so, but because the errors were committed by the Court below.

The Appellee is mistaken in saying that the Appeal has been taken upon all the grounds provided for in the Book of Discipline. Only five out of the six grounds of appeal specifically mentioned in Section 95 of the Book of Discipline have been alleged by the Prosecuting Committee.

If the Prosecuting Committee had been at liberty to consult its own wishes it would have presented a much shorter document, with fewer grounds of appeal and not so many specifications of error, but the Committee felt that the Constitution held it to a strict responsibility and compelled it, in taking the Appeal, to specify all the errors committed, however tedious their recital may be to the members of this Court.

In so far as the doctrinal issues involved in this case are concerned, I should be perfectly willing to submit the case to the Assembly, as it has been presented by my colleague, Dr. Lampe.

Many of the Appellee's statements and arguments have been already anticipated by my colleague. Some of the Appellee's propositions are hardly worthy of extended answer or denial. In any event, I shall not take the time of the Court to traverse many of them. Some of the statements made during his argument, however, require some correction, and these corrections I shall make as briefly as possible.

FIRST GROUND OF APPEAL. IRREGULARITY IN THE PROCEEDINGS OF THE PRESBYTERY.

The striking out by the Presbytery of Amended Charges IV. and VII., in spite of what was said yesterday, by the Appellee, was irregular and illegal.

(*a*) Charges IV. and VII. were not new Charges.

(*b*) The doctrines referred to in these Charges had not been retracted by the Appellee, but had been re-affirmed and republished by him.

(*c*) It was not in the interest or furtherance of justice that they should be struck out.

Dr. Lampe, in his opening argument, has already explained to you the views of the Committee as to these amended Charges IV. and VII.

CHARGE IV.—PREDICTIVE PROPHECY.

I shall now refer briefly to the statements concerning Charge IV., relating to Predictive Prophecy, which have been made by the Appellee during his argument in this Court.

I am sorry to say that this is not the first time that this passage from the Inaugural Address relating to Predictive Prophecy, and dealt with in amended Charge IV., has been under discussion in the Courts of the Church.

Kuenen may have shown that if we insist upon the fulfillment of the details of Old Testament Prophecy, much of it has been reversed by history. The Presbyterian Church does not accept this view, nor quote it with approval.

But the question is not what Kuenen may or may not have said or shown. The question is as to the categorical statement of the Appellee, which he has affirmed in four successive editions of the Inaugural Address, namely, that the great body of the Messianic prediction has not only never been fulfilled, but cannot now be fulfilled. But why? For the reason that we insist upon the fulfillment of the details? No. But, to quote the words of the Appellee, "for the reason that its own time has passed forever." This is similar to the case of one who might say the prediction about Nineveh was not fulfilled because God recalled His decree. Jesus Christ, in insisting upon the jots and tittles of fulfillment, sufficiently disposes of Kuenen's suggestion. And the Appellee's unconditional statement, with its additional reason, remains reaffirmed and unretracted.

Suppose that we do insist upon the fulfillment of the details of predictive prophecy, then our Bible, according to Dr. Briggs, becomes fallible, untrustworthy; its truth is not in the written word, throughout, but only in the essentials which are to be determined by each man for himself.

Whatever the meaning of the statement quoted from Kuenen may be, or whatever the orthodoxy of the Appellee's book on Messianic Prophecy may be, the statement of the Inaugural Address remains as he spoke and published it, is still reaffirmed and has never been retracted: "The great body of Messianic prediction has not only never been fulfilled, but cannot now be fulfilled, for the reason that its own time has passed forever."

At the time when Charge IV. was struck out by the Presbytery of New York, sitting as a Judicatory, the case had not yet come before the Court on its merits.

The alleged disclaimer of the accused, which was given as one of the reasons for striking out amended Charge IV., was nothing more than a plea of not guilty, introduced to affect the sufficiency and the form and legal effect of the indictment. But in the successive editions of the Inaugural Address, notwithstanding the alleged disclaimers, the words of the Inaugural, above quoted, still appear, unconditionally stated. They have never been withdrawn. And the Appellee now stands before this Court, reaffirming that the great body of Messianic prediction not only has not, but cannot be fulfilled, because its own time has passed forever.

Dr. Lampe showed to you yesterday that the dual authorship of Isaiah was asserted by the Appellee upon the naturalistic principle that a prophet must be limited by his own circumstances in making his predictions. According to the Appellee, one who might prophesy the invasion of the Assyrians could not foretell the captivity at Babylon. Under such limitations upon predictive prophecy, as are thus set by Dr. Briggs, it might well be asked, How could the ancient prophet of the Hebrew Monarchy foresee and foretell the advent of the Prince of Peace?

CHARGE VII. REDEMPTION AFTER DEATH.

I will now call your attention to the statements made by the Appellee during his argument before this Court concerning amended Charge VII., relating to his teaching, "that the processes of redemption extend to the world to come in the case of many who die in sin."

The disclaimers of the Appellee, with respect to the doctrine here charged, have been made before the

Directors of Union Seminary, before the Presbytery of New York, and again before this Court. But as my colleague, Dr. Lampe, in his opening argument, clearly proved, the doctrine of Redemption in the Middle State has been affirmed again and again in the Inaugural Address, and in the writings of the Appellee referred to therein.

Dr. Briggs claimed in your presence, yesterday, that his doctrine of Redemption had not been properly understood. It is upon his own definition of Redemption that amended Charge VII. may be most evidently proved. Redemption, according to Dr. Briggs, as stated by him yesterday, includes all the principal processes of grace. It includes Regeneration, Justification, Repentance, Faith, Sanctification and Glorification. But we are further informed by Dr. Briggs that the whole race of man is redeemed; and therefore the process of redemption must go on in every man. Every man must have faith and repentance, because the whole race of man is redeemed, and this, as Dr. Briggs informs us, cannot be accomplished by the selection of a limited number from the mass of men. It is, he says, only the irretrievably bad who are lost. It is therefore reasonable to infer, that a man who believes that we are justified by faith, and who believes that justification must precede sanctification, must necessarily hold that those who are unbelievers in this world, must believe in the world to come, otherwise they are never justified.

DISCLAIMERS TO HAVE BEEN EFFECTIVE SHOULD HAVE BEEN UNDER OATH.

The Appellee, in commenting upon his own refusal to take the oath or affirmation, before the Court below, unintentionally perhaps, presented an argument in favor of his being required to take such an oath, which reinforces the wise provision of Section 61 of the Book of Discipline. He asked, in substance, "Why the extracts from the Inaugural, unsworn to, should be good and competent evidence for the committee, and yet the defendant's extracts from the Inaugural should require his oath or affirmation for their verification?"

Is it not plain that if the defendant had taken the oath, and been examined, these questions of disclaimer might have been settled at the proper time, and a due renunciation, of the doctrine of Redemption after death, might then have been effective?

The difficulty has been that the case was on trial before a Judicatory of the Presbyterian Church, and not before the Directors of a Seminary. The case has been on trial under a certain code of procedure, and upon a document which has been often reaffirmed, in spite of the alleged disclaimers, which have never been properly submitted to that Court, in the form prescribed by the Book of Discipline.

SECOND GROUND OF APPEAL. RECEIVING IMPROPER TESTIMONY.

Although the improper evidence introduced by the Appellee with the approval of the Moderator of the lower Court, referred to in the second Ground of Appeal, was declared to be competent; the introduction of said evidence was accomplished in private, without notice being given to the Prosecuting Committee, or to the Judicatory.

A part of the evidence thus introduced consisted, upon the Appellee's own admission, of the writings of rationalistic and non-Presbyterian authorities, and it did not have those invincible qualities attributed to it by the Appellee. The Prosecuting Committee was only anxious that the Court should have a trustworthy stenographic record of its proceedings, and did not appeal because of the character of the evidence thus improperly introduced as it was not objected to upon that ground at the trial. The committee's objection then was, and the present appeal charges, that said testimony was improper because of the time, the circumstances and the irregular manner of its introduction.

It is undoubtedly true, as we saw from the portion of the stenographic report read by Dr. Francis Brown yesterday, that a protest was made by members of the Presbytery against the introduction of this evidence and the improper manner in which it was done.

It is also true that the protest was answered by a Committee appointed for that purpose, and that the Presbytery accepted the answer of the Committee, thus confirming the ruling of the Moderator and its own subsequent decision as to admitting the evidence referred to. All these details, brought out so clearly by Dr. Brown, demonstrate the truth of the Prosecuting Committee's position and confirms the allegations of the Appellant, set out in the Second Ground of Appeal and the specifications thereunder. There is no question as to the irregular and improper manner in which the said evidence was introduced, the fact that the Moderator ruled it in, and the Presbytery sustained his ruling, only shows that the error alleged, when once made, was, with all the facts before it, fully confirmed by the Presbytery and should now be overruled by this Assembly.

THIRD GROUND OF APPEAL. DECLINING TO RECEIVE IMPORTANT TESTIMOMY.

As the questions involved in the two specifications of error under this Ground of Appeal have already been sufficiently considered, when discussing the first and second specifications under the First Ground of Appeal, they do not require further attention at this time.

FOURTH GROUND OF APPEAL. MANIFESTATION OF PREJUDICE IN THE CONDUCT OF THE CASE.

The specifications of error alleged under the Fourth Ground of Appeal afford an instructive view of the composition and temper of the lower Court, where this case has so lately been tried. It is conceiveable that in a public assembly, where no judicial case was in progress, rash, prejudiced, and even unparliamentary language might be used by those taking part in its deliberations. But, in a Court, especially in a Court of the Presbyterian Church, which had been solemnly charged, so that the judges sitting therein might feel their responsibilities, it is incompatible with a fair hearing and fair decision, that such judges or jurors should be permitted to make appeals *ad populum* when grave issues are on trial before them.

It is possible that such exhibitions might be overlooked as the expression of feeling on the part of ill-balanced or excitable Ministers and Elders who were prevented by emotion from being judicial. But the law cannot take cognizance of such excuses as these. The blood of judges should not boil when one with whom they sympathize, has been fairly met in argument, nor should the blood of such judges boil at the citation of great Presbyterian authorities. To sum up a case against a defendant is not a fresh attack, and there is no injustice, not even seeming injustice, in answering properly, and logically, ill-considered and invalid arguments, even when made by one assuming to be a great scholar and theologian.

But some of the utterances set out in the first specification of error under the Fourth Ground of Appeal, cannot be justified by attributing them to the unbridled passion of inexperienced men. There is prejudice manifested when an eminent Minister describes a legally and carefully drawn indictment, as giving the "lie direct" to the accused. Trials cannot be brought to an end whenever the accused pleads not guilty, by denying or disclaiming the offence charged, nor should the blood of Presbyterian judges boil if Presbyterian doctrine is successfully defended in its Judicatories.

The decision of the General Assembly of 1892, referred to in the fifth specification of error, under the Fourth Ground of Appeal, was made in a judicial case, is final, and cannot be reviewed. But if it were to be reviewed, it would be found that more than one of those, who were then declared by the General Assembly to have manifested prejudice when sitting as judges, not only deliberated and voted at the recent trial, but again took the floor as advocates when they should have kept their places as judges.

Besides all this, in the trial of a Professor in Union Seminary for utterances published in an Inaugural Address, you find among the judges or jurors, as you may see fit to call them, named in the sixth specification of error, those who had in a manner, and in their official capacity, become responsible for the publication of the alleged errors, who had approved and published the Inaugural Address, and who justified themselves and their position, by voting to acquit the author of any offence in teaching doctrines, the publication of which they had previously approved.

Previous to the trial of Dr. Briggs in the Presbytery, the Board of Directors of Union Seminary had resolved to sustain him, saying "We will stand by him." At a subsequent meeting, the Board of Directors "considered "the action of the Assembly at Detroit, and decided that "it was due to our students to know what to count "upon for the coming year's instruction, and that "it was due to ourselves and Dr. Briggs that we "should be true to the promise we had made to stand "by him."

Notice of these two actions taken by the Board of Directors of Union Seminary was formally communicated by Dr. Hastings, the President of the Seminary, in behalf of the Board of Directors, to the General Assembly at Portland (see Minutes, 1892, pages 56, 57). After these repeated assurances on the part of the Directors of Union Seminary, "to stand by him," several of them went into the Court of the Presbytery as judges and were possibly unprejudiced, but it is a noticeable fact that each of them voted solidly upon each of the charges and specifications to acquit Dr. Briggs, thus fully redeeming the pledge that had been officially given for them, in advance of the trial.

I must here add a word with respect to the manifestation of prejudice in the final judgment of the lower judicatory, to which reference is made in specification fourth, under the Fourth Ground of Appeal. The words there quoted as expressing an earnest conviction that the grave issues involved in this case will be more wisely and justly determined by calm investigation and fraternal discussion than by judicial arraignment and process, exhibit a not altogether praiseworthy disregard of the Constitution of the Church and its mode of judicial procedure. In rendering a judicial decision it is not the part of an unprejudiced judge to suggest that debate about alleged offences is preferable to the execution of laws which he has vowed to maintain.

FIFTH GROUND OF APPEAL. MISTAKE OR INJUSTICE
IN THE DECISION.

The Fifth Ground of Appeal is concerned with mistake or injustice in the decision. It is my purpose to confine my argument under this head wholly to the legal questions involved in some of the specifications of error alleged to sustain the same. I desire to call your attention especially to one or two of these specifications, in order that their meaning may be perfectly plain.

The argument of the Appellee, with respect to specifications first and second, under this ground of appeal, deserves a moment's consideration. His argument was introduced with a gentle reproof to the Prosecuting Committee, suggesting that they should not reason incorrectly, or that, reasoning correctly, they should be sure of the truth of their premises. All question as to whether the specifications were relevant to the several charges or not was removed, not by the opinion or action of the Appellee, not by the action of the Prosecuting Committee, but by the action of the Presbytery of New York when it passed upon the sufficiency in form and legal effect of the amended charges and specifications.

The passages quoted in your presence by the Appellee, from his defence, were first spoken when the case was being tried on the merits in the Presbytery. Unless the several charges and specifications had alleged real offences, there would have been no case for the Appellee to defend before the Presbytery. While specification second, under this last ground of appeal, makes this perfectly manifest, it is possible that a few words may be necessary to correct the misapprehension of the Appellee, which he may have communicated to others.

Notice the nature of a charge in relation to the specifications cited to sustain it.

A charge alleges a certain offence, and cites the law against which the offence has been committed. The specification contains the necessary facts relied upon to prove the offence alleged. If the extracts from the Inaugural cited in the specifications, the utterance and publication of which the defendant fully admitted, did not prove the alleged offences, then the charges and specifications would have been insufficient in form and legal effect. When the sufficiency in form and legal effect of the charges and specifications had been sustained by the Presbytery, it was by that act, decided, that if the accused had spoken and published the words found in the specifications, he was guilty of the offence charged, otherwise he would not be put on his defence.

At that stage of the judicial proceedings it is still open for a judicatory to decide, that even if the alleged erroneous doctrine had been uttered by the accused, it was not an offence; or it might be decided that the utterance contained in the specification does not sustain the allegation in the charge.

If the Presbytery had decided these questions in this way, the charges and specifications would have been or should have been found insufficient in form and legal effect. But after striking out Charges IV. and VII., the Presbytery of New York found the remaining charges and specifications in order and sufficient to place the accused upon his defence (Book of Discipline, Sec. 22; Printed Document, p. 86; page 92 of this volume). What then remained for the Prosecuting Committee to prove? Simply that the accused had spoken and published the words from the Inaugural quoted in the specifications. The merits of the case involved simply the question of fact. But the fact was openly admitted by the accused that he had spoken and published the words quoted in the specifications. The proof was complete. The verdict should have been guilty, and each of the charges and specifications should have been sustained.

The case on its merits is a jury case. It is a question of fact, not of law. The peculiarity of the case before you, as well as in the trial below, is that the utterances of the accused, relied upon by the Prosecuting Committee to sustain the charges, have all been admitted by him. Did he utter them or not? That was the question on its merits. There was no question of fact but that. The facts were admitted, and the only course left to the Court was to bring in a verdict of guilty. It was gross error on the part of the Presbytery, under such circumstances, to acquit the accused.

From this it follows that had the Appellee conformed his reasoning to the laws of discursive thought, in the conduct of his defence, before the lower Court, he should either have declined to defend himself where no offence was charged or should have pleaded guilty to each and all of the several charges. The Appellee does not and cannot deny that the specifications relied upon to prove the charges are facts. But if he denies that they sustain the charges, he places himself in direct conflict with the decision of the New York Presbytery, which had already passed upon the sufficiency, both as to form and legal effect, of the charges and specifications.

The facts of which the Appellee complains, are quotations from his own writings. The logic of which the Appellee complains, is the logic, not of the Prosecuting Committee, but of the Presbytery of New York.

I will not occupy the time of this Court by making extended comment upon the remaining specifications of error under the Fifth Ground of Appeal.

THE FINAL JUDGMENT OF THE PRESBYTERY WAS CONTRADICTORY AND ILLEGAL.

There are, however, several points connected with the final judgment of the Presbytery, specified as errors under the Fifth Ground of Appeal, which the Appellee attempted to traverse in his argument, to which I must call attention.

The alleged disclaimers made by the Appellee were accepted by the lower Court, as grounds for acquittal, although, in fact and in law, they had no more force or effect than the formal plea of not guilty, which was subsequently made by him. The Inaugural

Address had been thrice republished and, in the preface to the third and fourth editions, the doctrines supposed to have been disclaimed in the answers to the questions submitted by the Directors of Union Seminary, and before the Presbytery, were specifically republished and reaffirmed by the Appellee. And he now stands before this Court, reaffirming and declining to retract or withdraw any part of the Inaugural Address.

The members of the lower Court, bound by their vows of ordination, had accepted and adopted the Scripture and the Standards. They were charged in this judicial case to decide whether the doctrines of the defendant agreed or disagreed with the Scripture and Standards. In the final judgment of the Presbytery they declared that the said doctrines were not out of harmony with the Standards, although at the same time they affirmed that they did not intend to say that they approved of the defendant's views, which they had declared to be not unorthodox.

So that, even assuming that the verdict of the trial Court should have been in favor of the accused (an assumption which the facts would not in the slightest degree justify), the decision and final judgment of the Presbytery of New York in this case is contradictory and illegal.

The lower Court was not called upon to express its views with respect to the Constitution, laws and discipline of the Church. Its final judgment should have been delivered as a verdict based upon the facts of the case. Undoubtedly the issue was somewhat confused by the fact that while the accused was before the lower Court, reaffirming and defending the Inaugural Address and admitting that he had uttered and published the doctrines alleged by the Committee to be erroneous, yet yet some of the advocate judges were pressing upon their associate judges the effect of so-called disclaimers, which did not and were not intended by the accused to disclaim or retract any of the errors charged.

But, in spite of the so-called disclaimers, in spite of the attempts to avoid a settlement of the questions at issue, without responsibility on the part of the judges, it is perfectly plain to any one who has read the specifications of error in this appeal, that the judgment of the lower Court was contradictory and illegal and should not stand. The grave issues involved in this case cannot be decided by occasional polemics concerning Presbyterian doctrine. The matter is one which must be determined by its courts according to the Constitution and discipline of the Presbyterian Church.

As I have already shown, the admissions of Dr. Briggs with respect to the passages of his Inaugural cited in the several specifications, settled all questions of fact which were at issue in the lower Judicatory.

But if one should be disposed to go farther and maintain that Mistake and Injustice in the decision implies mistake and injustice in dealing with the law and the evidence, I am prepared briefly to bring before the General Assembly the propositions which I think have been satisfactorily proved by the Prosecuting Committee in its opening argument and inadequately answered by the Apellee in his argument to which you have given such careful attention.

Some of the fundamental questions discussed by the Appellee, in the course of his argument, should, however, be now referred to.

If we begin with the statements of the Inaugural Address, to which the Appellee still adheres, the task is comparatively easy. The whole series of answers made by him to the positions of the Prosecuting Committee can be shown to be irrelevant.

I shall take up briefly and in their order the points, against which the Appellee argued so fully, but which the Prosecuting Committee have been able clearly to establish, from evidence furnished by Dr. Briggs in his Inaugural Address.

THE REASON AS A FOUNTAIN OF DIVINE AUTHORITY.

The Appellee has taught that the Church and the Reason are great fountains of Divine Authority. That he regards them as divine rules of faith, independent of the Bible, is shown by his explanations and illustrations. The proposition of Dr. Briggs that the Church and the Reason are sources of divine authority has been explained by him in your presence. He holds that Martineau, like Spurgeon, is a representative Christian whose loving certainty and joyous confidence repose not on an infallible rule of faith, but upon the metaphysical categories, the conscience and the religious feeling. This he still asserts, although Martineau has written as follows: "The blight of birth-sin, with its involuntary perdition; the scheme, of expiatory redemption, with its vicarious salvation; the incarnation, with its low postulates of God and man, and its unworkable doctrine of two natures in one person, the official transmission of grace through material elements in the keeping of a consecrated corporation; the second coming of Christ to summon the dead and part the sheep from the goats at the general judgment—all are the growth of a mythical literature, or Messianic dream, or Pharisaic theology, or sacramental superstition, or popular apotheosis." *

THE CHURCH AS A FOUNTAIN OF DIVINE AUTHORITY.

Dr. Briggs has also taught that Newman, finding the Bible inefficient, found divine certainty fixed upon the rock of the papal Church.

The defence of the accused in the lower Court, and again in your presence, was that there is a divine

---

* Martineau's Seat of Authority in Religion, p. 650.

influence which pervades the Church, which moves the reason, which gives efficacy to the sacraments. But the authority of God is something different from the divine influence; and the Bible and the Standards of the Presbyterian Church declare that divine authority is to be found in the Scriptures alone.

According to the Appellee, the whole race of man is redeemed, not only through the preaching of Christ as an objective reality, but by the Church, even if the Church be apostate, or by the Reason, even if the Reason deny the divinity of Jesus Christ. The fact that but one of these authorities is declared by the Appellee to be infallible, while all three are declared by him to be divine, is in no way reassuring, for unless the authority be infallible it cannot be divine.

Dr. Briggs' Doctrine of the Errancy of Holy Scripture.

The Appellee has taught, as the Prosecuting Committee has proved, doctrines which destroy the infallibility of Holy Scripture. The infallibility of Holy Scripture is adopted in the ordination vow of the Presbyterian ministry, and is plainly taught in the Standards. It is, in fact, the fundamental written law of the Church. If men are unwilling to believe that the inspired word as it came from God was without error, it is difficult to see how they can adopt the doctrine of infallibility for that word as we have it now. With this doctrine of the Appellee that Holy Scripture contains errors which may have been in the originals, it is impossible that the present Scriptures should be infallible. Unless the original Word was without error, it is impossible that infallibility could have been imparted to it by the long line of transcribers.

The mere technical question of the mode of inspiration has not been raised by the Prosecuting Committee, except in so far as it has maintained that whatever is inspired of God is true. And this position we hold to be essential, in accordance with the Constitution of the Presbyterian Church. Let me especially direct your attention to what this word of God is held to be in the doctrine of the Westminster Standards. In presenting, in evidence, the answer to the second question in the Shorter Catechism, Dr. Briggs seemed to me to lay especial emphasis upon the word "*contained*," as if the terms "Word of God" and "the Scriptures of the Old and New Testaments" were not co-extensive terms. Is it true that the Word of God is contained in the Scriptures of the Old and New Testaments, or that the Word of God is the Old and New Testament Scriptures? According to the Catechism, the Word of God is contained in the Scriptures; and in the light of the Confession of Faith, it may be seen what is meant by this. It is not the greater containing the lesser. The Confession of Faith (Chap. I., Sec. II.) says: "Under the name of Holy Scripture, or of the Word of God written, are now contained all the books of the Old and New Testament, which are these:" then follows the list of the books. If the Word of God is contained in these Scriptures, and these Scriptures are contained in the Word of God, how are we to explain the difference of statement except upon the ground that these terms are co-extensive.

AUTHENTICITY OF THE PENTATEUCH AND ISAIAH.

The questions of authenticity with respect to the Pentateuch and the Prophecy of Isaiah, present no difficulties of proof. That the Pentateuch is not from the hand of Moses, and that there are two authors to Isaiah are propositions which the accused has taught. And he has admitted in his defence, and before this Assembly, that these are his views. The Prosecuting

Committee, by reference to the New Testament, as well as the Old, with the Bible as their guide and not the speculations of men, has insisted that these are essential questions ; and that the doctrine here contradicted by the Appellee is essential doctrine.

The Presbyterian Church, to which we belong, is ready to debate this question of authenticity with its enemies. But the question of authenticity here, and as raised by Dr. Briggs, has an essential importance, not as a theory of criticism but as a question of dogma. And the dogma which is here imperilled is the Deity and absolute truthfulness of Jesus Christ. To deny or even to doubt His word is to offend against the very essence of Presbyterian doctrine.

DR. BRIGGS' DOCTRINE OF REDEMPTION AFTER DEATH.

Lastly, the doctrine of Redemption in another world has been taught by the Appellee, and the Prosecuting Committee was permitted to deal with this question only partially by the Court below. This fact was called to your attention when I referred to the error committed by the trial Court in striking out Amended Charge VII. But the last of the amended charges (Charge VIII.) alleges an offence which was admitted by the Appellee before the lower Court and has been reaffirmed by him in your presence. It is the offence of teaching that there is a continuation of the process of sanctification after death. As the Presbytery had found this Charge VIII. sufficient in form and legal effect to create an offence if proved, and as the accused in that Court admitted, as he has repeated here, that he holds and teaches the doctrine, the Presbytery should have sustained the charge, and the error it committed in not doing so, should be overruled and corrected by this Court.

Your familiarity with the great doctrinal issues involved in the amended charges and specifications is a sufficient reason why I should not unnecessarily occupy your time with them, so I have abstained from discussing them further than to reply to the argument of the Appellee and to give you a full understanding of their relation to the specifications of error alleged in the Appeal upon which this Court must shortly pass.

TOLERATION AND LIBERTY.

The question of tolerance and liberty, of which you have heard so much from the Appellee, is one into which I shall not enter. The question before us is a judicial question. The facts are before you in the doctrines of the Inaugural Address—doctrines which have been often reaffirmed by the accused, but never retracted. I ask you simply to judge of them in the light of the Holy Scriptures, in the light of our historic Standards, and with fidelity to the truth of Almighty God.

This case seems to me, Moderator, to be now before the General Assembly in a perfectly intelligible form. The Appellant has presented comprehensively its evidence and argument; and the Appellee has had full opportunity to be heard. It is now the duty of the Prosecuting Committee to leave this important case in the hands of the Supreme Court of the Church.

We close our work, as we began it, with a simple desire to have the doctrines of the Inaugural Address compared with those of the Presbyterian Church, with the object of deciding whether the teaching of Dr. Briggs, in that address, constitutes an offence or not.

The sympathies of every true Presbyterian must be with those who have erred and are deceived. But there is a higher standard of action than sympathy. There is loyalty to the Church, to the Word of God, and to the vows which we have made.

Every Presbyterian minister is a representative of his Church. If he teaches error, he teaches it in the name of the Church whose orders he bears.

It seems almost incredible that the Appellee, after reaffirming so often, the alleged erroneous doctrines for which he has been put on trial, should appear before this Court with a series of orthodox statements, for the utterance of which he is not and has never been on trial. The question is not whether he has once or twenty times taught what was orthodox. The trial is based upon the doctrines of the Inaugural Address, and upon those doctrines of the Inaugural Address which are alleged to be offences against Presbyterian doctrine.

There is no room for obscurity here. There is no reason for searching the works of the Appellee, published in the past, to reassure yourself, or to shake the position of the Prosecuting Committee. The question is this : Are the unretracted doctrines of the Inaugural Address, affirmed and published, reaffirmed and republished so many times, upon which are based these charges and specifications, are they in conformity with the Word of God and the Standards of the Presbyterian Church ? This is the question, and this only.

The array of authorities, many of them rationalistic writers, which the Appellee has cited in opposition to the Presbyterian doctrine of the Scripture, is without doubt imposing; and all scholarship is worthy of respect.

I am aware, however, that at the great universities of Europe, there are many jurists of the the highest learning, who defend monarchy, and are very scornful in the expression of their views of the popular institutions of the United States. But as a citizen loyal to the American Constitution, I do not regulate my loyalty according to the conclusions of foreign *doctrinaires*.

In like manner, those of us who are loyal to the Constitution of the Presbyterian Church, are not called upon to alter our views, with respect to our Presbyterian Constitution and doctrine, at the bidding of unbelievers, however high their position. Oxford Episcopalians and German Rationalists do not interpret the Presbyterian Constitution and doctrine; for Presbyterianism has a history and has claims which do not need the support of any one, seeing that the foundation is Jesus Christ as He is revealed in God's Holy Word.

X.

APPENDIX CONTAINING THE JUDGMENT OF THE GENERAL ASSEMBLY AND VOTE OF THANKS TO THE PROSECUTING COMMITTEE.

REPORT OF THE COMMITTEE APPOINTED TO FORMULATE THE JUDGMENT OF THE ASSEMBLY IN THE CASE.

"The Rev. George D. Baker, D. D., Chairman of the Sub-committee of the Committee on the Judgment in *Judical Case No.* 1, at the request of the Committee, made the following statement, which was ordered to be recorded, viz.:"

"When the Committee of fifteen convened this morning it was impressed with a sense of responsibility which seldom falls to the lot of men to bear. We all felt that the very first thing to do in all Christian love and courtesy, was to appoint a committee to call upon Dr. Briggs, and give him an opportunity to say whatever he might be pleased to say, in view of the distressing circumstances. There was a prayer in our hearts that Dr. Briggs might be led of God to say something which would relieve the painful situation. I regret to say that our hope in this regard was disappointed. Our interview was frank, kind and cordial to the last degree; but Dr. Briggs insisted strenuously, positively, irrevocably upon everything that he had said in the defense which he made when brought to the bar of this Court. At my request, he gave into my hands this statement, in his own handwriting, and bearing his own signature, which I will read:"

"COCHRAN HOUSE, June 1, 1893.

"*To the Rev. Dr. George D. Baker, Chairman of the Sub-committee of Committee of the Assembly appointed to formulate a judgment in the case of the Presbyterian Church, U. S. A., against Prof. C. A. Briggs:*

"MY DEAR SIR:—In accordance with your request I hereby state that your Committee called upon me and asked me if I had anything to say to them respecting the disposition of the case. I thereupon said that I adhered to all the positions taken before the General Assembly, and had nothing further to say, save that the Appellee reserves all rights, and that the General Assembly should take the exclusive responsibility for any further action.
"C. A. BRIGGS."

"When I interrogated him particularly with reference to the declaration he made to this Court, that he should continue under all circumstances to teach, so long as he lived, the doctrines to answer for which he was brought to the bar of this Court, he replied that he had only to reiterate the declaration, that whatsoever might be the disposition of this case, whatsoever action we might take this afternoon, with reference to it, he should still teach, as he has done heretofore, these doctrines which he sincerely believes. It was in view of this declaration, that your Committee took the action which is now to be reported by the Chairman."

"The Rev. Thomas A. Hoyt, D. D., Chairman of the Committee on Judgment, presented the following Report, which was adopted:"

"General Assembly of the Presbyterian Church in the United States of America, in session at Washington, D. C., June 1, 1893.

PRESBYTERIAN CHURCH IN THE
UNITED STATES OF AMERICA,
Appellant,
vs.
REV. CHARLES A. BRIGGS, D. D.,
Appellee.

On appeal from the final judgment of the Presbytery of New York.

This appeal being regularly issued and coming on to be heard on the judgment, the notice of appeal, the appeal, and the specifications of errors alleged ; and the record in the case from the beginning, and the reading of said record having been omitted by consent, and the parties hereto having been heard before the judicatory in argument, and the opportunity having been given to the members of the judicatory appealed from to be heard, and they having been heard, and opportunity having been given to the members of this judicatory to be heard, and they having been heard, as provided by the Book of Discipline, and the General Assembly as a judicatory sitting in said cause on appeal having sustained the following specifications of errors, to wit: all of said specifications of errors set forth in said five grounds of appeal, save and except the first and fifth under the fourth ground of appeal, on consideration whereof this judicatory finds said appeal should be and is hereby sustained, and that said Presbytery of New York, the judicatory appealed from, erred in striking out said amended charges four and seven, and erred in not sustaining on the law and the evidence said amended charges, one, two, three, five, six and eight ; on consideration whereof this judicatory finds that said final judgment of the Presbytery of New York is erroneous and should be and is hereby reversed; and this General Assembly, sitting as a judicatory in said cause, coming now to enter judgment on said amended charges, one, two, three, five, six and eight, finds the Appellee, the said Charles A. Briggs, has uttered, taught and propagated views, doctrines and teachings as set forth in said charges contrary to the essential doctrine of Holy Scripture and the Standards of said Presbyterian Church in the United States of America, and in violation of the ordination vow of said Appellee, which said erroneous teachings, views and doctrines strike at the vitals of religion and have been industriously spread; wherefore, this General Assembly of the Presbyterian Church in the United States of America, sitting as a judicatory in this cause on appeal, does hereby suspend Charles A. Briggs, the said Appellee, from the office of a minister in the Presbyterian Church in the United States of America, until such time as he shall give satisfactory evidence of repentance to the General Assembly of the Presbyterian Church in the United States of America, for the violation by him of the said ordination vow as herein and heretofore found.

And it is ordered that the Stated Clerk of this General Assembly transmit a certified copy of this judgment to the Presbytery of New York to be made a part of the record in this case.

It was also ordered that a copy be furnished to the Appellee, the Rev. Charles A. Briggs, D. D.

ATTEST,

WM. HENRY ROBERTS,

SEAL. *Stated Clerk.*"

(Minutes General Assembly, 1893, pp. 163–4.)

VOTE OF THANKS TO THE PROSECUTING COMMITTEE.

Upon motion of the Rev. William C. Young, D. D., the following preambles and resolution were adopted:

"*Whereas*, the Prosecuting Committee, of which the Rev. G. W. F. Birch, D. D., is Chairman, appointed in compliance with Sec. 11 of the Book of Discipline, has conducted the prosecution in the case of the Presbyterian Church in the United States of America against the Rev. Charles A. Briggs, D. D., in all its stages, in whatever judicatory, until the final issue has been reached, and,

"*Whereas*, The Presbytery of New York, at the close of its proceedings on the 4th day of November, 1891, when it passed the resolution dismissing the said case, took the following action:

"'*Resolved*, That a vote of thanks be tendered to the Committee for its diligence and fidelity,' and

"*Whereas*, The final judgment of the said Presbytery of New York, in the said case, entered on the 9th day of January, 1893, declared as follows: 'Accordingly the Presbytery, making full recognition of the ability, sincerity and patience with which the Committee of Prosecution have performed the onerous duties assigned them, does now, to the extent of its constitutional power, relieve said Committee from further responsibility in connection with this case.' Therefore be it

"*Resolved*, That the thanks of this General Assembly and of the entire Church are due to the members of the Prosecuting Committee for the diligence, fidelity, ability and Christian spirit in which they have performed the onerous and difficult duties devolved upon them." (Minutes General Assembly, 1893, pp. 166, 167.)

www.ingramcontent.com/pod-product-compliance
Lightning Source LLC
Chambersburg PA
CBHW030407230426
43664CB00007BB/780